YOUR MID-CAREER SHIFT

BY THE SAME AUTHOR:
Instant Business Letters
Make That Call
Managing Your Time

Your Mid-Career Shift

HOW TO CHANGE YOUR JOB AT 35+

Iain Maitland

Thorsons
An Imprint of HarperCollins*Publishers*

Thorsons
An Imprint of HarperCollins*Publishers*
77–85 Fulham Palace Road,
Hammersmith, London W6 8JB
1160 Battery Street
San Francisco, California 94111–1213

First published 1997
10 9 8 7 6 5 4 3 2 1

© Iain Maitland 1997

Iain Maitland asserts the moral right to
be identified as the author of this work

A catalogue record for this book
is available from the British Library

ISBN 0 7225 3260 1

Printed and bound in Great Britain by
Caledonian International Book Manufacturing Ltd, Glasgow

All rights reserved. No part of this publication may be
reproduced, stored in a retrieval system, or transmitted,
in any form or by any means, electronic, mechanical,
photocopying, recording or otherwise, without the prior
permission of the publishers.

Contents

Preface vii
1. **Changing your Job – at 35+!** 1
   Likely reasons for wanting to change 2
   Deciding what you want to do 5
   Recognizing what you have to offer 10
2. **Getting Everything Together** 15
   Learning about vacancies 16
   Drafting your job-search schedule 26
   Identifying suitable opportunities 37
3. **Creating Terrific Letters** 45
   Types of letter 45
   Gathering the information for your letter 59
   Presentation 60
   Style of writing 64
4. **Producing Sensational CVs** 69
   Personal information 75
   Education, qualifications and training 76
   Leisure activities 77
   Drafts and final versions 77

5 Making Application Forms Memorable 79
   Obtaining an Application Form 85
   Filling in an Application Form 87
   Returning completed forms 92
6 Perfecting your Telephone Technique 95
   Making phone calls 96
   Receiving phone calls 100
   Following up your phone calls 103
7 Impressing the Interviewer 105
   Preparing for interviews 105
   Self-presentation 112
   Handling the interview successfully 115
   Following the interview 125
8 Benefiting from Rejection 129
   No response 130
   The rejection letter 131
   Making changes and improvements 134
9 Being Offered That Job 137
   Accepting or rejecting the offer 139
   The company pension scheme 148
   Success at last 149

Afterword: Fighting Ageism in the Workplace 151
Further Reading 155
Useful Contacts 159
Index 163

Preface

In May 1996, I was asked to apply for voluntary redundancy at the college where I had taught for nine years. I did and soon found myself a 35-year-old mid-career job-hunter having to confront the misconceptions that so many employers have about the older applicant.

Whether the need to seek new employment is thrust upon us, or we have made the decision ourselves, the problems and the solutions are the same.

The unenlightened employer's view is that at our age we are likely to be out-of-date, reluctant to adapt and not as fit as we might be – and this has led many job-seekers to the defeatist conclusion that it's impossible for the over–35s to find work.

It is certainly not as easy as it once was to get a job, but that's true for everyone, and it has little to do with age. There *are* jobs out there, though, as the Situations Vacant columns clearly show, and the fact is that 35+ job-seekers often have a lot more to offer an employer than younger applicants. To begin with, your maturity and experience are definitely plus points, and proven reliability and dependability are also part of your stock in trade. Compared with the young job-hunter you are ahead already.

So, logically you are the choice of preference to a potential employer, but at 35+ you usually have to work harder to prove it. This book shows you how, and it covers the whole job search from start to finish, giving you practical advice on promoting your strengths at every stage, including action checklists, sample letters and CVs.

At 35+ I took stock of my situation, and by following the sequence of activities described – producing letters, CVs, application forms and making telephone calls that got me interviews – I won an appointment to a new job. It can be done. I did it – and you can, too!

1

Changing your Job – at 35+!

So, you're over 35 – perhaps 40, 45 or 50 – and you need to change your job, either through your own volition or through redundancy.

At one time or another nearly everyone wants to change jobs, and for all sorts of reasons, but take care not to make a hasty decision in the heat of the moment, as it is almost certain not to be in your best interests. The decision to make a job change must never be an emotional one, it should only be taken after cool and calculated consideration.

First, you should stand back and take a long, hard look at your situation. Calmly and closely examine the reasons which lie behind your wanting to change, and consider the possible consequences of making a mid-career shift. You must be clear in your mind exactly what it is you wish to do, and what you have to offer a prospective new employer.

If you are forced to move through no choice of your own – perhaps because of an impending round of redundancies or the closure of the firm you have been working for – then the decision has been made for you, but apart from that the way forward is the same.

Likely Reasons for Wanting to Change

One of the most common reasons for wanting to change jobs is a lack of opportunity for personal growth and advancement – in short, you have become bored with the job and you feel it is no longer challenging and stretching you. Maybe you have been meaning to move for months, or even years, but have not quite got around to doing anything about it.

Another reason for wishing to move is a lack of prospects in the company. Your ambitions are no longer being fulfilled by your current position and there is limited scope for promotion within the department or organization. Perhaps, in such circumstances, you believe you have no choice but to look for a job elsewhere.

It could be that the company you work for is in the process of reorganizing itself, merging with or being acquired by another company, and you suspect that your job may disappear as a result – and you want to jump before being pushed.

There are, of course, other reasons and quite often these are age-related, especially for those 35 and older who are reaching the middle of their careers and who are finding the rapid changes in technology harder to keep up with. This is particularly acute in companies shifting towards a younger and more aggressive workforce, and adopting new working practices incorporating part-time work and short-term contracts. This can lead to the feeling that a move must be made now, before it is too late. Perhaps no-one above 40-years-old has been promoted in your company for some time.

The Advantages of Changing

Inevitably, the advantages of change will vary from one person to another according to their individual circumstances. However, most people will find that the main benefit will be one of three universally applicable ones:

- Change can provide you with the opportunity to progress, either in terms of self-development or your career.

- A new job may offer different tasks and activities, challenges and targets to work towards. This may enthuse and invigorate you to work harder and better, and give you a greater sense of achievement.

- The move might be a step up the ladder to a better job with more money and improved terms and conditions, or perhaps a sideways step into another department or division, but one with better prospects for future advancement.

Alternatively, a change of job may be essential to maintain your current status and/or standard of living – all-important if you are trying to cope with the threat or reality of redundancy. However, it is vital that the sense of relief from going for and getting another job – any job! – does not overshadow what it is really like. You need to be sure that it is the right job for you, offering whatever it is you personally want from employment. Initially, you may simply be relieved to be working and at a comparable level, but that advantage alone may not be enough to keep you motivated and happy once the excitement of change has worn off.

If the job is the correct one – and only you can tell if it is – you should enjoy your work, perhaps more than you did before. Whatever it was that you were dissatisfied with – such as a lack of prospects, insufficient challenge, the replacement of more experienced employees by younger part-timers – try to make sure that the same problems don't plague your new organization, so you can now gain fulfilment without feeling threatened by the prospect of being overtaken and left behind.

The Disadvantages of Changing

Similarly, the disadvantages of change will differ from person to person depending on his or her particular situation. Nonetheless, the majority of people will discover that the key drawback for them will be one of the following:

- Whatever it is you are giving up may be considerable, most notably in terms of salary and security for your family. If you want to change jobs voluntarily, perhaps because of a lack of personal development or an absence of prospects, then you ought to think carefully about this, to decide whether or not it is worth leaving. Of course, you may not be moving by choice, having been notified of or suffered redundancy, in which case you will probably be acutely aware of what you are losing.

- Linked to this common disadvantage is the fact that the job you are going (or hoping to go) to may not really be better. Maybe it offers an improved salary and fringe benefits, but fewer prospects, or even none at all in the long term. Possibly, it provides you with challenging, more varied work, but this could be accompanied by increased responsibility and longer hours, with greater levels of pressure and stress involved. It is always very tempting to believe that all of the problems and frustrations that exist in your current workload, type of job or company will be resolved if you move elsewhere. This rarely happens in practice – you usually discover another, but this time unfamiliar, set of difficulties.

- If the prospect is daunting to you, probably the biggest disadvantage of making a move, whatever your age, talents or abilities, is the very process involved. You are going to have to go through the whole job-search/application/interviewing process again, in what is now a fiercely competitive and rapidly changing marketplace. It is not unknown for hundreds of people to apply for a job. Part-time and temporary work, job sharing and short-term contracts are increasingly becoming the norm, and only those applicants who accept this will be successful. You have the skills, knowledge, expertise and the resolve to see it through – but there is a lot of work to do! This book will guide you, but you must have the will to win.

Deciding What You Want to Do

Your planned job change may be within your chosen field, or it may involve a complete change of career. If it is to be a career change, whether the decision to move is yours or not, you need to decide beforehand exactly what it is you now wish to do. At 30, 40 and 50-years-old or more, you may have spent 20-odd years in the same position, company, trade or industry and be absolutely desperate to move. But, instead of just thinking about the type of work you want, it could be time for a complete self-inventory, a review of your personality, likes, dislikes and goals. Only after having established these can you conclude what it is you really want at this turning point in your life.

Your Personality

Begin by considering your general characteristics (both strengths and weaknesses), being as brutally frank as anyone can be when assessing themselves. To focus your thoughts, it may be a good idea to compile a list of 10 or more words or phrases which provide a full description of your personality. As an example, you might note that you are 'a natural leader', 'hardworking' and 'ambitious'. Try to see yourself as others do, listing both positive *and* negative aspects. Perhaps you 'do not suffer fools gladly' and are viewed as being 'serious' and 'lacking in humour'. Be blunt if you want this

TO GO OR STAY?

Changing jobs at any age is a big step, and one which needs to be thought about carefully beforehand. Answering these questions honestly may help you to decide what to do in your situation.

	yes	maybe	no
Are you bored in your current job?	☐	☐	☐
Are your prospects limited or non-existent?	☐	☐	☐
Are you being made redundant?	☐	☐	☐
Has another job opportunity arisen?	☐	☐	☐
Do you have other reasons for wanting to move on?	☐	☐	☐
Are your reasons for wanting to leave both serious and permanent?	☐	☐	☐
Will a change give you the chance to progress personally and/or careerwise?	☐	☐	☐
Will it enable you to maintain your current status and standard of living?	☐	☐	☐
Will you enjoy work more than you do now?	☐	☐	☐
Can you really afford to give up your current salary and security?	☐	☐	☐
Will a new job truly be better, in every respect, and on a long-term basis?	☐	☐	☐
Are you totally prepared to go through the whole job-hunting process, over and over again?	☐	☐	☐

For a green light to make the change, you should be able to say 'yes' to most of these questions. If you cannot do this, then it may be more sensible to stay where you are.

Figure 1.1 To Go or Stay?: An action checklist.

preliminary work to serve its purpose: to enable you to ascertain what's right for you in the future. By way of confirmation, ask a good friend to describe your personality.

Your Likes

Next, you need to contemplate what it is you like, and enjoy doing, by way of work. To do this fully, you might wish to compare notes on paper or on a computer screen under various sub-headings, such as 'trade or industry', 'organization', 'job', 'salary and benefits', 'terms and conditions', 'working environment' and 'location'. You may want to add others appropriate to you. Jot down everything you can think of. For example, under 'organization' you might record that you like working for a small family business or a large corporation – or perhaps you have no particular preference. Concerning 'colleagues', you could put that you like to work with other people, or prefer working alone. Maybe you want to work amongst people with a wide variety of interests and backgrounds, or you would rather mix with those who share your own interests. In making your wish list be as specific as possible.

Your Dislikes

Then, you should mull over your dislikes in relation to work. For easy reference, build up your notes beneath the same sub-headings – 'trade or industry' through 'terms and conditions' and on to 'location'. Again, make a note of anything that comes to mind. As an example, below 'tasks, duties and responsibilities', you might state that you do not want to take on too much responsibility any more – maybe you have had enough of leading people and making key decisions, and now just want a nine-to-five 'let's-go-home-and-forget-all-about-it' type of job. Similarly, under 'location', perhaps you no longer wish to work in a city centre, preferring a move to an out-of-town situation. You may have tired of working at a desk all day surrounded by computer monitors, phones and faxes and wish to make a change to a job which takes you out and about, or one maybe which is computer-free.

Your Goals

After assessing your personality, likes and dislikes as rigorously and as extensively as possible, you should be in a position to spell out exactly what it is you are looking for – the type of trade or industry and organization you want to work in, and the nature of the job and work you wish to do. Obviously, this has to be done in a pragmatic manner. Not surprisingly, many people would like to work a handful of hours each week from home and for a fortune, but relatively few are able to achieve this!

To clarify your thoughts, you may find it helpful to rework the notes that you made about your 'personality', 'likes' and 'dislikes', reorganizing them into three categories – 'essentials', 'desirables' and 'contra-indications' (aspects of the job which would automatically disqualify it from consideration). Perhaps it is essential that you earn a particular salary in order to maintain an acceptable lifestyle. Certain fringe benefits such as healthcare arrangements would be desirable, but their absence would not stop you from pursuing a job. Possibly you have to find employment within a certain locality, so anything outside of that region would need to be rejected immediately. Clearly, the more flexible you are during this process, the greater your chances of success are likely to be. Filling in the form given in Figure 1.2 could be useful at this point.

PROSPECTIVE EMPLOYMENT – THE KEY CRITERIA		
Essential Criteria	Desirable Criteria	Contra-Indications

Figure 1.2 Deciding What You Want to Do: A checklist form.

Recognizing What You Have to Offer

With your mind focused very clearly on your goals, you now need to be aware of precisely what it is you have to offer a new job, prospective employer and/or trade or industry. Having details about your strengths, weaknesses and general circumstances set out in front of you will prove to be invaluable later on when you begin to apply for jobs and have to write letters, compile curricula vitae, complete application forms, and so on.

This information can be used as a database for ready reference purposes, and as a checklist of points to include in and exclude from applications as appropriate.

Your Strengths

It is sensible to start by contemplating the strengths that you can bring to the specific type of work you want to do. Probably the best way of doing this is to make a note of 10 or more strengths that you can think of. To set your thoughts in motion, consider what you have to offer under various sub-headings – physical make up, achievements, abilities and personality, perhaps. You may be able to think of others that are applicable to you. For example, under physical make up, you might record that you have a smart appearance, speak well and are healthy. Similarly, beneath 'abilities' you could note that you have a broad general knowledge and are good with words, and at spelling, grammar and punctuation. Be realistic here, though, if you want this preparatory exercise to be useful when you are seeking work. Ask a friend to suggest some of your strengths as well, as this may reveal qualities of which you weren't aware.

Think, too, about the special strengths that you have because you are an older job-hunter. What are the advantages of being 35 plus? List those advantageous qualities associated with age – greater maturity, patience and financial responsibility, increased confidence when dealing with people, more extensive skills, knowledge and expertise and a proven track record, amongst others. The list is long – you have so much going for you! Be aware of it, and be ready to refer to these strengths when job seeking, creating terrific letters, producing sensational CVs and so on. Mentioning them as and when you can will help to build up a solid, positive impression.

Your Weaknesses

Following this, you should compile a similar list, but this time consisting of your weaknesses, so far as they relate to the job, organization, trade or industry in which you are planning to work. To gather your thoughts, it is a good idea to set out a number of subheadings, such as – 'physical make up', 'achievements', 'abilities' and 'personality', plus any others you can think of that are relevant to you. Under 'achievements', for example, you may note that you do not have certain formal qualifications, and possess limited experience in working with new technology in your field. Below 'personality' you might record – if you are as brutally honest as you ought to be – that you are a loner rather than a team player. This may be a weakness or a strength depending on the nature of the job you want to do. Again, ask a plain-speaking friend to comment, too – especially if you cannot think of many weaknesses!

Consider, as well, any weaknesses (real or perceived) related to your age. The only disadvantage is that older job-hunters are perceived to be set in their ways, reluctant and slow to learn, and less likely to be fit and healthy. You know these to be mistaken perceptions, and when you apply for jobs you must take the positive line by stressing your flexibility and your experience, maturity and reliability – as well as your determination to keep active. Your task is to convince the potential employer that in your case age is not a weakness.

When drafting lists of strengths and weaknesses, take into account that many strengths can be developed and weaknesses eliminated through hard work and effort. For example, formal qualifications may be gained via correspondence or adult education courses, and technology can be mastered through further training and practice.

Your General Circumstances

Invariably, there will be some features you can think of which are neither strengths nor weaknesses, but which need to be recorded somewhere — typically under a sub-heading of 'general circumstances'. Perhaps you might compile a hotch-potch of assorted notes referring to your possession of a mobile phone and fax machine, use of the Internet, and the like. At the moment, all these bits and pieces of information may seem interesting but not directly relevant. That view may change as you progress through the job-hunting process. See the suggested form given in Figure 1.3.

General Strengths	Age-Related Strengths (to promote)	General Weaknesses	Age-Related Weaknesses (to be overcome)	General Circumstances

Figure 1.3 Recognizing What You Have to Offer: A checklist form.

2

Getting Everything Together

Having built up a database of information about your reasons for wanting to change your job; and about your personality, likes, dislikes, strengths, weaknesses and general circumstances – and having established that a job change is right for you – it is time to start looking for new employment. To do this effectively you need to approach the task in the same professional way that you would tackle any major task at work.

To begin with, you should give thought to where you can best learn of vacancies, and the various merits of using the different, and often quite varied, sources of information. Then you need to draft a schedule of action so that you can apply yourself to the process in a systematic and thorough manner. After taking these steps you can move on to identify suitable opportunities.

Learning About Vacancies

There are many ways in which you can find out about vacancies, and you need to decide for yourself where best to concentrate your search. There are the situations vacant advertisements in newspapers and specialist journals. Also, you can contact and put out feelers to friends and associates; or make speculative approaches to selected organizations; or use agencies and consultancies who act as intermediaries between prospective employers and potential employees. A mix of tactics and sources is quite often a good idea.

Job Advertisements

Scanning advertisements is by the far the most common way of finding out about job vacancies. It is estimated that 95 per cent of all job-seekers use this method; and often as their primary source of information. At least you will know that your application will be accepted and read, even welcomed; which may not necessarily be the case with speculative approaches. Also, an advertisement will contain information about the company, job and the type of person required – essential for deciding whether you are well-matched to what is on offer, and a useful source of data if you do apply. Even if you do not, these details – combined with a general trawl through job advertisements – will help you to keep up-to-date with changes and developments within that particular firm, and the trade or industry at large.

However, it is important that you do not restrict yourself to searching for work purely through advertisements, as many would-be job changers do. Only 40 per cent of vacancies are filled in this way. It has to be said that often advertisements are placed in the situations vacant columns of newspapers and magazines some time after the decision to recruit has been made, and in many instances someone has already been pencilled in for the post. This is especially so in organizations operating within the public sector which are obliged to advertise vacancies by expectation or tradition, although the selection decision may be a foregone conclusion. Even if this is not the case, your application is likely to be in competition with dozens, if not hundreds, of others, thereby narrowing your chances of success, unless you can produce an exceptional application.

The national, local and specialist Press are not the only source of job advertisements. It is possible that opportunities are made known in your existing workplace. These might include memoranda circulated in wage packets or to heads of departments, or items in house magazines and newsletters and on company noticeboards. Externally, advertisements can be found on notices at factory gates, or can be heard about on the radio and through the Teletext pages on television. Each source tends to be well-known for its particular category and level of job advertisements, and each has its advantages and disadvantages.

When job-hunting, it is tempting to look everywhere and anywhere for employment, but this can be soul-destroying, simply because some sources of job advertisements are less suited to the older job-seeker, however good they are. It may be best to give priority to those that offer the best prospects for success. Sources are summarized in Figure 2.1 'Sources of Job Advertisements: A checklist for older job-seekers' (see overleaf). You may find it useful to look at this before going any further.

	Types of Job	Advantages
Memoranda	Tend to be used to fill part-time, temporary, administrative and junior positions.	Suggests vacancies may be taken in-house, which reduces competition and improves chances.
Internal Notices	Used primarily for part-time, short term, clerical and low-level positions.	Likely that vacancies will be filled from within, thus avoiding extensive, external competition.
In-house Publications	May be used to advertise middle-ranking and senior positions in this or other divisions of the company.	Limited competition if the jobs are to be taken in-house. Extensive background data available too.
Word of Mouth	Those of direct relevance to the particular job seeker, hopefully.	Possibility of substantial, inside information and a personal recommendation from the person providing the information.
External Notices	Tend to be used to advertise part-time, temporary, retail, factory and lower level positions.	Easy to monitor availability if sites are checked regularly.
Job Centres	Sales, clerical and lower level jobs in most instances. Some part-time and temporary opportunities.	Easy to access and keep up-to-date. Good source of help and advice, too.
Employment Agencies	Individual agencies specialize in different jobs, levels and sectors.	Personal, one-to-one service, and often a real desire to match job hunters with an appropriate job. Support services available, too.
The Press	All types, depending on local, national or trade orientation.	Easy to identify suitable publications, and access on appropriate days. Good information given about the jobs.
The Radio	Tends to be used for mass recruitment.	Can be listened to during free time; requires little effort to monitor.
TV (Teletext)	All types, but most often sales, clerical and computing.	Easy to check and keep up-to-date (if Teletext TV owned). Seen as a modern recruiting method, used by sharp job-hunters.

Disadvantages	Prospects
Likely to be circulated to everyone. Internal pressures may exist; to stand, not to stand, to back someone else.	Fair – if it is the type of job you want.
Jobs may be earmarked for a particular person; others not encouraged to apply.	Reasonable – if this is the work you want to do.
More likely to be advertised externally as well; so competition could be fierce.	Good – at least you will have a head start on outside applicants.
Some key information may not be passed on, or could be interpreted incorrectly.	Good – often worth pursuing vigorously.
Extensive competition; and jobs often filled on a first-come-first-served basis. May have to check daily, which is time consuming.	Mixed – Perhaps not a top priority.
All job-hunters use this source, so stiff competition. Quality of service can vary.	Mixed – perhaps better suited to those seeking junior and/or low grade posts.
Suitability and quality of agencies vary. Some charge for registration and assistance.	Considerable – if right agencies approached. A much underrated source.
All job-seekers use this source, so intense competition. Need to react promptly and well. Some jobs already earmarked at this stage.	Fair – if an excellent application is made, but an uphill struggle in many cases. Never use in isolation.
Difficult to note down information quickly enough, especially as advertisements unexpected.	Poor – used infrequently by recruiters. Often overrated.
Access depends on possession of teletext TV. Use by recruiters is still limited.	Good – you will be seen to be at the cutting edge!

Naturally, your search of the job advertisements will concentrate mostly on the media and other sources which specialize in the level of employment and the trades and industries that match your needs. Therefore, if you are a works manager, for example, you might look on factory gates and at local newspapers, whereas a management executive may concentrate instead on certain national newspapers, which advertise specific types and grades of job on particular days. Nevertheless, it can be beneficial to study some or all of the remaining sources just to keep yourself abreast of what is happening in the locality to firms and industry in general. It all helps to give you a broad picture of what is going on, and a better chance to spot opportunities that are worth following up.

Networking

This is the process of making yourself, your availability and your job requirements known to a network of contacts – whether family, friends or (more likely) business associates and other people suggested by them. As an older job-hunter you have a distinct advantage here – you've been around longer and know more people! A well-timed approach can sometimes result in your being individually considered for an up-coming vacancy, and there may be possibilities to gain interim work in a freelance capacity. Although suitable vacancies may not be available at the time of approach, networking still enables you to maintain and build friendly relations with prospective future employers, and to obtain feedback on your application, the firm's activities, the state of the market *and* perhaps expand your network through additional recommendations from your existing contacts.

As with job-hunting via advertisements, it is essential that networking is just part of your overall programme of job-search activities, rather than being your only avenue of approach. Your chances of success are much improved by adopting a broad mix of tactics instead of a favoured one or two. Networking tends to be popular because it is relatively easy and convenient to carry out; but it does have its shortcomings. It is important to be aware of the limits of each contact's knowledge, area of activity and ability to help you find a job. Very few people have the power to hire and fire, and most contacts will be able to do little more than introduce you to the right people. If you are too forward – asking friends for a good recommendation, or a job, even – then it may damage personal and business relationships, perhaps irreparably.

Networking can be carried out in a variety of ways, but the usual method is to write to your contacts. If you use the phone, be sure it is at a time which is convenient for the person you are calling. The least popular way – but one which can be used if you know contacts well enough – is to visit them in person for a face-to-face meeting. The suitability of each method will vary according to the particular situation and has its own mix of advantages and disadvantages depending on your circumstances, as indicated in Figure 2.2 'Making Contact: A checklist for mature job-hunters' (see overleaf).

MAKING CONTACT

It is debatable whether to contact people by phone, letter or in person during job-hunting activities. Although each and every situation is different and should be treated as such, it is useful to have some idea of the pluses and minuses of the various options.

Method	Pluses	Minuses
Phone	<ul><li>Quick and informal. Recipient may be more frank 'off-the-record'.</li><li>Older job-seekers able to converse more fluently and impressively.</li></ul>	<ul><li>Difficult to judge the 'right' time to call: when the recipient is free and willing to chat.</li><li>Contents and direction of conversation hard to predict – substantial preparation required.</li><li>Age issue may be raised, and needs to be handled carefully and in a positive manner.</li></ul>
Letter	<ul><li>Sender is able to decide on exact appearance, contents and style. Has total control.</li><li>Age and other potential shortcomings can be excluded.</li><li>Mature job-hunters have greater experience of letter writing than younger ones.</li></ul>	<ul><li>No chance of immediate feedback, nor opportunity to answer queries.</li><li>Difficult to know exactly when and how received, and what is then done with it – may be damaged in transit, lost or overlooked on arrival.</li></ul>
In Person	<ul><li>Prompt and immediate – shows confidence and positive attitude.</li><li>Allows the property, the person being visited and other aspects of the visit to be assessed.</li><li>Job-seekers of 35-plus have the experience and ability to convey a good impression.</li></ul>	<ul><li>Not easy to judge the 'best' time to visit – when the recipient is available and happy to talk.</li><li>Unlikely to be practical if the recipient is located some distance away.</li><li>Time consuming and requires substantial effort.</li><li>Outcome hard to estimate – needs extensive preparation.</li><li>Age immediately apparent – can lead to rejection if it is an issue.</li></ul>

Figure 2.2 Making Contact: A checklist for mature job-hunters.

Your network will consist mainly of those people who may actually be able to offer you a job, but it should also include those who may know of others who can provide you with work, either now or in the future, and are willing to give you their names and details or pass your information on to them. Also you may wish to get in touch with people who are well-informed about what is taking place in your area of activity, and can supply you with advice about what is worth pursuing. Time consuming though it can be to contact (and keep in touch with) your network, it is always worth building this into your job-search programme, as many jobs are filled in this 'who you know, not what you know' way. It is estimated that more than 50 per cent of jobs are gained by personal recommendation, rather than through response to advertising. Make sure you access this hidden jobs market.

'On-Spec' Approaches

In many respects, speculative approaches to specific individuals in authority within organizations you would like to work for are comparable to those you make to people you know within your network of contacts. If you make contact at an appropriate moment – when a job is about to become vacant or be created – you may be able to jump to the front of a queue of potential applicants, or even be appraised on your own without competition. Even if work is not available, on-spec approaches can still be advantageous as they serve to establish relations with would-be employers, generate discussions on prospective jobs and your suitability, and the ever-developing and changing marketplace in which you are seeking employment. Sometimes, they can lead to suggestions to get in touch with other people who may have opportunities available and are seeking staff with your blend of skills, knowledge and experience.

However, the main difference between on-spec approaches and networking – and it is a significant one – is that you do not personally know the people you are contacting on a speculative basis. Unless you are really thorough in your research, a proportion of approaches will be made to the wrong people; those whose job titles may imply they are responsible for recruiting for certain jobs, but whose roles do not include this. Even when you approach the right individuals within chosen organizations, there will be no existing goodwill, and you will have to work hard to overcome that almost automatic response of 'not another begging letter'. This is hardly surprising, since managing directors of companies are reported to receive, on average, about 50 on-spec letters each week.

Like networking, on-spec contact can be made by letter or by phone, and there is the alternative – although one which is used relatively infrequently in this approach – of going to see them, asking for a face-to-face talk about you, what you have to offer and the type of work you are looking for. How appropriate each of these methods is will depend upon the given situation. They all have their pros and cons, as highlighted in that 'Making Contact' checklist on page 22.

The people who are going to be placed on your list of on-spec contacts should be those responsible for recruiting staff for the type of work you want to do, in the companies you would most like to work for in your preferred trade or industry. Obviously, it is sensible to prioritize what might be a fairly lengthy list of names, putting at the top the ones who are most likely to help. Alternatively, you may decide to prioritize according to how much you wish to work for each particular firm – or a mix of these two approaches.

Agencies and Consultancies

Perhaps the least used way of finding a job is through those agencies and consultancies which act as intermediaries between an employer and a prospective employee. Only 10 per cent of job-hunters access this source. Using a go-between when looking for work does have its advantages. Some will be responsible for screening applicants and passing on candidates to be interviewed by the would-be employer themselves. Often, this screening is rather cursory in nature, but it may mean you can by-pass the letter/application form/telephone call stage, and go straight for an interview.

Also, many intermediaries will offer advice and assistance in various aspects of job-hunting, such as compiling a CV and interviewing techniques. You may find this invaluable. If there is nothing available now or you are unsuccessful this time round, then the majority of agencies and consultancies will retain your details on their register, and contact you as and when suitable opportunities arise.

Not surprisingly, there are disadvantages as well. Being granted an interview almost automatically may seem advantageous initially, but will appear less so if your hopes are subsequently dashed and you find out that nearly everyone who was only half interested or suitable was treated in this way. Some of these go-betweens will charge you for the services they provide – such as advising you how to write a letter of application and what to say in a phone conversation, and keeping your details on their database for future reference. You may be happy to pay for this if – and it is sometimes a big if – it leads to an offer of the right job in an appropriate company. Often it does not.

There are a number of different types of agency and consultancy – including job centres, employment bureaux and recruitment consultants – all of which you should consider contacting. There also exist executive search consultants, who might even get in touch with *you* if you are known to be very good at your job and they are 'headhunting' on behalf of another company for someone with your experience and abilities. Each type of agency or consultancy tends to deal with their own specific range of categories and levels of job, and naturally you will concentrate on those specializing in the area of employment you are interested in. For example, if you are seeking a sales job, you might use job centres, whereas a computer programmer would perhaps concentrate on employment agencies. See Figure 2.1 'Sources of Job Advertisements: A checklist for older job-seekers', pp.18–19.

If you have time, it is also useful to liaise with other less apparently relevant agencies and consultancies, so that you build up as much knowledge as possible about what is currently happening in the job market.

Drafting your Job-Search Schedule

To find the rewarding employment you seek, you must be prepared to devote a lot of time and energy to the quest – perhaps two hours each evening if you are in work, or three to four hours per day if you are not. Drawing up a plan of action can help you to use your time profitably and channel your energies in the most efficient way. You should also budget your working time, and keep records and notes which will be of use to you during your job search. Be sure to use your free time sensibly so that each day you are relaxed and ready to tackle the task with enthusiasm.

Your Working Time

To begin with, you should list all tasks that you need to carry out to learn about potentially suitable job opportunities. You can do this under four key headings – reading advertisements, networking, approaching organizations and using agencies. Each of these separate lists may be fairly lengthy. For example, 'reading advertisements' may include references to 'looking at the company newsletter', 'checking the noticeboard in the staff rest-room', 'scanning Teletext pages on television', and so on, as appropriate to your particular situation. A job can be found in all sorts of ways and from the most unlikely sources, so you need to do this original listing as thoroughly as possible, so that you do not overlook anything that is relevant to you, and might help you to succeed.

Having done this, you should go through each listed task in turn to decide how often it needs to be dealt with. For example, Teletext pages might have to be checked every day for changes and developments, the company newsletter once a week and the trade magazine once a month on publication. You may wish to attend to these tasks at specific times – perhaps scanning Teletext as soon as you wake up in the morning, the newsletter on Friday afternoon when it is printed and the trade magazine on publication on the third Thursday in the month, or whenever. Prioritizing will be necessary. For instance, you may have 20 contacts in your network, 30 organizations and 30 agencies and consultancies to contact, and you may wish to approach these in batches of perhaps five at a time, starting with the ones which are most likely to be responsive and working down the list from there.

This data – tasks, dates, times and so on – can then be transferred to your 'job-search schedule'. This can be a large piece of card, a diary or (preferably) a wall-chart, which shows the coming days weeks *and* months – be realistic, and plan to be hunting for at least three to six months to get the right job for you. Then note on it what you have to do each day, week and month, as appropriate. Do this in pencil so that you can amend errors and make other changes as you go along. It is up to you how you arrange and set out this schedule; the important thing is that you do it, as it will bring organization and structure to your activities. As you progress, you can also use it to note down interviews, which will occur with increasing frequency, it is hoped, as you become more adept at your approaches. An example of a job-search schedule is given in Figure 2.3 overleaf.

28 Your Mid-Career Shift

DAYS \ WEEKS	w/c	w/c	w/c	w/c	w/c	w/c	w/c	w/c	w/c	w/c	w/c	w/c
MONDAY												
TUESDAY												
WEDNESDAY												
THURSDAY												
FRIDAY												
SATURDAY												
SUNDAY												

Figure 2.2 Job-Search Schedule Form: An example.

To tackle the whole job-hunting process thoroughly, you may find it useful to transfer data from this (wall-mounted) schedule into a diary on a weekly basis. You can then work through each day's checklist of activities in turn. It is also sensible to have close at hand a plentiful supply of sticky labels on which you can scribble notes and reminders – 'Call Nick again in a month – may have some news then.' These can then be switched to the wall chart and diary at a later, more convenient, moment.

By way of a caution: it is tempting to become so involved with filling in charts, diaries and forms, that you do not do much else. You can end up spending all your time planning what you are going to do instead of actually doing it. Note what you have to record, quickly – then get on with job-hunting!

Records

Probably the easiest way of keeping proper records of your job-search activities is to do so under those four key headings of reading advertisements, networking, approaching selected organizations and using agencies and consultancies. You will find it helpful to draw up A4-sized forms for each area of activity which enable you to note, for example, where and when you saw a job advertisement, the job title and any reference number, the name of the company, the type of application made and the date and its progress from there – for example: 'rejection', 'invitation to an interview', 'an interview', 'rejection', 'offer'. Examples of forms for all of the different categories are given in Figures 2.4 to 2.7, pages 30–5.

30 Your Mid-Career Shift

adverts / progress	source	date	job title	company	type of application	date of application

Figure 2.4 Job Advertisements Form: An example.

Getting Everything Together 31

acknowl-edgement	rejection	invitation to interview	date of interview	letter of rejection/ offer	outcome	additional comments

contacts / progress	date of contact	type of contact	outcome	follow-up	date of contact

Figure 2.5 Networking Form: An example.

Getting Everything Together 33

type of contact	outcome	follow-up	date of contact	type of contact	outcome	follow-up

34 Your Mid-Career Shift

organizations / progress	reason for approach	date of approach	type of approach	response	follow-up	additional comments

Figure 2.6 On-Spec Approaches Form: An example.

agencies/ consultancies / progress	cause for approach	date of approach	type of approach	outcome	follow-up	additional comments

Figure 2.7 *Agencies and Consultancies Form: An example.*

The forms can then be put into four separate files, marked 'Advertisements', 'Contacts', 'On-spec Approaches' and 'Agencies and Consultancies'. You should keep originals or copies of all documentation relating to your numerous applications. As an example, you would retain the job advertisement cutting, a photocopy of the completed application form, notes made during a subsequent telephone conversation, and so forth. Doing this may take up your time and effort and use up space, but it will prove to be invaluable if you need to refer to something later on, perhaps immediately prior to an interview or in three months' time when a firm contacts you unexpectedly about a forthcoming vacancy. It happens, so you need to be prepared for it by keeping everything of any significance.

Assorted Notes

It is advisable to retain all of your job-hunting materials together for quick and easy reference. Therefore, you will find it beneficial to have another file which includes all the details you noted down earlier. With one form about your personality, likes, dislikes and goals and another one recording your strengths, weaknesses and general circumstances, these should complete the information needed to pursue a job-search programme successfully.

Clearly, it is important that you keep all your records and notes somewhere safe and secure. Ideally, you will have a separate area or room where you can attend to your job-search activities away from distractions. If you have a desk, telephone answering machine and fax machine, all the better. It is useful to have the sort of answering machine which you can call into whilst you are out to check incoming messages. Carry a phone card with you at all times in case a coin-operated telephone is unavailable.

Your Free Time

If you feel trapped in a dreary job or are unemployed, finding a new job is a high priority, but it needs to be kept in proportion. Two to four hours of intense, thorough activity each day for three to six months should be sufficient to get you the job you want. Don't forget that you have a lot to offer an employer – self-belief is a key ingredient in successful job searches. Use the rest of your time wisely – read a good newspaper to keep informed on both general news and business news, eat a proper breakfast, lunch and dinner to maintain your health and energy, and exercise regularly and get out and about, for a walk, a drink or a trip to the cinema. Forget it all for a while – and come back feeling refreshed and raring to go the next day!

Identifying Suitable Opportunities

If all goes well, you will learn from a range of sources about a large number of vacancies that currently exist or are to be created in the near future. However, you do not want to waste your time, effort and money on applying for jobs unless they will provide you with what you want, *and* you can offer what the respective employers are looking for. To decide which ones are worth pursuing, you need to research the trade or industry, firm, job and the type of employee required, for each and every vacancy that becomes known to you and seems to be potentially suitable.

The Trade or Industry

Begin by jotting down a list of questions you want answered about a particular trade or industry (or sector of it), the answers to which will enable you to judge if it is the right one for you. For example: What is the trade or industry? Who are the key players within it?

Who are the customers? Whereabouts are they? What are their wants and needs? What do they buy, when and how? Who are the main suppliers? Where are they, and what do they do? What are their main features, strengths and weaknesses? How are they doing? Who are the representative bodies? Whereabouts are they? What exactly do they do? Who else is involved in the trade or industry? What are the influences upon it, for good and bad? Is the trade or industry expanding, static or contracting? Perhaps most important of all, does it welcome the over 35s?

Most of these questions can be answered easily through your own knowledge or that of other people, such as business colleagues and acquaintances, customers and rivals – or even friends and relatives. The remaining queries should be resolved by simple research – reading the job advertisement carefully, if appropriate, studying local, national and trade newspapers, magazines and journals, perusing trade bodies' literature and working through local, national and trade reports, surveys and statistics from chambers of commerce, councils, government and the like. You may find useful reference books in libraries as well (see the Further Reading section at the end of this book).

The Firm

Next, you need to turn your attention to the business that may employ you, to calculate whether you are well-suited to each other. Again, the best way of doing this is to make a list of questions – such as: Who owns it? How is it structured? What do the various departments and employees do? How many people are employed there? Where is it based? Are there any other outlets? If so, where and how are they organized and run? What does the firm do exactly? What products and services does it offer? What are its goals? What is its reputation like? Is it a growing, static or declining business in terms of number of employees and turnover? What is its market share? Also, as important as any other question, is it known as a youthful, aggressive firm, or as one which accepts older employees, and in positions of responsibility?

You may be able to answer most of these questions from your own accumulated general knowledge, although you must be careful not to mistake biased opinions and gossip for facts and the truth. Other queries may be answered through straightforward research. Look at the job advertisement, if applicable, along with the organization's own literature, such as annual reports, sales brochures, catalogues and price lists – making sure you distinguish between statements of fact and sales hype. Talk to people who work (or have worked) for the firm, and customers, rival concerns and trade associations, too – although some of their comments may be rather subjective. Visit the business if you are able to, and look around. Check the local, national and trade Press for recent and up-to-date news and information. You may also find some helpful reference books in your local library.

The Job

There will inevitably be much you want to know about the job that you may be applying for and could be offered. List the questions you have – for example: What is the job title? Where is the job located? What is its purpose? Who would you be responsible to, and what would you be responsible for? What are the main tasks, duties and responsibilities? What standards need to be reached, and maintained? What are the targets? How does the job fit into the department and organization? What are the working conditions like? What is the social environment like? What are the salary and fringe benefits? What are the terms and conditions of the job? What are the prospects for transfers and promotions? Also, of key importance find out whether there are any stated or implied age restrictions on the job?

Of course, you may have some knowledge of the job already because you currently work in a similar capacity or are employed in the same organization and are aware of what is going on around you. This basic understanding can be developed through elementary research – reading the job advertisement, making preliminary phone calls to whoever is responsible for recruitment, looking at the firm's promotional materials, chatting to the person who is leaving (if possible), their colleagues, acquaintances and anyone else who has something relevant to say about this particular job, or comparable employment elsewhere.

Perhaps the most helpful source of information here is a job description, which should be provided to you by the business, on request. This document sets out key details of the job, such as its title, the job titles of those employees who the job holder is responsible to and for, plus its purpose, tasks and duties. An example is given in Figure 2.8 opposite. Although this is drawn up by the firm for its own reference purposes during recruitment and selection processes and beyond, it can be equally useful to you, enabling a much fuller understanding of the job to be built up.

	JOB DESCRIPTION
Job Title:	Sales Representative (East Anglian Region)
Responsible to:	Sales Manager (southern Sales, United Kingdom)
Purpose:	To maximize sales of nursery products and associated goods within East Anglia.
Tasks:	To call on existing customers in accordance with the monthly rota to obtain sales orders.
	To call on prospective customers as requested by them or by the Sales Manager to take sales orders.
	To submit sales orders on a weekly basis in accordance with company procedures.
	To maintain accurate and up-to-date sales records in accordance with company procedures.
	To attend monthly sales meetings at head office in London, and on other occasions as required by the Sales Manager.
	To complete any other sales-related tasks as directed by the Sales Manager.
Prepared by:	Peter Ramsden
Date:	28 June 1996

Figure 2.8 Job Description: An example.

The Type of Employee Required

You then have to consider precisely who it is the business is looking for to fill the vacancy. As before, the most sensible way of approaching this is to jot down all the questions you can think of that need to be answered. For example: What should the ideal employee be like physically (if appropriate) in terms of appearance, speech and health? What educational qualifications, training and work experience are called for? How about general and specific aptitudes – a good memory perhaps, and/or a head for figures? What about personality? What interests should they have, if relevant – literary or artistic ones perhaps? What about their general circumstances? In particular, is age an issue here?

If you already do a job of this nature or are familiar with it, you will probably have a good idea of the type of person needed to do it well. This knowledge can be increased by basic research – talking to whoever is in charge of recruiting, reading the company's promotional literature, speaking to the person who is departing and those people who come into contact with this or similar work on a regular or occasional basis. Perusing various publications may be of benefit to you as well.

By far the best source of assistance here is an employee specification, also known as a job-, person- or personnel specification. Sometimes, this will be given to you by the firm, if requested. It will specify the skills, knowledge, experience and other attributes needed to do the job effectively. Often, requirements will be grouped together in terms of essential and desirable criteria. Such a document may even include contra-indicators, and if any of these apply, a candidate will be rejected automatically. A recent prison sentence for a serious crime is a typical contra-indicator. An example of an employee specification is given in Figure 2.9. If such a document is unavailable, even after being requested, you should be able to calculate its contents by looking at each part of the job description in turn and asking yourself what qualities would be required to carry out that task, duty or responsibility properly.

EMPLOYEE SPECIFICATION	
Job Title:	Sales Representative (East Anglian Region)
The Job Holder:	Must be of Smart Appearance
	Must speak clearly without speech impediments
	Should have previous experience of face-to-face selling
	Should have some knowledge of the nursery trade
	Must have a telephone and facsimile machine
	Must reside in or close to East Anglia
	Must have five years' driving experience
	Must have a clean driving licence
Prepared by:	Peter Ramsden
Date:	28 June 1996

Figure 2.9 Employee Specification: An example.

The Decision: To Apply or Not

Having discovered all you need to know about the trade or industry, firm, job and the type of employee required, you should stand back, mull over all this information and ask yourself two questions. The first question: Is this what I want? You need to consider whether this opportunity suits your personality, matches your likes and dislikes and will fulfil your goals. The second question is: Can I offer what the firm wants? You must contemplate whether your strengths, weaknesses and general circumstances are likely to be acceptable to the organization, or not. If either of the responses is 'no', then it may be advisable to look elsewhere, rather than waste everyone's time, effort and money by pressing on. If the answers are 'yes', you should proceed – and you also now have a huge database of background information to use during the application process. You will find this invaluable as you go ahead.

Do be especially conscious here that if the trade or industry and firm is particularly youth-orientated, then you are going to have to work that much harder to overcome the stereotyped image of older job-hunters, and succeed. Your time and energy may be better employed directed towards more receptive organizations in other sectors. Similarly, if a job advertisement makes it clear that the type of employee required should be a certain age then – unless you are in or within a few years of the suggested range – you will find it difficult to be accepted for what you are, rather than what you are perceived to be. Your time is valuable, so concentrate instead on more promising opportunities.

3

Creating Terrific Letters

As an older job-hunter you really have a great chance to get off to a flying start when writing letters. After all, no-one knows how old you are – unless you give the game away by stating your age or using outdated words and expressions – so you can set out to make such an impact that, by the time you meet, any possible age disadvantage may well be discounted. Start by considering the types of letter that might have to be written, before going on to think carefully about gathering information to put in them, composing the contents and submitting letters in the most effective manner.

Types of Letter

The most common type of job-hunting letter is written in response to an advertisement, and it will usually be sent with a curriculum vitae detailing your skills, knowledge and experience to date. However, your comprehensive job-search programme will also involve other types of letter – in particular those to contacts in your network, to organizations you would like to work for and to agencies and consultancies acting as go-betweens. All of these types of letter must be considered individually prior to contemplating the more general dos and don'ts of letter writing.

Letters to Job Advertisers

Letters must be sent to job advertisers *only* if the advertisement states that applications should be made in this way. If you submit a letter when the advertiser has asked you specifically to apply for and complete an application form or telephone a particular person, then it is likely that your letter will be disposed of straightaway. The advertiser does not have the time nor the inclination to study applications which differ from the norm, and from job seekers who cannot follow clear instructions. So, always do precisely what the advertisement indicates you should do. Also, it is important to note that some advertisers want letters of application; others require letters with curricula vitae, timetabling your life to date. A letter of application may be two pages long, and fairly detailed. A letter with a CV is no more than a covering letter, perhaps highlighting one or two key points, with the remaining information in the accompanying curriculum vitae.

Both types of letter should follow a similar sequence of points. Begin by stating why you are writing, what job you are applying for and where you saw the advertisement for it. This helps to immediately focus the reader's attention, telling them exactly what the letter is about. Also, bear in mind that larger employers will inevitably be advertising numerous jobs at the same time, so if you do not specify the one that you want, you may find that your letter goes into a centralized pool of on-spec enquiries received by the personnel department and will not be considered on this occasion. Indicating where the advertisement was seen can further help to identify the vacancy, and enables the advertiser to judge how effective that source of advertising has been.

Next, you should provide some concise information about yourself; ideally, your background and general strengths, which should be those that are best associated with this job, company, trade or industry. In a letter of application, these details may span two or three paragraphs, each dealing with a separate point (or linked ones). In a much briefer, covering letter, you should do no more than mention two or three of your main attributes in one succinct paragraph; these will act as a taster of what's included in your curriculum vitae and, it is hoped, will persuade the reader to keep on looking through your letter and the CV that has been submitted with it.

Often it is a good idea to follow this by stating why you want the job – perhaps it is an upward move either within your own company or another one, or a sideways move which will lead to further, accelerated progress in due course. Lots of positive (and complimentary) words and expressions can be used here, with mentions of opportunities to progress, achieve, fulfil potential and the like. Even if you want the job for what might be considered to be negative reasons – you've just been or are about to be made redundant – you should still concentrate on the major attractions of this job, company, trade or industry and how it can fulfil, develop you, and so on. At this stage, you do not want to draw attention to anything remotely negative, weak or detrimental. Don't give them the chance to reject you. Keep this paragraph bright, upbeat and enthusiastic.

You should indicate what it is you can bring to this post – in effect, matching very specific strengths to the particular requirements of the job. In a letter of application you might do this over three or four paragraphs, showing how each requirement tallies with some practical experience from your past; probably obtained from your current or most recent employment. For a covering letter, you might simply summarize those specific qualities that you possess which relate directly to the job you are applying for. Again, these will highlight what is set out in your curriculum vitae, and may keep the reader's interest in the prospect of what will be found within it.

The final paragraph – of either version of this letter – must state what you want to happen next; to be telephoned for a discussion or to be written to with an invitation to an interview. Be bold here – make it clear what you want! Encourage the reader to concur by referring to that supporting and explanatory CV and/or giving your telephone number or enclosing a stamped, addressed envelope, as appropriate. Make it as easy as possible for the reader to respond as required, by providing whatever is needed to generate that response. A suggested letter of application and covering letter are reproduced in Figures 3.1 and 3.2 below.

Dear Mr Jacobs

I write to apply for the post of companies researcher, as advertised in today's Daily News.

At present, I am working as a researcher/writer at Hopkirk and Sons, a small market research agency in Felstone, Suffolk. This involves researching local firms via direct contact and additional field and disk research, and producing sales brochures and associated literature for them. I am responsible for approximately 12 projects each year, and for co-ordinating all aspects of researching and writing them, including the use of freelance researchers on an 'as and when' required basis.

To do this job successfully requires self-initiative, the ability to work well with people, to organize and schedule tasks in an efficient and effective manner and not least, to work to tight deadlines. Excellent writing skills are needed, too, in order to produce high quality publications. I have received five commendations for my work in the past year, copies of which are attached for your attention.

I am applying for your job because I am looking to progress from working on local accounts to those of a national and international nature. I have done all that I can do in Suffolk and am now seeking to develop my potential further. I believe that this job in a growing company such as Matthews and Corbett offers me that opportunity.

I possess the skills and expertise to make a success of this job. I have more than the two years' research and editorial experience that you are looking for, and in relevant areas. In the past six months I have worked on projects for 'Harlows', 'Greersons' and 'Parkinson-Betts', amongst others. I am also fully familiar with relevant source materials for companies; part of my job involves visiting Companies House on a regular basis, for example.

My spoken and written English are excellent; an example of one of my company brochures is enclosed, for which I won an Anglia Business Writing Award in 1995. I am also fluent in both French and Spanish. My wife is French, and I have been studying Spanish at adult education classes over the past three years, and completed my diploma in July. A copy of this is attached.

I would like to meet you to discuss this vacancy and my application for it in more detail. I am free all next week, and would be happy to come to London to see you whenever it is most convenient for you.

My telephone number is 01832 821 616, and I look forward to hearing from you shortly.

Yours sincerely,
Malcolm Fox

Figure 3.1 Letter of Application: An example.

Dear Miss Pergelly

Re: Sale Representative Vacancy (Home Counties)

I write to apply for the above vacancy, as advertised in Office Equipment News *published today. As requested, I enclose my curriculum vitae for your attention.*

As you will see, I am an experienced sales representative in the trade, having worked for an office equipment wholesaler for the past five years. I am, of course, very familiar with your company and products.

I am looking to change jobs because of the forthcoming merger between Abbots and Baileys which is causing considerable uncertainty at the moment, with numerous redundancies being anticipated by the workforce.

I note from your advertisement that the successful applicant will cover Southern England and be responsible for servicing existing accounts and generating new ones. I already cover this territory, and service 125 accounts. The company had 48 accounts in this area when I joined them.

I very much want to work for Denehams because it is a dynamic, growing company, and the job offers me the new challenge that I am seeking. I trust you will wish to take the matter further, and will call me shortly. My telephone number is 01716 600060.

Yours sincerely,
Tessa Hutton

Figure 3.2 Covering Letter: An example.

Letters to Contacts

Letters to contacts within your job-search network may be sent if you feel this is likely to be more productive in the first instance than a telephone call, or a face-to-face meeting – often it will be, as it can be difficult to make contact with a busy person by phone and/or arrange a meeting for what may be little more than a general conversation at this time. Although these letters can be divided into two categories – to those people you know and to others who have been recommended – the approach should be much the same (except in their tone, which may vary somewhat between friendliness and formality).

Start by explaining why you are making contact. For instance: to ask to be considered for a job which you understand is about to be created or become vacant in that company; to seek information on prospective opportunities there or at similar organizations; to request your details are circulated to their associates who may be able to help you; or to seek names and addresses of people whom you can subsequently approach for work. Do ensure that you begin in a clear and businesslike manner – too many letters from younger applicants tend to be vague and circumspect, with their writers apparently too embarrassed to say what they want: a job! As a result the recipient is unsure of what is required, and does not respond as anticipated.

If you are writing to ask to be taken into consideration for a job, then the rest of the letter should be along similar lines to that to a job advertiser – information about you, why you want the post and what you can offer. In contact letters of a more general nature you should explain what type of position you are seeking, and in which kind of organization, trade or industry. The more specific you are, the easier it will be for the recipient to think of possible suitable opportunities, associates who may be in a position to assist, and so forth. It is usually unwise – unless you know the contact really well

– to indicate why you are job-hunting. Avoid creating questions and concerns where none exist. If the recipient is that interested, they can contact you.

After stating what you are looking for, sketch out what you have to offer – one or two paragraphs summarizing your specific strengths as they relate to this type of job, company, trade or industry. These will serve to refresh a known contact's memory and give them some key facts to pass on to their associates. Also, they will act to highlight your main strengths to those people who do not know you personally – contacts of contacts – and who wish to find out more about you. If you then put a curriculum vitae in with your letter, these new contacts can build on this knowledge, by reading about what you have done to date.

Conclude in much the same way that you would in a letter to a job advertiser, setting out what you want to be done now – to meet to discuss a soon-to-be-created post, to chat on the phone about potential opportunities, to circulate copies of your CV to their contacts, or to fax you a list of useful names and telephone numbers. Always help them to assist you by indicating you are free to meet at a time which suits them, and even including copies of your curriculum vitae for circulation purposes. Suggested wording for this kind of letter is given in Figure 3.3 opposite.

Dear Jeremy

I write to ask you for a favour – would you be so kind as to pass on my details to anyone you know who may be looking for a copywriter?

As you will be aware, Thousetts is in the process of closing down and I will be looking for alternative employment from 1 June. Ideally, I am seeking work as a copywriter in an organization within our industry, although I would be happy to change if the right opportunity arises. I am also flexible on both location and salary.

To give you some facts and figures to pass on – I have worked for Thousetts for nine years, and have been involved closely with the award-winning 'Kingfisher' advertising campaign (1994) as well as the hugely popular 'Domino' and 'Retruch' advertising campaigns in 1995 and 1996 respectively. I won the company's 'UK Copywriter of the Year Award 1996', following two successive years of commendations.

To make it easier for you to help me, I enclose 10 copies of my curriculum vitae for circulation. Please let me know if you need any more. Meantime, my grateful thanks for your assistance.

Yours sincerely
Debbie Riseborough

Figure 3.3 Networking Letter: An example.

Letters to Selected Organizations

'On-spec' letters are probably the hardest job-hunting letters to write. Large companies receive dozens of them each day, and nearly every one fails to progress beyond a cursory glance and a standard 'we'll-keep-it-on-file' response. Usually, this is because 'on-spec' letters are little more than circulars, written to nobody about nothing in particular! You are going to get your letter read through by writing specifically to the person who is responsible for recruiting for that type of job, in that department or company. Most 'on-specs' end up in the bin because they are addressed to the company or the wrong person, who is unlikely to be bothered to hand it on to the right person.

As with the other examples, open your letter by outlining why you are writing – in essence, to enquire about current or future job opportunities in that department or organization. Try to prevent that almost automatic 'Not another circular!' response by indicating you have written because of some development or change that has taken place within the company *and* about specific vacancies rather than 'anything that is going'. Perhaps the firm has just announced plans to expand or diversify, so a reference to that shows intelligence, interest and enthusiasm in the business, which may persuade the recipient to go on reading. Asking about particular types of job – especially those likely to be generated by the development or change – can have a similar effect on the reader.

Following on from this initial paragraph, you should state what qualities you can offer a job like this. Given that you do not know the reader (and do not, therefore, necessarily have their goodwill) *and* that they are busy and will dispose of your letter as soon as their interest flags, it is sensible to be exceptionally brief and to the point here – summarizing your particular strengths in short sentences over one succinct paragraph. As with the other types of letter that you might be writing, these concise comments may act as a taster,

Creating Terrific Letters 55

persuading the reader to take a look at an accompanying curriculum vitae. Even if they don't, they are still short enough to encourage (or at least not dissuade) the reader to go on, rather than losing interest in a mass of endless text.

Just in case that specific type of job is unavailable, but other related ones are or might be, you could add another paragraph, again concentrating on what you have to offer, but this time in more general terms. The comments in this paragraph would show how you were well-suited to employment in this company, trade or industry. One or two of these comments may spark off an idea that 'so-and-so is looking for someone like this' or something similar, and your letter might be passed on. Make your comments as brief and succinct as those in the preceding paragraph so that the reader is not discouraged from reading on to the end.

Finish your letter along similar lines to those written by you to job advertisers and contacts – saying what you would like to happen next, and making it easy for the reader to act in the way that you want. So, provide your phone number if you wish to be telephoned; a stamped, addressed envelope for a written response; and copies of your CV if you want these to be studied, retained on file, or handed over to other people within the firm. You may also wish to indicate that you will telephone them at a later date for a discussion. This can be an effective tactic, but it needs to be phrased politely and diplomatically since you do not want to sound demanding and pushy. A suggested 'on-spec' letter is given in Figure 3.4 overleaf.

Dear Mr Lloyd-Davies

I note from the latest planning applications to Tendebury District Council that Hansons has applied to extend its factory space and wonder whether this means you will be recruiting more operatives in the foreseeable future.

I am seeking full-time, permanent employment as a production line worker, having been employed previously in this capacity at Butt and Sons Limited from 1983 to 1994 when it ceased trading, and I have been on temporary, short-term contracts at Watermans since then.

To be offered these contracts on a regular basis, I have had to prove that I am a fast and accurate worker, and flexible, too. On occasions, I have worked for Watermans as a processor and packer, and would be equally interested in applying for these types of vacancy should they arise in your company.

I enclose a copy of my curriculum vitae for your perusal, and hope that you will grant me an interview so that we can discuss this matter further. I attach a first-class, stamped addressed envelope for your reply and look forward to hearing from you in due course.

Yours sincerely
Liza King

Figure 3.4 On-Spec Letter: An example.

Letters to Agencies and Consultancies

Letters to intermediaries such as agencies and consultancies can be categorized in two ways – ones that are sent because you are aware these go-betweens are acting for a particular employer who is seeking to recruit for a specific job (or jobs), and others that are sent on a speculative basis in the hope that the intermediaries can help you by finding employment on your behalf. If you are applying for a known job, your letter should unfold in much the same way that it would if you were writing to a job advertiser.

Speculative letters to agencies and consultancies should begin by outlining why you are writing – to find a specific type of job, perhaps in a particular type of company, trade or industry. This will focus the reader's attention straightaway. If they work in this field – and they will do if you have done your homework – they should read on to see if they can help you, and therefore themselves.

Next, provide some key data about yourself, your background and your strengths in general terms, as you are not pursuing a specific job in a given company, trade or industry at this stage. You might do this over two or three paragraphs; the first one concentrating on your background, and the others on your strengths. Alternatively, you may prefer to write a shorter letter enclosing your curriculum vitae, and this could be the wiser course of action, as agency and consultancy personnel might be inundated with correspondence, and ready to reject at the first sign of waffle. If you do this, write one paragraph summarizing two or three of your major strengths, which you hope will encourage the reader to take a look at the more detailed CV enclosed with your letter. Supplying a curriculum vitae also gives the agency or consultancy something to keep on file or to circulate, as appropriate.

As with the other letters, the final paragraph should express how you want the recipient to respond. If you ask them to phone you, be sure you are in to receive the call, or at least switch on your answering machine if you go out. Respond promptly to any letter as this shows your enthusiasm. See Figure 3.5 for a suggested letter to an agency.

Dear Ms Ginaska

I understand that you specialize in recruiting secretarial staff on temporary, short-term contracts for firms in the City and wonder whether I can come to see you to discuss possible job opportunities in this field.

In brief, I have just moved to this area after eight years of living in Bowditch, Lancashire, where I worked as a personal assistant/secretary for the senior partner of a solicitor's practice, Jackaman, Jones and Meldrew. I am fully familiar with all office practices and am up-to-date with computer programmes and the Internet which was introduced into the practice last year to ensure instant access to clients in the United States.

At this stage I simply enclose my curriculum vitae for your attention, and hope that you will telephone me 01917 747176 once you have looked at it, so that we can arrange a meeting within the next week or so.

Yours sincerely
Brenda Pilkington

Figure 3.5 Letter to an Agency: An example.

Gathering the Information for your Letter

Having become familiar with the various types of letter and their general content, you can now get down to compiling the specific information which you want to include.

It is a good idea to jot down some notes on why you are writing. Obviously, your overall aim is 'to find the right job', but this is too vague and generalized a goal for your letter, whoever you are writing to. So, put down something specific which you can work upon and develop – 'I am writing to apply for the post of administrative assistant, as advertised in *The Evening Echo* of 7 July 1997', for example, if you are writing in reply to a job advertisement.

When writing to contacts in your network, chosen organizations and agencies and consultancies, you will need to state as precisely as possible what type of job you want and, if appropriate, the type of company, trade or industry you wish to work within. Clearly, this information can be obtained (if necessary) or checked from that database of knowledge you built up earlier when you were deciding what new career you wished to pursue. Again, it is worthwhile jotting down some notes which can then be built up and polished. For example: 'I am seeking a sales agency in the north-west region, preferably for a well-established manufacturer operating in the nursery goods trade, or associated industries.'

Whatever type of letter you are writing and whoever to, your strengths must be stressed, perhaps in a brief, summarized form in a covering letter sent with a CV, or in more detail with a letter of application to a job advertiser. Again, this information can be drawn from your database of information compiled when you were listing what you had to offer. Sketch out some general background strengths along with two or three more specific ones relating to the job in question. Also, record some supporting evidence: an example of how you showed initiative in your last job, for instance.

Avoid giving clues about your age through reference to jobs that you held some time ago, or to the length of your employment at a particular firm – it's easy to do this inadvertently. Concentrate instead on the suitability of the work, what you have learned from it and given in return, rather than dates and durations. Ignore your age until the interview, by which time you hope to be so far ahead of your rivals that it will be less of an issue!

Presentation

You must pay special attention to the appearance, layout and style of your letters. Even though the information you are giving is relevant and appealing, if it is not presented in a clear and businesslike manner it is unlikely to be given the attention it deserves.

More often than not, the envelope will be your first point of contact with whoever you are writing to – and it may well be your last if it is a cheap and scruffy one with a misspelt name and address scrawled on it. Use good quality envelopes which convey a clean, crisp businesslike image. White envelopes are generally preferable, but if the nature of the job you are applying for merits it – advertising, for instance – the use of coloured envelopes could be appropriate.

Make sure that the address (name, job title, company, street, town and postcode) is correct in every respect. An incorrectly spelt name may cause irritation or offence, and an inaccurate address or postcode could lead to a delay in delivery. If in doubt, telephone the company to find out – don't leave it to chance. If you make a mistake, tear up the envelope and start again.

Always use first-class post – it is not unknown for some employers to reject automatically all those letters with second-class stamps, on the assumption that this indicates a lack of enthusiasm for getting the job.

If your envelope is the first point of contact, it will be followed closely by the writing paper – so it is important that this conveys an equally impressive image. Spend a little extra money on watermarked, A4-sized paper which looks classy and professional. Ideally, it should match the envelope in which it is placed so that an impression of neat co-ordination is given.

Type or write your letter according to requirements. A job advertisement may state specifically that letters of application should be handwritten and, of course, you should follow such an instruction if you want to be considered seriously for the position. When no indication is given, the choice is your own, and if you can type or use a computer competently you will be able to make your letter look better. However, be wary of asking someone else to do the typing for you – as some 'experts' will advise – since this implies to the recipient that you can type, which may have potentially embarrassing consequences if that assumption carries on into your employment.

In most instances when no stipulation is made, a handwritten letter is acceptable – but make certain that it is neat and legible and that the lines of writing do not slope upwards or downwards, as often can happen. Be wary of writing by hand if you have an old-fashioned writing style, as this can date you and may lead to rejection if age is an obstacle. Whether typed or handwritten, be sure that your spelling, punctuation and grammar are correct.

Your letters must be laid out neatly, and contain various key ingredients. First and foremost, it is worthwhile having a hundred or more letterheaded sheets of paper run off by a local desk-top publisher or printer, with your name, address, telephone and fax numbers (as appropriate) printed across the top; either in the centre or to the left or right, as preferred. Choose a simple and discreet typeface to create a calm and dignified image, rather than using brash typography (the sort many younger applicants select) which is likely to make you seem over-confident and self-important. Your letterhead can make all the difference to the way in which your letter is initially perceived, so take the trouble to ensure it is suitable.

References are included in some letters – 'Our ref:' if you are sending one out, and/or 'Your ref:' when you are responding to someone who has written to you and used a reference. It is unwise to use 'Our ref:' in any of your job-search letters (as various job-seekers have been known to do) because this suggests you are sending out hundreds of them. This may well be the case, but you don't want to advertise the fact! Each recipient of your letters should be given the impression that you are writing to them alone – that way you've a much better chance of being considered seriously. Do include 'Your ref:', though, when replying to anyone who has written to you, using a reference. This is not only courteous, but makes it easier for them to find earlier correspondence, and to file it away afterwards. References are usually placed three to five lines below the letterhead.

The date should be typed or written next, and in full – for example: 2 February 1997. Then, two to three lines below this, put the recipient's name, job title, address and postcode, taking care to ensure they are wholly correct and match the those on the envelope. Putting 'Mrs' instead of 'Miss', 'Carol' when it should be 'Carole', and so forth, can make you seem careless and uninterested.

It is surprising how many job-hunters put 'Dear Sir', 'Dear Madam' or 'Dear Sir or Madam' in their letters. Such a greeting shows that you haven't taken the trouble to find out exactly to whom your letter should be addressed, and it gives the impression that your letter is little more than a circular, sent out by someone with no more than a passing interest in the job or company. If you are writing to a person you know well and are on equal terms with, then just their first name can be used, such as 'Dear Rajesh' or 'Dear Sophie', but should you not know the addressee well, use the formal greeting, such as 'Dear Mr Munglani' or 'Dear Miss Wilkins'. Usually, the greeting is placed two to three lines below the name and address.

You should state the subject matter of your letter between the greeting and the text. If you are replying to an advertisement, this may be something like 'Re: Practice Manager Vacancy', or if it is a letter to a contact, prospective employer, agency or consultancy, it could, for instance, be 'Re: Administrative Job Vacancies'. This helps to focus the reader's attention on your letter and tells them what it is about; so make sure you sum up the contents succinctly in two or three words only. To make it stand out, if your are typing your letter, this heading can be put in bold type, or if writing by hand it can be written in capitals or be underlined.

Next comes the text of your letter – and by now you should know what facts you are going to include – about the job vacancy, you and your suitability for this position. Ideally, the text should consist of short and concise paragraphs (typically dealing with one key statement each) and of roughly equal length, so that they appear well-balanced and easy to read. Start your first paragraph one line beneath the subject matter heading, and leave one line gaps between the subsequent paragraphs.

Most of the job-hunting letters that you send will be relatively short; more often than not just a single page long. However, if you have to use a second (continuation) sheet, you should ensure that you use plain paper which matches exactly that of your letterhead paper. About six lines from the top of the paper put the page number, date and the recipient's name on three separate lines down the left-hand side. Then leave another three lines before starting the next paragraph. It is inadvisable to go beyond one continuation page.

At the end of your letter, put 'Yours sincerely' ('Yours faithfully' usually follows a 'Dear Sir' or 'Dear Madam' greeting which, hopefully, you will have avoided). This should be placed one line below your final paragraph. Add a clear and legible signature, rather than a flamboyant squiggle or a rushed scrawl. Allow a space equal to about five or six lines for your signature. Then type or write your name.

Most likely there will be an enclosure, such as a curriculum vitae, to go with your letter. If so, you should indicate that this document has been included with your letter by referring to it in the text, and adding 'Enclosure', 'Enc', 'Enclosures' or 'Encs', as appropriate, two lines under the last entry.

Should you be sending a copy (or copies) of your letter elsewhere – perhaps to a contact who was kind enough to put you in touch with the addressee – you should add their names, two lines below. For instance: 'Copy: Mr Steve Barham' or 'Copies: Mrs Janet Wilson, BMA Monitors, Mr Dan Hudson, IM Consultancies' (each name on a separate line).

There are three main formats you can use for your letter. These are known as 'blocked', 'semi-blocked' and 'indented'. In a blocked format everything is ranged left against the left margin (which is perhaps half-an-inch in from the edge of the paper, with the same margin on the right-hand side). The semi-blocked format has any references and the date ranged right for filing and retrieval purposes, while the rest is ranged left as in the blocked format. The indented format is the same as either the blocked or semi-blocked formats (as preferred) except that the first lines of the paragraphs are all indented by some five to six spaces. Most people use the blocked format these days, so stick to that to avoid creating an antiquated image of yourself.

Style of Writing

The appearance and layout of your job-search letters should persuade recipients to look at them, but it is often the style of your writing that will encourage them to read on to the end, and study any accompanying material. If you are trying to avoid revealing your age because you feel it might be considered a weakness, then you need to take care not to use old-fashioned words, expressions and phrases.

Keep your letters short and to the point. Use plain language which will be readily understood, and avoid technical terms and trade jargon when writing about your recent work activities unless you are sure the reader is fully familiar with them.

Inject some personality into your letter. Be sincere and take a friendly but courteous 'please' and 'thank you' approach, but without being servile or ingratiating. Write in your own (up-to-date) words so that it reads like *your* work rather than a standard letter copied from a book (such as this!), and be wary of incorporating humour as your sense of fun may not match that of the recipient.

The Draft Letter

Using the information that you have assembled, first produce a draft letter. Concentrate on including everything you wish to say, and put it in a logical order. Don't worry too much about its exact appearance, layout and style at the moment – these can be dealt with later on when you are writing out your final polished version.

Once you have written your draft, it is a good idea to put it aside for a short while. When you come back to it you will in effect be seeing it afresh, and will consequently be more likely to spot any obvious flaws – for instance: some part of your background which you omitted to mention or explain properly, strengths which would be better placed in a different order so that those which are more relevant to the job in question are given more emphasis. Your draft may also benefit from being read by a respected colleague who can appraise it in a more objective manner than yourself. Be prepared to listen to constructive criticism – however embarrassing it may be – and act upon it, making amendments to your draft as and where necessary. It is tempting to believe that, because you are older and used to writing letters, your first effort will be perfect; but this is rarely so for anyone. You might find that you will have to draft and redraft your initial effort several times before you are completely satisfied with it.

The Final Version of the Letter

Once you are happy with your amended draft, the time has come to prepare the final version of your letter, paying heed to the layout advice above. Once done, check it thoroughly for spelling, punctuation and grammatical mistakes – it is surprising how often something slips through between the draft, its amendment and the final copy. Use a spell check facility, a dictionary and/or an informed colleague as a double-check! Watch out, too, for typographical errors, perhaps where your finger has touched the wrong key on the word processor, or the right one twice. If there are any mistakes – however minor – you should produce another, corrected version. Errors reflect badly on your competence, and enthusiasm for the post.

Despatching your Letter

Many experts claim that it really does not matter how job-search letters are sent, just so long as they arrive at the required time and in good condition.

Normally you would send it by first-class post, but if the company you are writing to is not too far away, you may consider delivering it by hand. This would also give you the chance to see what the firm's premises (and your prospective work environment) look like. An alternative is to send your letter by fax machine. The immediacy of this method is attractive, but you will forego any benefit that may come from the trouble you have taken over choosing quality paper for your letter and enclosures. For help in making a decision about this, see Figure 3.6 opposite and overleaf.

SUBMITTING MATERIAL

It can sometimes be difficult to know how best to submit material during job-hunting activities – whether by post, fax or in person. Even though each set of circumstances will differ from the other, and should therefore be considered individually, it is helpful to have an idea of the main pros and cons of the alternatives available to you.

Method	Pros	Cons
Post	Likely to be the most convenient, especially if the recipient is some distance away.	Might be delayed by strikes, heavy seasonal usage of the system, could go astray.
	Relatively inexpensive in most instances.	Might be damaged in transit, creating adverse impression.
	Importance can be enhanced by the use of recorded or registered delivery.	Difficult to know when and how it is received, and what is done with it thereafter.
	Recipient cannot know the age of the sender.	Unlikely to be distinctive, and may be placed at the bottom of a pile of similar envelopes and packages.

Method	Pros	Cons
Fax	Conveys an image of a professional, up-to-date job-hunter.	Some of the documents may not be transmitted clearly, making them hard to read.
	Creates an aura of importance: to be looked at straightaway.	Other (three dimensional) documents cannot be submitted via this method.
	Fast and easy to send at a specific time.	Materials may be separated from other applications, and occasionally not considered.
	Recipients cannot know the age of the sender.	Assumes both recipient and sender have access to facsimile machines.
In Person	Guarantees a safe delivery, and at a chosen time.	May not be practical if recipient is based some distance away.
	Enables premises and other aspects of employment to be seen and assessed.	Time consuming, and requires some effort.
		Recipient will know the job-hunter's age, which may lead to automatic rejection if age is an issue.

Figure 3.6 Submitting Material: A checklist for job-seekers of 35-plus.

4

Producing Sensational CVs

Curricula vitae play an integral part in most job-search activities. You need to know how to compile them effectively and how they can be adapted and used for different situations.

A curriculum vitae (curricula vitae is the plural) is, in a way, a brief timetable of your educational and working life so far. It would normally run to one or two pages, detailing various key aspects of your career to date; not least your achievements, strengths and suitability for the job in question.

Most job applications – whether in response to advertisements or unsolicited – will involve curricula vitae. Job advertisers ask for CVs because they tend to be easier to refer to than potentially lengthy letters, and can make the job of shortlisting less time consuming. For this reason they must be well structured and organized. Jobseekers generally prefer curricula vitae because they are in control of what is included and excluded, and they can set them out to convey the most favourable image.

How to Compile your CV

The key to a successful curriculum vitae – one that makes readers respond in the way that you want them to do – is its adaptability. Quite simply, your standard CV must be adapted for each and every application. Clearly, you need to promote your strengths, so if one of your qualifications, training courses or jobs is particularly relevant to an application it should be given greater priority and emphasis. Likewise, you need to play down anything that might stand in the way of your getting an interview. So, if you feel you might be discriminated against because of your age, marital status or dependants, omit references to them. You are under absolutely no obligation whatsoever to include anything that might remotely be held against you. Sell yourself on your strengths! Take a look at the examples of format and content of a standard CV and an adapted one for an older job-hunter in Figures 4.1 and 4.2.

CURRICULUM VITAE

Personal Information:
Susan Jones
50 Brightwell Close, Thretford, Surrey KP17 4LF
01464 81243

35 years old
Married, two children, Michael (8), Sophie (4)

Education, Qualifications, Training:
*Thretford Secondary School, Abbey Road, Thretford, Surrey KP17 3BZ,
September 1973 to July 1980*
O-Level English Language 'A' Grade June 1978
O-Level English Literature 'A' Grade June 1978
O-Level Commercial English 'B' Grade June 1978
O-Level History 'A' Grade June 1978
O-Level Geography 'C' Grade June 1978
O-Level Physics 'D' Grade June 1978
O-Level Chemistry 'D' Grade June 1978
A-Level English Literature 'C' Grade June 1980
A-Level History 'D' Grade June 1980

*Thretford Adult Education Centre, Bury Road, Thretford, Surrey
KP17 0YD*
A-Level Business Studies 'C' Grade June 1996
A-Level Economics 'C' Grade June 1996

Surrey College, High Road East, Millward, Surrey KP14 9YS
NVQ 3 Diploma Information Technology and Data Processing
Distinction June 1996

Work Experience:

1996—
Gerrard Smiths (freight transportation), Ranleigh Road, Thretford, KT17 8PO (01464) 89900.
Receptionist (part time) dealing with visitors, answering the telephone and other general duties. Seeking full-time employment.

1980–88
Hobsons Limited (industrial storage and transportation), Valley Industrial Park, Thretford, Surrey KT17 5XX (01464) 83710
Clerical Assistant, general office duties, £5,000 per annum, 1980–84. Promoted to:

Assistant Office Supervisor, supervisory/administrative duties, £6,500 per annum, 1984–85. Promoted to:

Office Supervisor, supervising office staff of eight/administrative duties, £8,500 per annum, 1985–88. Left to have family.

Leisure Activities:
I organize the pre-school activity group at St John's Church in Maidstone Road, Thretford, Surrey. This runs on weekday mornings from 9.30 to 12 o'clock.

I also run the C-Kers Youth Club for 11 to 16 year-olds at the church on Friday evenings.

I am the treasurer of the parent-teacher association at Thretford Primary School, Beecroft Avenue, Thretford, Surrey.

Figure 4.1 Standard CV: An example.

SUE JONES
50 Brightwell Close, Thretford, Surrey KP17 4LF
01464 81243

Education, Qualifications, Training:
Thretford Secondary School, Abbey Road, Thretford, Surrey KP17 3BZ
Thretford Adult Education Centre, Bury Road, Thretford, Surrey KP17 0YD
Surrey College, High Road East, Millward, Surrey KP14 9YS
NVQ Level 3 Diploma, Information Technology and Data Processing (Distinction)
4 A-Levels, Business Studies, Economics, English, History ('C', 'C', 'C', 'D' Grades)
7 GCSEs, Commercial English, History, Geography, Physics, Chemistry, English Language, English Literature ('A' Grades mainly)

Work Experience:
1996–
Gerrard Smiths (freight transportation), Ranleigh Road, Thretford, KT17 8PO.
Receptionist, dealing with visitors, answering the telephone and other general duties, as required.

Previously
Hobsons Limited (industrial storage and transportation), Valley Industrial Park, Thretford, Surrey KT17 5XX.
Office Supervisor, supervising office staff of eight and miscellaneous office duties, previously employed there as Clerical Assistant and Assistant Office Supervisor.

Leisure Activities:
In my free time I run the C-Kers Youth Club for 11 to 16 year-olds at St John's Church in Maidstone Road, Thretford, Surrey. I do this on Friday evenings during the school year.

I also like to keep fit and healthy and visit the 'Gym and Trim' in Henley Road, Thretford, Surrey on Tuesday and Thursday evenings – lifting weights, using the rowing machine, etc.

Figure 4.2 Adapted CV for an Older Job-Hunter: An example.

The phrases used in your CV should be vibrant and lively, rather than reading like a shopping list. Include such upbeat words as 'achieving', 'capable', 'creating', 'effective', 'efficient', 'experienced', 'initiating', 'organizing', 'qualified', 'resourceful', 'successful', 'trained' and 'versatile'. Quantify your comments whenever possible. 'I improved output' is a positive statement, but the addition of 'by 25 per cent during the two years I was in charge' puts it into perspective and gives a hard, factual edge to what might otherwise sound vague.

It needs to be said that whatever you state in your CV must be truthful. It is fine to arrange things so that your strengths are brought to the fore and any weaknesses are less evident or even omitted, but you must never exaggerate or lie. Should you do so, it can backfire in a thoroughly embarrassing way. For instance, you could be asked to produce the certificates to prove your claimed qualifications, or your former employer may be asked to confirm what you have listed as your achievements while with that company. If any of your statements are proved to be untrue, it is inevitable that you will be deleted from the shortlist or, if uncovered at a later stage, you may be dismissed straightaway.

Presentation

Your CV should be on quality A4 paper which matches your covering letter. It should be typed, double-spaced on one side of the paper only, and be no more than two pages long. If you cannot type, ask a friend or colleague to do it for you, or go to one of the desk-top publishing firms trading in most shopping centres nowadays, some of which will be able to laser print it for you. Whatever you do, never submit a grubby photocopy, as it is likely to end up in the wastepaper bin.

The main headings for the information you must include in your curriculum vitae are: 'personal information', 'education, qualifications and training', 'work experience' and 'leisure activities'.

Personal Information

Full personal information usually comprises your name, address, contact phone (and, perhaps, fax) number, date of birth, marital status, number and ages of children, health status, and whether or not you are a holder of a driving licence. You may not wish to include all of this in your CV – your date of birth and ages of any children being obvious items for exclusion at this stage.

Telephone and fax numbers should be those where you can be contacted most easily – at work if this is acceptable (perhaps you have a direct line or are under notice of redundancy and are being encouraged to find alternative employment) or at home, if not. Do invest in an answering machine if you include a home phone number and you are often out, so that messages can be left for you.

The inclusion of such information as your date of birth, marital status and the number and ages of your dependants is an area of concern and, as mentioned above, it is perhaps best left out. In theory, firms are not allowed to discriminate against applicants (or employees) because of their sex, marital status or race and are encouraged not to do so on the grounds of age or disability either. However, in practice, there is no guarantee that this will not take place, and it is difficult to prove that it has, especially at such an early stage of the recruitment (and selection) process.

Education, Qualifications and Training

Under 'education, qualifications and training' (or a similar title) brief chronological information may be given about schools, colleges, universities and training courses attended, listing exam results such as GCSEs and A-levels, and qualifications such as NVQs, diplomas and degrees.

School, college and university information may need to be checked carefully before inclusion as it is likely to relate to 15, 20, 25 years ago or more, and may have lost some of its relevance since employers are going to be more interested in what has happened recently. Nonetheless, they do need to be referred to, albeit with little more than one line summaries in most cases. Be careful not to give your age away here, though. Omit details and dates if age might be held against you. Remember, strengths in, weaknesses out!

Much the same applies to information concerning qualifications and training courses. You may have to look through old records for certificates and other verification and those obtained and/or attended many years ago may be of secondary importance now. Again, brief, one-line entries are all that is needed. Concentrate on more recent information, especially that which shows initiative and enthusiasm – such as training courses attended voluntarily in your own time.

When listing your career history, the best approach is to start with the present time and work back. This way the potential employer will see the most relevant information first, rather than starting at the first job you did after leaving school. Here you will include the names of the companies you have worked for, your job titles and responsibilities.

Jobs which you had some time ago, and which are not really relevant to the job you are seeking now, should be mentioned only briefly – perhaps not at all if age is an issue. Instead, give greatest emphasis to your most recent employment.

Leisure Activities

Under 'leisure activities' you will list your hobbies, sports interests, membership of clubs or societies, posts of responsibility and trust and any voluntary work. Indeed, include anything which indicates that you are healthy, a team player, capable of taking responsibility and being trusted.

Drafts and Final Versions

Your first attempt at drafting a curriculum vitae will not be perfect: no-one could expect it to be. Nevertheless, it is often hard to spot imperfections immediately after it has been written. So, as with your job letters, it is advisable to put it away for a short while and come back to it. Any shortcomings will then be more readily apparent to you – maybe you missed out a course you attended, or included too much about your hobbies, making it sound as though you are more interested in them than your work. Show your draft to someone else whose views and opinions you value, and take account of their comments, however unwelcome they may be, and make revisions until you and they are happy with the content and order of things.

It is surprising how many job-seekers spend ages preparing and revising their curricula vitae, and then fail to check over the final copy for mistakes. Do spend a few minutes on the elementary – but essential – task of thoroughly reading through the curriculum vitae for any mistakes in spelling, punctuation and grammar, referring to a dictionary or a reliable and informed colleague for a second opinion, if necessary. If there are any faults then you must do it again – nothing will destroy your chances more quickly and emphatically than an error-ridden curriculum vitae.

5

Making Application Forms Memorable

Many job advertisements, and especially those placed by large companies, will state that people interested in the vacancy should complete an application form.

Such forms have a similarity of purpose in that they are designed to focus on key aspects of an applicant's background, knowledge, skills, experience and suitability for the job in question. There are, however, different ways in which they are put together – some forms are short and structured, containing a series of very specific questions, whilst others are much longer and open-ended, giving applicants the opportunity to express themselves more fully.

The main advantages of an application form to a company advertising a vacancy is that from the outset the company 'forces' a response to the questions that it wants answered, and the standardized format in which the required information is given makes it easier for checks and comparisons to be made in the process of drawing up a shortlist of applicants. When you complete such forms you cannot omit or gloss over tricky areas, as you might do with letters or curricula vitae. For the older job-seeker this inevitably means that your age has to be declared at the start. An option to discount the application form and send your CV instead is most unlikely to exist.

The information, such as personal details and education and career history, that you will be asked to supply on an application form is naturally the same as that which you prepared for your CV, but the major difference is that you will have less scope to present it in the way you want, and you will *have* to answer the questions listed and in the order that they are asked. Any uncompleted 'boxes' will be plain for all to see, and will doubtless result in rejection.

It is quite likely that there will be questions about your health status, whether you are in possession of a clean driving licence and whether you have a criminal record. You may well also be asked to say why you want the job, what you will bring to it and what your required salary is. And, finally you will probably have to sign a declaration that all information given is correct to the best of your knowledge.

An example of an application form is given in Figure 5.1 opposite.

Making Applications Forms Memorable

Application for Employment at Smith and Jones Ltd Private and Confidential	Complete this form in your own handwriting Return it to: The Personnel Officer, Smith and Jones Ltd, 6–12 High Street, Endsleigh, Warwickshire ES10 3AB
Position Applied for:	Source of Application
Title:	Date of Birth:
Surname:	Place of Birth:
Forename(s):	Marital Status:
Full Address:	Have you been employed by the company before? If so, give details:
Telephone Number:	Dates of Employment:
Do you have any restrictions on geographical mobility? If so, please give details:	Do you hold a valid driving licence? Are there any dates when you are unavailable for interview? When would you be available to start work, if your application is successful? Do you require a UK work permit?

References (Please note: References will not be taken up until after an offer of employment has been made and accepted by the applicant)

1. Name	2. Name
Address	Address
Occupation	Occupation

82 Your Mid-Career Shift

Medical History. Have you had any of the following conditions. Please circle where appropriate:	Have you ever had a serious illness or injury? If yes, please provide details.
Epilepsy, Fits, Blackouts Migraine, Dizziness	Have you been treated at hospital at any time? If yes, please give details.
Anxiety, Depression, Asthma, Hay-Fever, Eczema	Are you currently receiving treatment of any kind? If yes, please supply details.
Diabetes, Psoriasis, Dermatitis	
Bronchitis, Tuberculosis, Heart Attack, Stroke	Do you suffer any disablement?
Rheumatism, Dyslexia	
Ear or Throat Infection, Recurrent Episodes of Diarrhoea	Are you on the disabled persons register? If so, what is your number?
Recurrent Absence from Work for any Reason	

Positive responses to the above questions may necessitate further medical enquiries or an examination. In these circumstances, an offer of employment could only be made subject to a satisfactory result.

Education and Training

	Name and Location	From	To	Examinations Passed (with grades and dates)
Schools				
Colleges, Universities				
Other Education, Training				

Please provide details of any Membership/Grade of professional institutions/specialized training you have had:	Details of interests, hobbies, activities:
	Membership of clubs/societies, and positions of responsibility:

Previous Employment (Starting with the most recent employment)					
Name and Address of Employer	Position Held	Salary	From	To	Reasons for leaving

What notice are you required to give your present employer?

What skills and experiences do you have which make you suited to this vacancy?	Please add any further information You may wish to give in support of your application here or on a separate sheet of paper.
Have you ever been convicted of any offence before a court of law? If so, please give details:	I certify that the information given is correct. Signature　　　　　　Date

84 Your Mid-Career Shift

Interviewer's Notes

Interviewer's Signature   Date

Figure 5.1 Application Form: An example.

Obtaining an Application Form

It may seem unnecessary to have to explain how to obtain an application form, but an increasing number of firms are now recruiting on the basis that only a given number of application forms will be distributed – typically to the first hundred applicants. Thus, you need to act quickly and follow instructions given in the advertisement to either write, phone or call in for a form, and then return it promptly. Companies have to shortlist somehow – especially as hundreds of applicants have been known to apply for just one job – and whether it seems fair or not, this is one of the ways in which they sometimes do it.

If your job-search schedule is sufficiently comprehensive and thorough, you will be seeing or hearing of job advertisements on the day they are made public. If you are asked to write in, put your letter in the post on the same day with a first-class stamp or deliver it by hand, making it clear what job you are applying for, where you saw the advertisement and requesting an application form to be sent to you. Also ask for further information about the company and job, such as sales literature and a job description, as what you learn from this will help to demonstrate your interest should you be called for interview. An example of such a letter – brief, to the point and following the usual guidelines for writing job-search letters – is reproduced in Figure 5.2 overleaf.

Dear Mr Catlow

I write further to your advertisement for a project manager in today's Daily Echo.

I am extremely interested in applying for this post, and would be grateful if you would forward an application form to me, by return.

Any additional information, such as a job description and company literature would be appreciated, too.

I look forward to your response.

Yours sincerely
Tasmin Bellows

Figure 5.2 Letter Requesting an Application Form: An example.

If you are asked to phone for an application form you should do so immediately so that you are one of the first to receive it. It is possible you will have to leave your request on an answer machine, so be prepared for that. If your call is answered in person bear in mind that it is likely to be someone working in an administrative capacity rather than the person who will be conducting the interviewing, so just concentrate on asking for the form and any supporting data. A suggested dialogue for this type of call is given in Figure 6.2 on page 99.

Prompt action is just as important if the job advertisement states that application forms should be collected personally, especially as the number of forms available may be limited.

Filling in an Application Form

As soon as you have got an application form for a job you want to apply for, it is advisable to photocopy it, so that you can practise completing it.

For the most part it will be self-explanatory. To recap: it will be a matter of filling in the boxes as instructed with your basic personal information, educational record and career history. However, where there is scope, concentrate on promoting your strengths, and give prominence to those of your qualifications which are specific to the job sought.

If reasons for leaving a previous job are asked for, and it was because of dismissal or redundancy, then you have no option but to state this, but if there were extenuating circumstances, add a note saying '*Please refer to additional information attached', and include an explanation.

There may be a number of ancillary questions related to your health, to check that you will not be off sick regularly. As usual, answer questions honestly, adding explanations as appropriate. Perhaps you have suffered from a serious illness, but have now recovered fully, and have a doctor's certificate to prove it. Health is always a tricky topic. You should not feel obliged to apologize for having been ill, but it is understandable that an employer wants to check.

Questions about your leisure activities are quite likely to feature somewhere on the form. A potential employer may want to see that your outside interests are compatible with the job. For example, there would be an advantage if a prospective sales representative for sports goods actively participated in sport. Never hesitate to stress how lively and active you are, especially if you suspect you might be discriminated against because of age. If you are a 40-year-old active tennis player, for instance, and the job in question calls for physical stamina, then you will surely have an advantage over younger applicants who may be less active – those perhaps who list their leisure interests as the cinema and reading, etc. Take care, though, not to overdo things and give the impression that your leisure interests are likely to be more important to you than your job.

There may also be a question about your membership of clubs, societies and professional bodies, or about work you may do for your local community. It is perhaps best just to include those of relevance to the job, or which serve to corroborate your good character.

You may be asked about your possession of a clean driving licence and whether you have a criminal record. As always, answer these questions truthfully – after all, if they are important, the would-be employer will request sight of your licence or permission to check you out with the local police authority; which happens automatically nowadays if you are applying for a job which involves contact with children.

The question 'What is your required salary?' (or something similar) is a difficult one – too high and you may be discounted immediately, too low and you may find you sell your services too cheaply. You should know what you want and have some idea of the minimum and maximum salary available. Perhaps you could say, 'I am seeking a salary within the advertised range, subject to discussion.'

It is possible that you might be asked about your availability for work – either in terms of when you could start and/or where you would be prepared to go. If you are currently in work, you may be expected to give a week's notice or longer, and should state this on the form – perhaps adding a comment like 'but I would wish to give my employer a little more time if requested, so that I can reallocate my tasks and responsibilities fully and depart with minimal disruption and inconvenience', as it shows you in a good light. If you are out of work you might suggest a date in perhaps two week's time or thereabouts. Don't seem too keen, as you may appear desperate and unwanted, which is off-putting and will make it harder for you to negotiate a good financial package, if or when successful. If asked, where you would be willing to move to, you need to bear in mind that the more flexible you are, the better your chances.

At, or towards the end of the application form, you will be asked to give the names and addresses of (usually) two people who can confirm that what you have stated is true. Before completing this, be sure to contact your chosen referees to ensure that they are happy to provide written or verbal verification on request and that their references will be positive and enthusiastic ones. Ideally, your listed referees will be people of importance and respectability, and who know you and your work well.

Additional Information

In most instances, the last page of an application form will include a request for 'additional information' such as: 'Tell us about yourself', 'Explain why you want this job', 'Outline your suitability for this post', or something similar. The rest of the page will be blank. It has to be stated that you do not *have* to complete this. Indeed, the form may imply that it is optional, but you can be certain that if you don't your application will go straight into the wastepaper basket 99 times out of 100.

In many respects, this one (or possibly two) page statement is similar to the contents of a letter of application. Depending on what exactly you have been asked, you might summarize those general strengths which are most closely associated with the job, company, trade or industry; perhaps a paragraph for each with an explanation and an example demonstrating how the strength was used in your last job. Your reasons for wanting the job should sound positive – 'an upward move' – and use upbeat expressions like 'a chance to progress', 'to fulfil my potential', etc. Comments on your suitability for the post should focus on your specific strengths so far as they relate to the particular requirements of the job in question. As a guide, refer to the sample response given in Figure 5.3 overleaf.

ADDITIONAL INFORMATION

(Use this space to outline your suitability for the post)

I believe I am the right candidate for this position because I fulfil all the key criteria that you are looking for. In particular:

I have proven management experience in an appropriate retail organization.
I am currently working as an assistant store manager for 'Barlows' – a regional company owning a chain of grocery stores in East Anglia. I have worked my way up from Saturday assistant at Eyke, Suffolk, to assistant manager at Woodleigh in Norfolk, where I have been for two years. Woodleigh is the biggest store in the chain, with a full-time equivalent staff of 20 and an annual turnover of £800,000.

I have a hands-on approach to management.
The role of assistant manager at Barlows is a 'see-it-do-it' one: it is my job to work between the manager and staff on the shop floor, dealing with situations as they arise, whether an unexpected stock delivery, a shoplifter in the store or a customer being taken ill. I have to be there, making on-the-spot decisions to deal with them.

I am capable of working under pressure in a physically demanding environment.
Working in a fast-moving grocery store such as Barlows means I am used to working under sustained pressure – getting goods shelved quickly, calling in staff as required, co-ordinating them, dealing with 101 tasks at the same time, AND doing them well. When necessary, I unload, move and shelve goods. I work out at

> the local gym twice a week and play golf on Sundays, which helps me to maintain my fitness and stamina.
>
> **I am determined to succeed.**
> Having been an assistant manager for two years and having stood in for the store manager when he was on leave, I am now looking to progress to become a store manager, AND in a growing, go-ahead company where there are opportunities for promotion on a nationwide basis. I am willing to move anywhere in the country for the right job: and I am convinced that the job is with you.
>
> I certify that, to the best of my knowledge, all information given in this application form is correct.
>
> Signature:
> Date:

Figure 5.3 Additional Information: An example.

If you have included any 'see additional information' notes anywhere in the form, you will now have some more writing to do. Naturally, you are only going to add extra comments if the basic facts about your age, last salary, reasons for leaving and the like have to be given and, if left unexplained, would put you at a disadvantage. You should certainly not draw attention to your perceived or actual shortcomings unless you have to. Whatever you put here should generally comprise a clear and concise statement developing, wherever possible, into a summary of your attributes, so far as they relate to the work. Examples of various statements are given in Figure 5.3 which you may find helpful.

Returning Completed Forms

Clearly, it is essential that your completed application form is as perfect as it can be, so you should spend time looking carefully at your photocopied form before making adjustments, switching the details over on to the original and carrying out last minute checks on this prior to returning it to the organization in question.

Do concentrate on getting the contents of the photocopied form exactly right, making sure than each box is filled in and every question answered. If you leave one blank or unanswered – especially if it relates to a key criterion so far as the prospective employer is concerned – then your application may be discarded automatically. Keep your comments – most notably in that 'additional information' section – brief and to the point in just the same way that you would in a letter or curriculum vitae. Try to fill up each box or blank page to give the impression that you are keen, enthusiastic and attempting to tell them as much as possible. Continue writing and re-writing until you are convinced that your form is as good as you can make it.

Put your completed, photocopied form to one side for a while – even if it is only for 30 minutes or so – before taking another look at it. You may then be better placed to notice any shortcomings and/or imperfections. You may also find it beneficial to have the form perused by a respected colleague, friend or family member as they will view your numerous answers and statements far more objectively than you could ever do. Do take note of what they have to say, and make additional adjustments as you see fit.

Satisfied with the contents of your photocopy, you should then transfer everything across to the original application form. You need to be especially careful here, following any instructions detailed on that form such as completing it in your own handwriting and/or in block capitals and/or in black ink, or typing out your responses. If you do not, then your application may be deleted from the list automatically. You must also take care to make sure that the data are switched over properly. When copying text – and particularly material which you are extremely familiar with – it is surprisingly easy to miss out a word or write the same sentence twice. Probably the best way of avoiding this common problem is to do it very slowly in a quiet and peaceful room where you can concentrate fully without distractions and interruptions.

Finally check it very carefully. Any spelling, punctuation and grammatical mistakes will reflect badly on your expertise and commitment, so watch out for these.

There are two key criteria for returning application forms; it must be done promptly (and certainly before any advertised closing date) and as stated in the job advertisement. See also Figure 3.6 'Submitting Material: A checklist for job seekers at 35-plus', pp. 67–8.

6

Perfecting your Telephone Technique

As a mature job-hunter, you will be that much more confident and experienced in using the telephone than many younger applicants will be, and this will stand you in good stead if you have to call, or expect to be called by, would-be employers, contacts, agencies, consultancies and the like. You are going to sound calm, in control and able to converse fluently – just the sort of person they are looking for! Build up this advantage by considering the numerous types of call that may have to be made, contemplating how to plan and manage calls and thinking about what needs to be done afterwards, to consolidate your chances of success.

Some job-seekers spend months looking for work without ever using the telephone, whilst others see it as an important part of their job-search programme. If you are job-hunting effectively, then you should be using it regularly, but selectively, to make outgoing calls to job advertisers, contacts, chosen organizations, agencies and consultancies. You may have to phone for application forms, too. Also, you could receive incoming calls enquiring about details given in a letter, curriculum vitae or application form and, hopefully, inviting you to interviews.

Making Phone Calls

The secret of successful telephone calls is preparation, as indeed it is for most job-hunting activities. You need to know something about who you are going to talk to, the best time to contact them, and have it clear in your mind what you are going to say.

What you have found out about the person you are going to speak to will affect how you address and talk to them. It is important that you do not automatically address a younger person by their first name as some older job-hunters are inclined to do. This can seem patronizing to them, especially if they are the employer, and you are the prospective employee. In general, it is wise to adopt a slightly detached, formal approach. Do not assume your expertise in a particular area is greater than that of the person you are speaking to, simply because you are older than them. It may not be so, and even if it is, they might not wish to be made aware of it.

It is sensible to ensure that you will not be disturbed whilst making your call. This is perhaps an obvious point, but it is one which many job-hunters seem to ignore, to their cost.

Some job-seekers prepare by drafting lengthy notes including scripted opening comments, lists of questions and stock answers; but then perform badly, sound stilted and stumble over their material, especially when the other person departs from the script! It is far better to jot down a loose and flexible checklist of key points to be included at one stage or another. As a more confident and relaxed speaker, this should be sufficient for your needs.

Only telephone in response to an advertisement if invited to, and ask to be connected to the extension number and person stated, and no-one else. Some firms screen applicants and produce a shortlist of candidates for interview by talking initially on the phone rather than requesting letters, CVs and so on; primarily because it enables them to raise direct questions which might otherwise by avoided, and to assess more easily attributes like speech and the ability to converse. Typically, the conversation will consist of the prospective employer asking the applicant a short series of questions relating to the main qualities of the ideal employee sought. If an adverse answer is given, the conversation will be drawn to a close shortly thereafter. If all goes well, the applicant may be asked to complete one of the limited number of application forms available, or to come in for an interview. The extract of a telephone conversation in Figure 6.1 below shows how to deal with age-related questions.

'... that's fine. Tell me, Ms Thomson, why are you seeking a job which is at a lower level and pays less than your last job?'

'Because I want to move into a growing sector of the industry and work within an up-and-coming company like yours. I need to take a step back in order to go forward.'

'So you'll be moving on soon then?'

'No. Obviously, I'm ambitious and looking to progress and take on new challenges, but from what I've seen, you provide plenty of opportunities for growth here. Hopefully I can develop with you, and put something back in.'

'And how would you feel about working for someone younger than you?'

'I'd be happy. I've never thought of age as an issue, to be honest. They're there because they have the skills and expertise to do the job. I'd hope to learn from them.'

> 'You would be older than many of your colleagues, too. Is that a problem?'
>
> 'No, I've been working as part of a young team at Hershaws, and we all work well together. We get on well too, playing badminton and squash on Friday evenings.'
>
> 'You keep fit, then?'
>
> 'Yes, I play badminton and squash, and a round of golf on Sunday mornings. It keeps me sharp.'
>
> 'Fine, now let's move on to something else. Tell me ...'

Figure 6.1 Handling Age-Related Questions: An example of a telephone conversation.

Probably the easiest call for a job-hunter to make is one requesting an application form; although this should be done only if it is stated specifically in the job advertisement. Calling for a form, when the advertisement requests that you write in, may be held against you. Quite simply, the applicant phoning in just needs to leave their details on an answering machine or with the person taking the call, and to ask for any other data that can be provided about the work or firm, so that these can be used for research purposes. A sample dialogue is given in Figure 6.2.

> 'Bresslaws. Maria speaking. How can I help you?'
>
> 'Hello. I'm ringing with regard to the advertisement for a polisher in today's *Daily Times*. Can you send me an application form, please?'
>
> 'Yes. Can you give me your name and address?'
>
> 'My name is Andrew Horton: H-O-R-T-O-N. The address is 15 Burleigh Road, Wick. That's B-U-R-L-E-I-G-H Road, Wick. The postcode is WK2 3TT.'
>
> 'We'll get one in the post to you this afternoon.'
>
> 'Can you send me a job description and any other information about the job and company at the same time, please?'
>
> 'We'll see what we can do. Thank you.'
>
> 'Thanks very much. Goodbye.'

Figure 6.2 Telephoning for an Application Form: An example.

Phone calls to contacts in your network, and other prospective companies and agencies, should only be made if this is a more fitting approach than a letter or a face-to-face meeting. See Figure 2.2 'Making Contact: A checklist for mature job hunters', page 22. Usually, the applicant will lead this conversation, politely and courteously outlining their general and specific strengths and the nature of the work they are pursuing. If appropriate, they may then be asked various questions similar to those covered by a job advertiser and if tackled successfully, will be invited to perhaps send in a letter and/or a curriculum vitae, complete an application form or come along for a discussion.

Receiving Phone Calls

Very occasionally, a potential employer to whom you have sent a letter of application, a curriculum vitae or a filled in application form may telephone you for clarification or expansion of some details which were stated by you, or perhaps excluded unintentionally (or intentionally, as the case may be!) Essentially, the conversation will consist of a number of questions about those areas which are most closely related to the employer's requirements for the job in question. Not surprisingly, the answers should be similar to what ought to have been stated in the first place; a basic statement, further details, if necessary, followed by an example linking a strength to one of the key criteria for the position. If received favourably, an invitation to an interview may conclude the conversation.

Ideally, of course, all incoming calls of this kind will be from prospective employers who have been sufficiently impressed by your application and now wish to invite you in for a face-to-face interview. Invariably, this will be no more than the briefest of calls, with the would-be employer suggesting a date, time and place for the interview. It is important that you do not try to lengthen the conversation unduly – to obtain further data about the job, your chances of success and so on – as the caller will inevitably find this distracting and annoying. A suggested dialogue for this type of conversation is given in Figure 6.3 below.

'277015. Jack Hargreaves speaking.'

'Hello, Mr Hargreaves. This is Stevenson's Bakery. I'm ringing about your application for the baker's job. Are you free to attend an interview on Monday afternoon at two-thirty?'

'Yes, of course. I'd be delighted. Can you tell me who will be interviewing me and where?'

'Yes, it will be Amanda Stevenson, the owner, and the interview will take place here at the main bakery in Ryders Grove.'

'That's fine. Thanks for your help. I'll be there at two-thirty on Monday.'

'Goodbye.'

Figure 6.3 Telephone Invitation to an Interview: An example.

Make use of a telephone answering machine, or an answering service, for when you are out, but be sure that the response message on your machine is a formal and businesslike one. Prospective employers are not going to be impressed if they are confronted by a humorous message, even though it might be a source of amusement to your friends.

Whether making or receiving phone calls, always have a pen and paper to hand. It is also advisable to have details of your job application nearby and copies of letters of application, curricula vitae, etc. so that you can refer to them quickly if necessary. This may be especially important if you are rung by a possible employer querying something that was included or omitted from your CV or application form.

Managing Phone Calls

Whether making or receiving calls, you should be ready and able to manage them competently. Most conversations will proceed along broadly similar lines – so you should know how to start one properly, when to speak and listen, how to ask questions and answer them and finish the conversation in a polite and businesslike manner.

Make sure you have the correct name (and pronunciation) of the person you are calling, and that you know their extension number, if appropriate. Such a call might go something like this: 'Good morning, could you please put me through to Mr Sidney Potts on extension 623 – thank you. Mr Potts? Hello, my name's Nikita Patel. I'm ringing with regard to the information management post that you advertised in today's *Echo*. I'd like to talk to you about it ...'

It is essential that you are clearly heard, so speak up and into the mouthpiece. It is surprising how many people do not. You should sound like the type of person they want to employ, by using positive, upbeat language and sounding keen and enthusiastic.

Listening carefully to what is being said to you is equally important, so that you can answer any questions correctly and effectively. Take care not to talk over the top of the other person's comments, as this can cause offence. It is surprisingly easy to fall into this trap in your eagerness to describe your strengths.

Have a checklist of the questions you wish to put during the conversation. Pose each question at the appropriate time in a direct and polite manner, and keep the conversation as succinct as you can.

When answering questions, be direct and to the point. For example: 'Yes, I've three A-levels – Business Studies, C grade; French, B grade; and German, B grade.' This is sufficient and requires no further explanation unless asked for. Only expand on an answer if it otherwise shows you in a bad light. Such as: 'No, I'm 41, but I have the vigour, enthusiasm and drive to do this job, and the knowledge and experience from my work at Hammonds to make it a success. I've increased productivity by 12 per cent in the last year here. Let me do the same for you.' Whenever possible, promote your strengths and link them to the criteria sought.

Following Up your Phone Calls

It is rare that a telephone call made during a job-search schedule does not need to be followed up one way or another. Usually, something can be done to advance your prospects of success.

If your call has been successful, you will probably have been asked to submit a formal letter of application, a CV or completed application form, or to come for a selection interview. Send or deliver in person whatever has been asked for as promptly as possible, so that you are seen to be keen and enthusiastic and will be considered whilst you are still remembered in a positive light. It is sensible to acknowledge a request to attend an interview with a concise letter, along the lines of the sample given in Figure 7.1, page 106. This is courteous, and it will act as a reminder for the prospective employer.

Should you have been contacted by a would-be employer enquiring about details provided in your application form or CV, and you feel in retrospect that your answer was not as good as it should have been, then you may wish to follow it up with a letter of explanation, and perhaps supporting documentation. An example of such a letter is given in Figure 6.4 below.

Dear Miss Siddle

Thank you for your telephone call concerning my application for the job of computer programmer.

I am aware that I am above the preferred age range for the job, but feel I am ideally suited to it nonetheless. I have worked in the computer industry since 1984, and am fully up-to-date with developments, particularly your system, which is identical to the one I helped to install at my last company, Bradburys.

Also, I have recently completed a six-week advanced training course in computer installation and systems procedures at the prestigious Montgomery Training Centre in Edinburgh, subscribe to various trade and general consumer magazines and am on the Internet at home to keep abreast of developments in the United States.

With these points in mind, I hope you will call me on 01992 929100 to invite me to an interview, or e-mail me on ...!

Yours sincerely
James Dawson

Figure 6.4 Letter of Explanation: An example.

7

Impressing the Interviewer

If you have written job-search letters, compiled curricula vitae, completed application forms and used the telephone well, you should be one of the selected handful of candidates to be asked to attend an interview for the job in question. To have got this far is a considerable achievement. Typically, only six to 10 candidates are chosen to be interviewed from amongst the hundreds of applicants for a job. To go one step further and be offered that job, you need to approach this advanced stage of the selection process both carefully and thoroughly.

Preparing for Interviews

It is courteous to acknowledge an invitation to an interview, even if you are not asked to do so. A sample letter is given in Figure 7.1 overleaf.

Dear Mrs Rigg

Thank you for inviting me to an interview for the post of Head of Resources at 11.30 am on Wednesday 26 August at your Head Office in Dalston Road, Eastwick.

I am pleased to confirm that I will be attending this interview and will bring my work samples with me, as requested.

Yours sincerely
Jay Hammond

Figure 7.1 Letter Acknowledging an Invitation to an Interview: An example.

You will already have conducted some research into the company, job and type of employee required, when making sure they were right for you before you submitted your original application. Even so, you ought to refresh your memory now to convince both yourself and the interviewer that you really are well matched. Mull over the numerous questions you asked yourself when you first identified this as a suitable opportunity, and peruse the notes you made as you discovered the answers to these questions. Similarly, check out the details you recorded about yourself when you were deciding what you wanted to do.

Armed with this all-important information, you should go on to think about the interview, the interviewer and the questions you will face. You will almost certainly be attending either a 'one-to-one' or a 'panel' interview. 'One-to-one' interviews are those which involve one interviewer, usually the head of the relevant department or the personnel manager in a larger concern, and one applicant – you, on this occasion. 'Panel' or 'board' interviews consist of several interviewers facing the one applicant. Perhaps you will sit opposite three to six interviewers, including the firm's personnel manager, the appropriate head of department, a specialist in your field and trainee interviewers sitting in to gain experience in interviewing techniques.

The majority of selection interviews – regardless of how and where they are run – will follow a similar pattern. They begin with introductions and gentle questions to ease the interviewee into the conversation. Then will follow cut and thrust questions designed to establish whether the applicant is suited to the job, and there will be an opportunity for the applicant to ask equally searching questions about the company. Proceedings will then be concluded with a rounding up of the discussion, an agreement on what was said and will happen next, plus farewells. How long it will last in total will vary according to what needs to be covered and individual circumstances. Thirty minutes is the norm; although an hour or more is not unusual.

Not surprisingly, interviewers vary from one to another. Some are experienced and competent, others less so. More often than not you will have to face just one interviewer and, hopefully, they will be trained and capable of carrying out the interview in an efficient manner. If so, they will be well prepared, the interview will start at the agreed time, and your letter, CV, application form or notes from a telephone conversation will be on the desk between you. You should be sure to bring several copies of your CV along, in case the interviewers need them for reference. The interviewer will work to a loose and flexible plan, knowing what topics have to be discussed, and which questions should be asked and answered. You will sense that you are being guided through this plan, with your comments kept to the point, and notes being made about what you say.

Various types of question will arise during your interview, and you need to be able to respond properly to them. 'Open' questions begin with words like 'what', 'how' and 'why', as in 'What do you do in your spare time?', 'How did you handle that situation?' and 'Why do you want this job?' They are asked frequently, and should be seen as an opportunity to put across your knowledge about the firm and this post, to talk through your qualities and show how well suited you are. 'Closed' questions such as 'Did you get along with your boss?' and 'Did you like that job?' allow only a 'yes' or 'no' response, and are used to check facts and keep nervous interviewees talking. It is sensible to treat these like open questions, answering along the lines of 'Yes, I did because ...' Tell the interviewer about yourself and those terrific strengths you have!

Limited questions start with words such as 'who', 'when', 'where' and 'which', as in 'Who did you work with at that company?' and 'Which area were you responsible for?' Your answers will therefore be short and limited and not very informative, unless you tackle the questions as open ones, and answer them accordingly! 'I worked with Kulvinder Kang. I learned a lot from him, and we worked together well.' Hypothetical questions revolve around what you would do in a given situation – 'What would you do if ...' and 'How would you handle ...' If you are well-prepared from your earlier research work, you should be able to work out what the 'ideal employee' would do, and respond accordingly. 'I'd approach the task calmly and logically. First, I'd look at the situation, assess the various options and then I'd ...'

Two types of question which should not be asked – but may be by nervous and/or incompetent interviewers – are 'leading' and 'multiple' ones. Leading questions are those which signpost the answer that should be given, such as 'Do you have initiative?' and 'Are you fit enough to do this job?' Clearly, the answers are obvious. If asked a leading question, give the 'right' answer, but then add to it to stress your strengths. 'Yes, I have initiative. As an example of this, at my last job I had to ...' Multiple questions involve several questions being rolled into one. 'What are your hobbies? Do you belong to any clubs or societies?' These are easy to answer. Deal with each component question, one at a time.

Probably the easiest way to research the type of interview you will be facing is simply to ask someone at the company about it – ideally the person who has invited you to interview. Hopefully, they will also be the same person who is going to interview you (or will at least be involved in some capacity), so that you can learn more about the interviewer and their capabilities at the same time. Preparing properly for the types of question you may have to answer means thinking about what you might be asked in your specific situation, contemplating how they could be phrased and then deciding how you will respond. The checklist of age-related questions given in Figure 7.2 below may help to start you thinking along the right lines. You could practise answering them with a friend acting as the interviewer.

All sorts of questions may be asked during an interview, most of which will concentrate on and develop from your letter of application, curriculum vitae or application form, and can be answered easily. Age-related questions may be trickier to handle. Here are some key questions, and some suggestions for your answers.

Q. *Why are you applying for a job which was advertised for someone younger than you?*

A. Because I'm right for it. You're looking for someone who is ... I have the required skills, knowledge, expertise ... For example ...

NB. Match what they want with what you have to offer, and give examples as proof. Emphasize your health and vitality by mentioning physical activities whenever possible. Avoid highlighting your age by NOT talking about lengthy experience.

Q. Why are you applying for a job which is not as good as your present/last one?

A. Because I wish to progress ... In a go-ahead firm ... Growth trade or industry ... One step back, two steps forward.

NB. No negative comments here about impending redundancy, unemployment or the need to work, nor criticisms of your old company or sector, as these reflect badly on you. Lots of positive, lively words and subtle compliments are required – and show you're still young enough to be ambitious too!

Q. How do you feel about working for someone younger than you?

A. Fine ... Never thought of age as an issue ... Judge people by who they are and what they've done, rather than age ... Will get on well ... Will learn from them.

NB. Again, lively and upbeat comments needed here. Be careful not to make your response sound like a none too subtle dig at those people who DO view age as an issue. Appear friendly and jolly, as someone who is ready to fit in ANYWHERE.

Q. How do you feel about working with people younger than you?

A. Happy! Always fitted into a team easily ... For example ... Always got on well with everyone ... As an example ...

NB. Another buoyant answer required. RECENT examples of teamwork and what 'we' did and 'we' achieved together are helpful. Avoid emphasizing the age element as this can convey a 'them and us' attitude. Concentrate instead on a we're-in-this-together answer.

Impressing the Interviewer 111

Q. Aren't you too old for this job?'

A. No! I'm right for it because ... You want this from an employee ... I can offer you this ... For example ...

NB. Perhaps surprising, but a terrific question, giving you the opportunity to sell your strengths and show your suitability for this job. You may even want to stress some of those special strengths that come with age – stability, maturity and so on. Give examples where possible – recent, lively and active ones; modest, too, if appropriate.

Q. Won't your age be a disadvantage in this job?

A. No! It gives me a great advantage because ... Special strengths ... Examples.

NB. Another excellent opportunity to show how good you are. Refer to those special, age-related strengths that are most associated with this job, and are likely to impress the interviewer (I've settled down and am here to stay; I won't be moving away in a year or two's time). Concentrate on what YOU have to offer, not what YOUNGER applicants cannot offer (this would make you sound defensive) and emphasize how old you are. Only old people moan about 'The Younger Generation'!

Figure 7.2 Age-Related Questions: A checklist.

Self-Presentation

Nearly everyone who is seeking a job, transfer or promotion tries to convey the best possible image of themselves – writing a smart and informative letter and curriculum vitae and completing an application form carefully and neatly. However, too often candidates let themselves down at the interview, failing to realize that they are being seen and judged by their prospective employer over a sustained period and will be assessed not only on what they say, but how they look, speak and behave during that time. Therefore, you should pay special attention to your appearance, speech and manner, working out what you are going to do beforehand.

Smart dress – suit and tie for men, and jacket, blouse and skirt for women – is usually a sensible choice as it shows respect and acknowledges the importance of the occasion. Nevertheless, your appearance can vary according to what is considered acceptable by that particular firm. An employee in an advertising agency, for example, may be allowed or even encouraged to dress more fashionably than someone working behind a counter in a bank. Dress to suit the situation, erring on the cautious side if in any doubt. Make sure you feel comfortable in what you are wearing. An itchy new shirt or blouse, tight trousers or skirt and pinched shoes feel unpleasant, putting you on edge and distracting you from what you are doing.

It is also worth stressing here that how you dress can make you look younger, and often substantially so if it is done with care and discretion; not a bad idea if you believe your age may be a negative feature on this occasion. Having a flattering hairstyle, shaving off a beard (if relevant) and wearing reasonably modern and up-to-date clothing can help to create a more youthful impression. Be very careful not to take this to excess though. A teenage hairstyle on a mature person, inexpertly dyed and/or unrealistically dark hair on an older face, and clothes which would look more appropriate on your children will only serve to make you seem undignified, and even desperate.

Personal hygiene is associated closely with your appearance, and must be considered too. There is little point in wearing suitable clothes if they are stained and grubby, and you have body odour and bad breath. No employer will want to take on a dirty person who will alienate colleagues and customers, no matter how perfect they may otherwise seem to be. So – wash your hair, have a bath or shower, clean your teeth, use a deodorant, scrub your nails and then put on clean clothes and polished shoes. Keep away from smoking, drinking alcohol and eating immediately before the interview to help to maintain your cleanliness. All obvious points, maybe, but not everyone takes note of them.

Of course, you may be in the building for an hour or more, talking to your prospective employer before and after the formal interview has been conducted, so you should contemplate your speech. Often, how you speak is as relevant as what you say. Make sure that you are heard properly, by holding up your head, opening your mouth wide and speaking in a clear, firm voice. Vary your speech patterns to maintain interest in what you are saying, talking slightly more quickly to convey enthusiasm and more slowly to emphasize key points. Avoid confusing slang, offensive bad language and irritating expressions such as 'actually' and 'you know' – all such language will create a poor impression.

As with your appearance, the way you talk can show your age, and you may not wish to draw attention to this if it is likely to be perceived as a drawback. There are two main areas of concern here. Many people tend to use the expressions which were popular during their youth (for example, 'with it') throughout their lives, which can not only date them but also confuse the interviewer if they are no longer in common usage. Some people try to over-compensate for their age by using the latest expressions of teenagers ('cool', 'wicked', 'chill out', 'no worries'), which makes them look foolish, especially if these are not used in an appropriate context. So, keep it short and simple.

How you look when you talk is of some significance. If you seem bored, the other person will be as well, or they might even be offended. Your facial expressions should match what you are saying, in order to support the points you are making. Try to appear serious, sincere or enthusiastic as and when appropriate. Look at the person as they speak, and when you reply. Avoiding eye contact, staring at your feet and/or out of the window make you seem uninterested and shifty. Don't hold their gaze for too long, though, as this can convey a rather manic image. Listen to what is being said instead of dwelling on your last reply or what you will say next. Otherwise, you may mishear, and give a nonsensical response.

Think about your body language during the interview. You need to ensure that it backs up what you are saying, does not irritate the interviewer, and makes you look calm and in control at all times. Achieve this by keeping relatively still for most of the time, leaning slightly forward in your chair to convey interest and enthusiasm, and making neat and tidy movements as and when relevant. Be conscious of – and avoid – any annoying mannerisms you may have, such as tapping your feet, fiddling with a pen or waving your hands around as you speak. Do not hunch up in your seat or lounge about at the other extreme; these will make you look tense or overconfident, neither of which will impress.

You may find it helpful to take a clipboard and paper or a notebook into the interview with you, so that you can jot down points raised, as and when relevant. This will also give you something to occupy your hands and will make you appear well prepared and professional in your approach (as long as your note-taking does not disrupt the flow of the conversation). Make sure you use a pen with plenty of ink and have a spare one (just in case), *plus* a copy of your letter of application, curriculum vitae, etc. You may be unfortunate enough to come across an incompetent interviewer, and being able to help them out by providing a copy of a mislaid document may get the interview off to a promising start.

The Trial Run

It is essential that you arrive at the right time and place – an obvious point, perhaps, but one which some candidates ignore to their cost. Do check exactly when and where it is being held, referring to any notes you may have made after a telephone call or looking at your letter of invitation and a map, as appropriate. If in any doubt, pick up the phone and ask for confirmation of the precise details. This is better than turning up late and flustered, which simply makes you appear foolish, causes embarrassment and may even mean you have to wait until everyone else has been interviewed before you are seen. If you have never been to this particular place, carry out a trial run at the same time on an earlier (equally busy) workday to see how long it takes to get there. Allow an extra 30 minutes travelling time on the day itself, just in case you encounter delays or have difficulty parking.

Handling the Interview Successfully

As an older job seeker of 35-plus, the interview itself may not be as nerve-racking and daunting as it is for younger people, many of whom tend to be either lacking in self-confidence or, at the other extreme, too confident to the point of brashness. Nonetheless, you may not have attended an interview for some time, so it is wise to think through what might happen and how you will respond on arrival and during the preliminaries, questions, answers and conclusion.

If you allow extra travelling time and then arrive at the premises with something like 20 minutes or so to spare, go for a walk or find somewhere to sit and read through your notes for a while. Go in with about five minutes left – you do not want to spend too long waiting around inside, as this can make you feel increasingly tense and nervous. Should you be delayed, possibly by traffic, do telephone the company if you can, leaving an explanatory and apologetic message, and an estimated time of arrival. Although a delay will probably create a negative impression, letting the firm know what is happening will at least limit the damage done to your reputation.

When you enter the building you should be greeted by a polite and friendly receptionist who will note your name and details, and direct you to a waiting area where your fellow candidates may be sitting and perhaps talking amongst themselves. You might be offered a cup of tea or coffee, depending on how long you are likely to have to wait. It is wise to refuse this, in case the interviewer comes to meet you early, and you still have your hands full. Sit down and take the opportunity to remove your coat (if appropriate) and put any bags on the floor. Holding bags on your lap makes you seem timid and nervous. Don't forget to take any valuables into the interview with you. Thefts happen everywhere, even in the most attentive organizations.

It is advisable to acknowledge any other candidates, but with no more than a polite and courteous smile, a nod and a 'good morning' or whatever, but be reluctant to enter into conversation with them. Many younger candidates seem self-confident to the point of arrogance and – although this often covers nervousness and a lack of detailed preparation – their brashness and exaggerated stories of previous interviewing experiences can be distracting. Ignore these – you are here on merit; more experienced and competent, calmer and better prepared than they are, so you're going to get this job! Instead of chatting, concentrate on checking your appearance. If you have a small mirror, look at your hair, eyes, nose, mouth and teeth to ensure they are clean. Make certain your clothes are still neat and presentable, buttons are fastened, and everything is tucked in.

Attempt to relax by breathing in deeply and counting under your breath. It can also be a good idea to prepare a greeting for whoever is going to take you to the interview room, so that you know what you are going to say when spoken to, instead of standing there speechless or stammering out a nervous or even nonsensical reply such as 'Goodnight' as some stressed candidates have been known to do. Try not to keep rehearsing the greeting, though, as it might come out back to front when you eventually say it, which will make you appear nervous. Loosen up – you have no reason to feel tense or inferior to anyone else.

It is most likely that someone in authority will come to meet you when the interview is due to begin. Be ready for this, making sure you are not so engrossed in your own thoughts that you have to be spoken to several times before realizing they are there. As appropriate, stand up, smile, introduce yourself and shake hands before picking up your overcoat and bags. Fold your overcoat over your arm and hold your baggage in that hand, so the other is free for opening doors or whatever. Follow the person's lead as they guide you to the interview room.

Be prepared to make small talk as you walk along a corridor or travel up in a lift. You may be asked if you had a good journey, found the premises easily or know the area at all, depending on circumstances. At the very least, you will have to exchange pleasantries about the weather. See these questions and comments for what they are – a relatively painless way of passing the time rather than walking along or standing in awkward, embarrassed silence. Clearly, the person you are with is not that interested in your journey or the weather, so avoid lengthy and/or detailed responses. Just say enough to nudge the conversation on a little, until you reach the interview room.

On arrival the person who has taken you there will hand you over to the interviewer. Smile, shake hands and thank that person for showing you the way – be polite and courteous to everyone and at all times, as you never know who is going to have some input into the selection decision. It may just be that one person you were a little brusque with! Then smile, shake hands and introduce yourself to the interviewer. Wait to be shown to your seat rather than sitting down uninvited. This can appear rather ill-mannered, and may be embarrassing if you sit in the wrong seat.

Questions and Answers

With at least a 30-minute interview ahead of you, the range of questions that may be faced is considerable, although the majority of interviews will contain many, broadly comparable ones, grouped loosely together into several categories, and dealt with in turn; often they will correspond with the sequence of information set out in your letter, CV, application form or telephone call. Various, preliminary questions may be asked before focusing on education, qualifications and training, employment, personality and miscellaneous matters including your leisure activities, and ending with an invitation for you to ask questions.

Try to answer each and every question raised. Listen to the question and consider what it is the interviewer wants to know. Contemplate what you have learned from all your research to date and give a reply which shows your strengths, and substantiates them, whenever possible. As an example, your interviewer may ask you to 'describe your current job' and you believe that this has been raised to see if you have the required experience to do *this* job. Thus, you should think over the two posts, discussing those aspects of your present position which are similar to this one and supporting your comments with descriptions of various specialized activities so that it is obvious you are truly familiar with them.

Do not criticize anyone when answering questions. Of course, it is human nature to blame others when things have gone wrong – bad trainers are the cause of poor course results, your departmental manager disliked you and blocked promotions and so forth – but such critical statements tend to reflect badly on you, making you seem small-minded and even obsessive. The interviewer will think you cannot face up to your failings. If asked directly, so that the answer is unavoidable, admit to your shortcomings, but then show how you have worked to remedy them (and hopefully, successfully). These efforts will then be seen as a strength, and be remembered more than the original weaknesses.

However well the interview is going, avoid becoming over-confident. In particular, do not drop names – 'Pat, my old boss', 'Joel, the MD' and the like simply make you sound self-important and pretentious. Also, try not to give examples of situations, perhaps in your last job, where you and you alone resolved a major problem or whatever, as these can make you appear vain and ridiculous. Try to be modest, and show you're a team player! Equally significant, *never* become over-familiar with the interviewer – that 'Lou – may I call you Lou?' approach can cause offence. You should aim to create a friendly and professional, but slightly detached, relationship, and can do this by keeping your physical distance, referring to them in formal fashion, and saying 'please' and 'thank you' when relevant (but not to excess).

Always tell the truth. Naturally, you will be selective in what you say, promoting your positive rather than your negative features so far as possible, but you must avoid exaggerating, and outright dishonesty. Experienced interviewers will probably be able to recognize when you are making up an answer as you go along, and even contradicting yourself. Certificates may have to be produced at some stage and previous and current employers could be approached for references, often via informal, off the record telephone conversations. By lying, you run the considerable risk of being found out, either straightaway which is humiliating or later on when you have got the job – which could lead to instant dismissal. If the only way you can succeed is by being dishonest, then this indicates you are not as well suited to the job as you thought.

Make sure that everything you say is relevant and kept to the point. Hear the question, work out your answer, say what you have to say and shut up! Being asked to describe your last job is an invitation to do just that, and briefly; not to give a lecture on the shortcomings of the firm, trade or industry you worked in. Similarly, it should not be seen as an opportunity to go on and on and on, repeating the same facts over and over again in different ways. Irrelevant and/or repetitious information will not only irritate and annoy, but may restrict both you and the interviewer from covering all the topics and questions that need to be dealt with in the time set aside for this interview.

Try to avoid becoming impatient at any time, and certainly do not show it if you feel this way. Allow the interviewer to complete each and every question before responding to it, even if you are sure you know what is going to be asked. Butting in makes you sound rude and arrogant, *and* foolish, if you misjudged what the question was going to be about.

Never get involved in a heated exchange with your interviewer, even if you disagree vehemently with and/or are upset by something that is said. Some interviewers will attempt to provoke you – to see if you stay calm and reasonable under pressure – by making controversial statements and/or querying your answers. Whether staged for effect or genuine, stand up for yourself, working through your comments or restating them in a cool and collected manner, without becoming aggressive or angry. Lose your temper – lose that job!

Stay calm, regardless of what happens. If someone enters the room or the telephone rings, pause, recall what you were talking about and resume when the interviewer indicates you should do so. If you do not know the answer to a question, say so rather than looking blank-faced or talking nonsense. Depending on the circumstances, ask the interviewer to tell you, or indicate that you will investigate and find out, as appropriate. Most of all, don't worry about these questions and answers. You are here on merit – in the top six or so of one hundred or more applicants – and because the interviewer believes you are potentially suitable for this job. Thus, you have no real reason to be tense or nervous. You know you are well matched – you just have to prove it!

The Conclusion

Having begun with preliminary, settling-in questions and then gone on to deal with education, qualifications and training, employment, personality and miscellaneous matters in turn, the interviewer will start to draw the interview to a close by asking you if there is anything you want to query or know about. You should take this opportunity to raise various questions about any key areas of concern which have not been covered fully or at all. A checklist of possible questions is shown in Figure 7.3 overleaf. Finally, the interviewer will conclude the interview by doing something along the lines of thanking you for attending, rising from the chair, smiling and offering their hand to you for a handshake. This will often be accompanied by a comment about when and how they will be in touch and a question such as 'Can you find your own way out?' It's time to go!

Most interviewees will have some questions to ask towards the end of their interview, typically about the exact pay and benefits package on offer. As an older job-hunter, you may wish to raise various, specific questions because of your age:

Q. What is the salary?

NB. More often than not, minimum and maximum figures will have been indicated in the job advertisement and/or associated literature, with the exact salary being subject to negotiation, usually at this late stage of the interview. It is likely that the interviewer will not have a precise sum in mind and – if you are the right person – will be prepared to go up towards that maximum figure. However, as an older job-seeker, you should be more concerned with the total package on offer, including health-care arrangements for example. So, it is wise not to be too trenchant or tough on negotiations here as this may make the interviewer less willing to be flexible elsewhere on other, equally important aspects of the deal. Reach an agreement by discussion, not negotiation.

Q. What is the total remuneration package?

NB. You do need to establish *exactly* what you will be entitled to – company car, performance-related bonuses, interest-free loans, health insurance, share options, non-contributory pension scheme, and the like. These all have a real monetary value, boosting your 'pay' substantially. As important, and without drawing attention to your age, you should find out if you are excluded from any benefits (perhaps because of your age). 'Are there any benefits I will not be entitled to upon joining?' is a question that can be asked at this point.

Q. Can I transfer my existing pension scheme to this company?

NB. When moving from one company to another, you can either (a) leave your pension behind to build up until retirement, (b) transfer it to the new employer's scheme (assuming they will accept it) or (c) transfer it to a personal pension plan (although this might then affect your entitlement to join a pension scheme run by your new employer). Check your options now – and later with your old employer and an independent financial adviser – before reaching a decision based on your very specific, individual circumstances. There are various advisory organizations that can help. See 'Useful Contacts' at the end of the book.

Q. Can I join your company pension scheme?

NB. In an increasing number of cases, a recruit's automatic right to join a company's pension scheme (albeit perhaps after a year or two's service) ceases if they are over 30. If they are older than that upon recruitment, joining the scheme is at the employer's discretion. Discover the position now, and then take independent advice about the best way of preparing for and providing for your retirement – again referring to the organizations listed in 'Useful Contacts'. Job-hunters often overlook the significance of having a pension as part of their overall package. It becomes more important, even crucial, the older you are. (See also Chapter 9 under 'The Company Pension Scheme', pp. 148–9.)

Q. Am I eligible to join the company's health insurance scheme (assuming that they have one)?

NB. As with a pension scheme, your entitlement to health-care protection may be at the company's discretion if you are above a certain age upon joining; 30 or 35 years old in many instances. It is advisable to try to secure this entitlement within your remuneration package – without creating the impression that you expect to be ill! – as it becomes increasingly important as you get older. Although you do not need it yet, you may do one day, so get protected now!

Q. What further training facilities are available to me?

NB. Don't forget you are still trying to sell yourself and get that offer – and a desire to better yourself, progress, fulfil your potential and so on will always impress (assuming that the company is a go-ahead one with room for career advancement to take place). So, ask this question because you want to know the answer, and get the job! (Also, you do want to check that you will not be discriminated against because of your age – 'Can anyone in the company apply for these courses?' may be a useful question here.)

Q. What leisure and fitness facilities are available at the company?

NB. Again, you would like to use these facilities and you also want to keep conveying the image of a fit, healthy and young candidate. Never miss the opportunity to stress how active you are, albeit subtly.

Q. Where do you see my future in the company?

NB. This question serves several purposes. You will probably want to join a firm where you can be transferred and promoted in due course, rather than being shunted sideways or out. You need to identify prospective opportunities now if this is the case. Also, you want to show commitment, ambition and a get-up-and-go attitude to succeed, and such a question suggests these attributes to the interviewer. You're not going to just tick over until retirement – you wish to make a real contribution whilst you're there.

Figure 7.3 Your Questions: A checklist for the job-seeker at 35-plus.

Following the Interview

You should always follow through on each and every interview, rather than simply putting it out of your mind once you have left the premises, and are travelling home. There is much to be gained from reviewing the interview; in particular, thinking about your performance and what you have learned from the occasion. Also, you must write a thank-you note to the interviewer as soon as you arrive home, posting it straightaway so that you will stand out from the crowd.

As you journey home, review your performance at the interview. Were you as well prepared as you should have been? Did you arrive on time, and deal with the preliminaries properly? Were age-related and other questions handled successfully, and answered in an effective manner? Did you speak clearly and competently, as and when necessary? Did the interview draw to a close in a pleasant and diplomatic way, without embarrassment and/or ill-feeling being generated? In short, do you feel you have done the best you can, better than anyone else and enough to be offered the job, transfer or promotion? If not, what could you have done better?

Also, contemplate what you learned at the interview. Did you find out anything new about this company that you want to work for, or progress within? Perhaps you were impressed by its efficiency or taken aback by the number and nature of its young and aggressive employees. Did you discover something more about the job? Maybe some of the interviewer's comments or questions gave you a greater insight into the work you would be doing, if successful. Did you uncover anything else about the type of person needed to do the job? Possibly, the interviewer probed you about requirements you had not thought of, and considered. You may decide that your personality, strengths and weaknesses are more – or less – suited to the post than you believed originally.

Think, too, about what you have learned of interviews from this occasion; it might have been the first interview you have attended for many years. What was the interview itself like? Perhaps it was a one-to-one interview, which was relaxed in manner and easy to handle. Alternatively, you might have faced a panel interview, which could have been more formal, and nerve-racking. How did you feel about the interviewer? They may have been calm and in control, leading the conversation on in a professional manner, or nervous and inexperienced, which meant that you had to help to move it on in the right direction. What were the questions like? Hopefully, these included plenty of open ones so that you were able to promote your strengths. If they contained others – such as closed and limited ones – you will have had to work harder with developing your answers.

Obviously, this overall view of what has happened will be of benefit in a variety of ways. Assessing your specific performance may enable you to decide if you have a chance of being offered the job and, if not, should highlight areas which need to be worked upon and improved prior to your next selection interview. Mulling over what you have learned about the organization, post and type of employee needed will allow you to judge whether you really want the job, if it is offered to you. Furthermore, the whole experience will stand you in good stead on any future occasion, if appropriate, giving you more experience and confidence in dealing with different types of interview, interviewer and questions.

The Thank-You Letter

It is a good idea to send a letter to the interviewer once you arrive home after the interview. In it, you should thank them for seeing you, restate your interest in the job, summarize your qualities and indicate what you want to happen next – the offer of that job, hopefully! Post this letter off by first-class post that same day or deliver it in person on the following one, if possible. Such a letter may distinguish you from the other candidates, remind the would-be employer of your strengths – including your courtesy and efficiency – and it might just tip the decision in your favour. An example of a good follow-up letter is given in Figure 7.4 below.

Dear Ms Chang

Re: Assistant Technician

Thank you for seeing me this afternoon with regard to the above post. I was very impressed by all I saw, especially the friendly and pleasant working environment.

I believe the practical experience I gained during my five years at McGowers would stand me in good stead in the job, and that I would fit in well as a hardworking member of this industrious team.

I hope that you will decide to offer the job to me, and look forward to hearing from you in due course. My telephone number is 01903 674 717.

Yours sincerely
Ben Hisani

Figure 7.4 Post Interview Thank-You Note: An example.

Having reviewed the interview and sent your letter, you should then put this particular application out of your mind – at least for the time being – and continue with that job-search programme which you sketched out and timetabled soon after you decided to change your job. It is absolutely imperative that you do not send any further letters or make telephone calls to the company asking for an update or a decision. If you are still being actively considered then such contact will only serve to irritate and annoy, and may well cost you the job.

8

Benefiting from Rejection

Anyone who is job searching – whether they are 16, 36 or 56 – has to accept that they will almost certainly be rejected, and perhaps over and over again. This happens to everyone, whatever their age or qualities. It is an extremely competitive market and it takes time to succeed. However good you are, rejections can take place at various stages of the recruitment and selection procedure. Sometimes you will not receive a response when you reply to job advertisements or contact people in your network or at selected organizations, agencies or consultancies. On other occasions, you will be rejected formally after you have applied for a job by letter, CV, application form or telephone or following an interview for the post. Whenever you are rejected, you need to learn from it so that your chances of success are improved in the future.

No Response

If you do not receive a reply to communications then the obvious question you need to ask yourself is 'Why?' With a job advertisement it may be that you are unsuitable for the position. Think back over the questions you asked yourself about the trade or industry, firm, job and the type of employee required when you identified this as a suitable opportunity, and look at the notes you made when answering them. Compare these alongside the details you recorded about your personality, strengths and weaknesses to judge if you are as well matched as you once thought. Probably not; in which case it is advisable to be more selective in future, concentrating your time and efforts on those opportunities with greater prospects. Alternatively, a reply may not have been sent because the firm has been inundated with approaches or is ill-organized and rude – which means you may not want to work for them anyway!

If a contact in your network did not respond, it is possible that they could not help you this time around and are too busy to reply. On the other hand, more worryingly, they may be fed up with your constant chasing. You could try to find out by making a brief phone call, but if the lack of response is not for the first reason then your call won't be welcome. If you believe the latter to be the case, then the better course may be to delete them from your list (at least for the time being).

A lack of response from a chosen organization, agency or consultancy can probably be attributed to the fact that they have no vacancies available which would be suitable for you, or your communication has been addressed to the wrong person and it has not been handed on to the right one. In the case of go-betweens, perhaps they help to recruit for different types of jobs, companies, trades or industries from those you are looking for. Again, do find out why, perhaps making a short telephone call to them to check the position. Often, they will feel awkward and embarrassed about not having replied, and may be more communicative as a result of this than they would normally be with job-seekers who cold-called them. Maybe they can then join your network of contacts! If you have made mistakes – writing to inappropriate people, for example – then learn from this, and avoid making them again.

Think specifically about your age being the cause of rejection. Check back over your application to see if you mentioned your age or indicated it through stating the dates of early employment, for example. If so, this may be the reason why you did not receive a response – although no-one is going to admit it, in case this leads to arguments and even bad publicity for the firm. If not, then unless you gave away your age through using dated expressions, you have probably been treated the same as everyone else – rudely! In the circumstances, that may be reassuring.

The Rejection Letter

Those rejections which follow the submission of a letter of application, a curriculum vitae or an application form will be formal and will invariably consist of a bland and rather vague letter such as the one shown in Figure 8.1 overleaf. Specific reasons for rejection will not be given as these tend to encourage applicants to get in touch to convince the prospective employer to change their mind, either by persuasion or argument. Also, such statements could leave the company open to claims for unfair discrimination, if rejected applicants felt these were unjustified and that they had been discriminated against because of their sex, marital status or race. They would be angry, too, if age had been stated as an issue. Neither use this letter as a cause for complaint to the would-be employer, nor screw it up in disgust and throw it away without a second thought. Use it as part of your learning process.

Dear Mr Rae

Thank you for your letter and curriculum vitae concerning the post of Data Processing Manager.

We have considered your application carefully but regret to inform you that on this occasion you have not been successful.

We would, however, like to take this opportunity to thank you for your interest and wish you every success for the future.

Yours sincerely
Pat Baker
Personnel Officer

Figure 8.1 Letter of Rejection: An example.

Following receipt of a rejection, mull over all those notes you made earlier about the trade, industry, company, job and type of person required and your personality, strengths and weaknesses. Maybe you are applying for posts which are ill-suited to you. Perhaps you are over- or under-qualified for them, for example, and might be better advised to devote your energies to pursing more appropriate positions. Also, contemplate how well you are actually applying, whether by letter, curriculum vitae, application form or telephone. Possibly you *are* ideally suited but are not putting over your strengths well, or disguising your weaknesses properly. It could be that you need to spend some time improving your approaches. Consider, also, whether age might have played a part in the decision.

Within a week or so of attending an interview, you should hear from the company. If you are rejected – typically with a letter as bland as that one reproduced in Figure 8.1 – you should look back over your job application and the interview in particular to try to work out the reason for this. Logically, if you have got this far, then the trade, industry, firm, job and type of employee required must be fairly well matched to your personality, strengths and weaknesses. Realistically, you will have been turned down because there was just one job and perhaps six to eight candidates, so only one person could be successful and on this occasion someone did that little bit better than you. You might not have performed well at the interview, being hesitant or even argumentative. It may be that time needs to be devoted to polishing your interviewing skills. Again, consider whether age was a significant issue, or not.

It can be beneficial to contact the interviewer for their comments about your rejection if – and it is sometimes a big if – you believe they will be receptive to this. Only you can tell. As few (if any) interviewers will want to put anything down in writing – just in case it is subsequently used against them, perhaps in an unfair discrimination claim at an industrial tribunal – it is usually best to telephone them for their views. They might tell you, which will be helpful next time around, enabling you to avoid making the same mistakes again.

Stay calm and polite if they are vague or prefer not to discuss the matter. They could be embarrassed, too busy or simply unwilling to give each and every candidate a blow-by-blow account of their performance. No-one is going to say you were discriminated against because of your age, for example. Becoming argumentative and angry is not only unreasonable, but will make it difficult for you to apply there again if another, suitable job ever arises.

Rejection is often seen as a setback, especially when it occurs frequently, and/or at a late stage in the selection process, after an interview has been conducted. However, it should be stressed that you must not view it in this way, particularly if you have only just started job-hunting. If you have made mistakes – and everyone does to begin with – see it as a learning process. Be philosophical about it, too; you may have done everything absolutely right, but it is a highly competitive market. By far the likeliest reason for rejection is that someone had already been earmarked for the job before it was even advertised. It is estimated that over half of all job vacancies are filled in this way. So, don't despair. The best candidate does not always get the job. You just have to make sure you do next time around.

Making Changes and Improvements

Having asked yourself why you were rejected on each occasion that it occurred and having identified the reasons for it, you will want to move on to make changes to your job-search programme and improvements to your application and interviewing techniques. Even though you probably did extremely well and were an outstanding candidate who was just pipped at the post, it is still worth doing this. It will give you the edge next time around!

Think again about where you are learning of vacancies. In retrospect, perhaps you are missing out some key sources of advertisements for older job-hunters, and/or have inappropriate names on your list of contacts in your network, chosen organizations, agencies or consultancies. Maybe you are approaching people incorrectly – in person rather than by letter, so that they can see you are older straightaway. Consider redrafting parts of your job-search schedule. You might be spending too much time concentrating on one job-hunting method to the detriment of others, or are failing to keep complete records and notes so that people are being contacted too often, or not at all. Possibly, your answering machine is switched off when you are out, and you are missing calls. Contemplate, too, how well you are identifying suitable opportunities. In all likelihood, you are not being thorough enough with your research and are sometimes applying for unsuitable jobs.

If you are progressing further – but not to the interviewing stage – then you may need to improve your application techniques. Mull over your letter-writing ability and be sure you understand fully the different types of letter than need to be written. Similarly, review how successfully you are dealing with curricula vitae and application forms. Perhaps you are not emphasizing your strengths and overlooking your weaknesses as you should be doing, which is a common cause of concern amongst most job-seekers. You might be revealing your age on those occasions when it might be seen as a liability. You don't always have to! Think once more about how competently you are using the telephone when applying for work. Maybe you are not handling calls as professionally as you ought to be doing, or are failing to follow through after the calls have been made.

To be turned down after an interview has been conducted is especially disheartening, particularly if you feel that it went well. Perhaps you cannot do any better, but it is certainly sensible to look again at your interviewing tactics to ensure you really are doing as well as you possibly can. Consider how you prepare for interviews. It may be that you have been trying to look younger, but have taken this a bit too far. Contemplate how you have been handling interviews. You might not have anticipated some of the age-related questions, and stumbled over your answers. Think about what you do following interviews. It is not unusual for candidates to chase would-be employers for a decision, thus losing out to another, equally excellent candidate who is not so demanding.

9

Being Offered That Job

In due course you will be offered a job and will receive a telephone call from the prospective employer, or perhaps a letter such as the one shown in Figure 9.1 below, within a few days of your successful interview. You then need to decide whether you are going to accept the offer or reject it, and, given that you accept, subsequently going on to change your job – at 35-plus!

Dear Ms Fox

Further to our recent meeting, I am pleased to offer you employment as a receptionist/office assistant at our Head Office. You will be responsible to Mrs Daphne McCoy, our office supervisor. This offer is subject to suitable references being received from your referees and the completion of a satisfactory trial period of three months.

Your hours of work will be 9 am to 5 pm from Monday to Friday inclusive. You will have a one-hour lunch break between 1 pm and 2 pm.

Your salary will be £800 per month, paid on the 15th day of the following month into your bank account.

You will be entitled to 20 days paid holiday each year, plus statutory holidays. These must be taken in accordance with the staff rota as detailed in the accompanying staff handbook. Our holiday year runs from 6 April to 5 April.

All other terms and conditions of your employment are noted in the staff handbook which you are asked to read before accepting this offer.

Please confirm within seven days whether you wish to take up this offer of employment. If so, will you inform me when you will be able to start work and also give me permission to contact your referees.

I look forward to hearing from you.

Yours sincerely
Janice Paxton
Administrator

Figure 9.1 Letter Containing an Offer of Employment: An example.

Accepting or Rejecting the Offer

It is very tempting to accept the first job that you are offered, especially if you are thoroughly tired of your existing one, are under notice of redundancy or have been out of work for some time. In such a case, a job – any job! – may be a financial and perhaps even a psychological necessity. However, if you feel you have a choice – maybe you are employed in dull but otherwise satisfactory work – then it is wise to step back and contemplate carefully whether or not this is the right job for you after all. Consider again the pros and cons of changing your job and its possible consequences, if this is really what you want and (not least) that you actually do have what is needed to do the job effectively. See Figure 9.2 'Rejecting or Accepting Job Offers: An action checklist for mature job-seekers' overleaf.

	Yes/Accept?	No/Decline?
Is this job well suited to my personality?	☐	☐
Does it match (most of) my likes?	☐	☐
Does it avoid (most of) my dislikes?	☐	☐
Will it enable me to achieve my goals?	☐	☐
Does it meet all of my essential requirements?	☐	☐
Most of my desirable requirements?	☐	☐
Absolutely none of my contra-indications?	☐	☐
In short, is it the right job for me?	☐	☐
Are my strengths well matched to the job?	☐	☐
AND the special strengths that come with age?	☐	☐
Are my weaknesses largely irrelevant with regard to this job?	☐	☐
AND the particular weaknesses that are perceived to come with age?	☐	☐
Are my general circumstances strengths rather than weaknesses here?	☐	☐
In short, am I right for this job?	☐	☐
Shall I accept it?	☐	☐

You need to think carefully about rejecting or accepting a job offer. Answering the following questions may help you to reach the right decision:

Figure 9.2 Rejecting or Accepting Job Offers: An action checklist for mature job-seekers.

Should you choose to decline – and some people will say this is brave, others foolhardy – then you ought to reject the offer in a pleasant and courteous manner, briefly explaining your reasons if these will not cause offence. Never criticize the job, nor the company offering it to you. If in doubt about what to say, give a bland, non-specific reason for turning it down – as in the example of a letter rejecting a job offer in Figure 9.3 below. It is advisable to reject in writing rather than over the telephone or (even worse) in person, as these methods might lead to an argument and ill-feeling. Always be conscious that you may wish to apply for another position at that firm at some point in the future, so you need to avoid upsetting anybody now.

Dear Ms Parkinson

Thank you for your letter of 12 June offering me the post of research assistant in your research and development department.

On careful reflection, I have decided not to accept your offer because I feel the job is not the right one for me at this stage in my career.

Thank you for the offer. I was extremely flattered to receive it.

Yours sincerely
Tony Banks

Figure 9.3 Letter Rejecting a Job Offer: An example.

In all likelihood, though, you will decide to accept the offer. If so, you will probably have been asked in the letter offering you the job to supply details of perhaps two referees who can vouch for the information given by you or, if already provided in an application form or at an interview, to grant permission to approach them. Thus, you will need to forward those details or give that permission. References should normally be produced by people of some independence and standing and who know you and your work well. Choose such people as current and/or former employers, tutors on leisure and/or qualification courses, rather than personal friends and relatives. They may be approached in writing along the lines of the letter given in Figure 9.4 below – or by telephone for a more informal, off the record reference.

Dear Neville

Reference Request: Private and Confidential

Jane Richards of 17 Ambefield Crescent, Kington-St-Mary, Suffolk BE12 0PS has applied to us for the post of personal assistant to our Marketing Director and states that she held a similar position in your firm from 1 June 1993 to 30 October 1996.

As such, we would be grateful if you would be so kind as to answer the following questions, and provide any other information that you think may be relevant to us. All information supplied will be treated in the strictest confidence.

How long was Jane Richards employed by you?

In what capacity was she employed?

What did her job involve?

How would you rate her in relation to:

a) ability to do the job
b) conduct
c) honesty
d) time-keeping and attendance
e) health

What were her reasons for leaving your employment?

What was her salary at the time?

Would you re-employ her?

Additional comments:

A stamped, addressed envelope is enclosed for your reply.
We thank you for your assistance in this matter.

Yours sincerely
Clive Bowkey
Personnel Manager

Figure 9.4 Letter Requesting a Reference: An example.

Either way, your referees will invariably be asked to comment on your present or earlier work – in particular, your job title, duties and responsibilities, length of employment, pay, abilities, conduct, honesty, time-keeping, attendance, health and reasons for leaving. They might even be asked to state whether or not they would re-employ you, which should produce an interesting answer! Make sure you nominate referees who can not only comment on those areas but will do so favourably.

As stated before, you should, out of courtesy, always check beforehand that people are happy to have their names put forward as a referee and let them know when you have done this so that they are prepared for a letter or phone call. After references have been provided, you ought to send a concise thank-you letter like the sample given in Figure 9.5 below. This is both polite and sensible, making it more likely that they will be willing to do it again in future.

Dear Raj

Just a brief note to thank you for giving such a good reference about me to Jack Preston at Norbury House.

As you know, I applied there for the job of researcher and have now been offered this position – and I'm sure your reference was a great help.

Thank you again for your assistance.

Yours sincerely
Peta Robertson

Figure 9.5 Thank-You Letter to a Referee: An example.

Clearly, satisfactory health is important for any post – no employer wants to recruit someone who is continually sick – but for the vast majority of jobs, the completion of general health questions on an application form and an acceptable reference from a current or former employer should be sufficient proof of this. However, if the job is particularly vigorous and/or physically demanding, then the offer may also be subject to the provision of a medical report which indicates that you will be able to do the job correctly. Under the terms of the Access to Medical Reports Act 1988, the would-be employer may ask for your written permission to contact your doctor for such a report.

Alternatively – and more likely – you will be asked to attend a medical examination at the firm's in-house centre. Hopefully, you will not have a problem with this – especially as you are a lively and active over-35, ready to show how fit and healthy you are!

Dear Mrs Davison

Thank you for your letter of 17 August offering me the post of works manager. I am delighted to accept this offer.

I am pleased to confirm that you may now approach my current employer for reference purposes. I am able to start work on 1 September, as discussed at our meeting.

I look forward to working at Hemingstone and Sons and await your instructions concerning the commencement of employment.

Yours sincerely
Douglas Smith

Figure 9.6 Letter Accepting a Job Offer: An example.

You can accept the job offer either by telephone or in writing, with a letter along the lines of the one set out in Figure 9.6 – it is up to you. Often, your choice will be determined by the nature of the offer itself. You may be asked to telephone to confirm your acceptance or to write with permission to approach your referees and your doctor. However you respond, it is important to bear in mind that this is an offer, which usually implies that it is subject to some negotiation. Knowing you are their first choice from so many applicants puts you in a good position to push for a better salary, improved fringe benefits and so on – so telephone or write to take up the offer and negotiate terms and conditions. Get the best deal that you can, because you deserve it. A checklist of areas for negotiation is given in Figure 9.7 below.

Being the first choice candidate for a post puts you in a strong position when it comes to negotiating. Here are some of the key areas which you may be wise to negotiate over until you have obtained a satisfactory, or even an excellent, job package.

		Excellent	Satisfactory	Non-Satisfactory	Poor
Pay:	Rate	☐	☐	☐	☐
	Frequency	☐	☐	☐	☐
	Method	☐	☐	☐	☐
Fringe Benefits		☐	☐	☐	☐
Hours of work		☐	☐	☐	☐
Breaks:	Length	☐	☐	☐	☐
	Frequency	☐	☐	☐	☐
	Timings	☐	☐	☐	☐
Working Environment		☐	☐	☐	☐
Working Practices		☐	☐	☐	☐

		Excellent	Satisfactory	Non-Satisfactory	Poor
Holidays:	Entitlements	☐	☐	☐	☐
	Pay	☐	☐	☐	☐
	Method of Selection	☐	☐	☐	☐
Sickness:	Entitlements	☐	☐	☐	☐
	Pay	☐	☐	☐	☐
Discipline:	Rules	☐	☐	☐	☐
	Procedures	☐	☐	☐	☐
Grievances:	Rules	☐	☐	☐	☐
	Procedures	☐	☐	☐	☐
Appeal:	Rules	☐	☐	☐	☐
	Procedures	☐	☐	☐	☐
Pension Arrangements		☐	☐	☐	☐
Notice Periods:	Employer	☐	☐	☐	☐
	Employee	☐	☐	☐	☐
Other		☐	☐	☐	☐
Other		☐	☐	☐	☐
Other		☐	☐	☐	☐

Of course, some areas will be negotiable and others non-negotiable, especially in larger firms, but it's certainly worth trying to improve what's on offer as much as possible!

Figure 9.7 Areas for Negotiation: A checklist.

The Company Pension Scheme

Company pension schemes are usually worth joining because your employer will contribute to the scheme on your behalf, and will often provide a whole range of benefits on retirement, including health care protection and life insurance cover. Many employers' schemes operate on a 'final pay' basis, providing you with a pension of about two thirds of your final salary on retirement – subject, of course, to the amounts and duration of contributions. This type of scheme has two main advantages – your pension will keep pace with a growing income and you will have a good idea in advance of what your retirement pension will be, and can therefore take steps to remedy the situation if it is not going to be enough for your needs.

Other schemes work on a 'money purchase' basis, whereby you build up a personal fund of assets derived from investments made with the money that you and your employer have paid into the scheme. The pension that you receive on retirement depends on how much has been paid in, how well the investments grow and what they can buy you as and when you retire. As 'final pay' schemes are relatively complex and costly for employers to run – they have to ensure there is enough money available to fund pensions, and have to make up the difference if there is not – these 'money purchase' schemes are becoming more popular. They are riskier, though. Some may produce a more substantial income, some may not.

What you receive on retirement will depend on how much has been contributed and for how long – and if you have changed jobs regularly you will almost certainly not have enough building up for a satisfactory pension. Once you start work you must check to see what you will be entitled to – and do this once a year to monitor the situation. You can boost the amount you will get from a company scheme by making 'additional voluntary contributions' (AVCs) which accrue on a 'money purchase' basis and then enable you to buy extra benefits on your retirement. Pensions are a complex area – and complicated further by their highly individual nature – and you do need to take expert advice as soon as possible. See 'Useful Contacts' at the end of the book for sources of help.

Success at Last

So you've made it. You contemplated your reasons for wanting to change, decided what you wanted to do and recognized what you had to offer. Then you learned about vacancies, drafted a job-search schedule and identified suitable opportunities, subsequently applying for them by letter, curriculum vitae, application form and telephone, and attending interviews. You benefited from rejection, made changes to your job-search programme, and improvements to your application and interviewing techniques, as and when necessary. You've now got the job that you want in a suitable firm, trade or industry and can look forward to a challenging and rewarding workload over the coming months and, hopefully, years. You've changed your job at 35-plus!

Afterword

Fighting Ageism in the Workplace

You've got the job! You now need to look to the future, establishing yourself in your new post and working towards a transfer or promotion in due course. You're old enough to have the skills, knowledge and experience to make a terrific success of this job, but young enough to retain the drive and ambition to progress even further still. To achieve greater success, you may need to be constantly aware of ageism in the workplace, and have to wage a subtle war against it on an ongoing basis. Here are the key steps to success:

- Be seen to keep up-to-date.
  Keep upgrading your expertise by reading the latest in-house literature plus books and magazines, and going on company and external training courses. Make sure that you can talk about changes and developments in an unbiased and informed way.

- Show a willingness to initiate change.
  It is important that you are not perceived to be the type of person who adheres to old systems and procedures, and is

reluctant to change. Be prepared to suggest changes and actually implement them as and when appropriate. Never indicate a resistance to change.

- **Stay fit and healthy.**
  Monitor your health and weight on an ongoing basis, taking regular exercise to stop you becoming run down and flabby. Use the company facilities when you can so that you are seen to be keeping fit. Be careful not to exercise to excess, though, as a red and straining body has the opposite effect: making it look as though you're past it!

- **Be a team player.**
  Make an effort to mix with all of your colleagues: old and young alike. Become a team member so that you enjoy the friendship and support of everyone. Socialize with them out of work, too, so that you are seen as 'one of us'.

- **Treat younger colleagues with respect.**
  Superiors must be treated exactly the same, whatever their age. Be seen to like and respect them, listening to their views and learning from them. Workmates and subordinates should be spoken to as equals regardless of whether they are older or younger than you. It's a cliché, but if you show respect for other people, they are far more likely to respect you in return.

- **Stay true to yourself.**
  Don't chase youth – having a dramatic, youthful haircut, wearing the latest teenage fashions and pretending you like current pop bands. Such actions will only serve to accentuate your age and make you seem foolish. You've moved on from this to the next, equally fulfilling stage of your life.

- Highlight your strengths.
  Whenever possible, show the strengths that you possess, and particularly those that come with age – calmness when faced with a tight deadline for completing work, maturity when coping with an angry customer or business contact, etc.

- Disguise your weaknesses.
  Never draw attention to your weaknesses, especially those that might be associated with age. Try to dispel some of the myths attributed to age, such as a lack of flexibility. Show you are flexible by welcoming new work practices, adjusting your hours and covering for colleagues, as and when required.

- Ignore your age!
  Don't make an issue of your age, by talking about what happened so many years ago, your experience and so forth. Be seen for what you are – a skilled and knowledgeable person rather than as an old one. If you appear to ignore your age, everyone else is more likely to as well.

Further Reading

An A–Z of Career Jobs (paperback), Diane Burston (London: Kogan Page Limited)
   Detailing more than 350 careers and jobs, this is a useful reference source for everyone who is considering a career change. It is full of up-to-date information on employment issues.

Answer the Question: Get the Job! (paperback), Iain Maitland (London: Century Business)
   101 of the most popular questions asked at interviews, and suggested answers – essential reading for every interviewee!

Coping with Change at Work (paperback), Susan Jones (London: Thorsons)
   Help and advice on recognizing and managing the ongoing changes that are taking place around you all the time. Essential reading before and after a mid-career move.

How to Know your Rights at Work (paperback), Robert Spicer (Plymouth: How To Books Limited)
   This book looks at your employment rights and responsibilities – ideal reading when you are starting a new job.

How to Negotiate Your Salary (paperback), Alan Jones (London: Century Business)

When it comes to negotiating, this practical guide tells you all you need to know to obtain the package you want, and deserve. It is worth a cover to cover read to boost your chances of a successful conclusion to your move.

How to Win at Interviews (paperback), Iain Maitland (London: Century Business)

An introductory text about selection interviews, containing numerous suggestions for success.

How to Write a CV That Works (paperback), Paul McGee (Plymouth: How To Books Limited)

Clear and practical advice, set out in an easy-to-read format. A helpful and highly informative book for all job-seekers.

Instant Business Letters (paperback), Iain Maitland (London: Thorsons)

Ready reference text, giving immediate access to 201 standard business letters – from which more personalized letters can be developed.

Make That Call! (paperback), Iain Maitland (London: Kogan Page Limited)

Short and pithy advice on making and receiving 101 difficult telephone calls, including those made and received when job-hunting.

Managing Your Time (paperback), Iain Maitland (London: The Institute of Personnel and Development)

A useful guide which may help you to budget your time more effectively whilst job-hunting.

New Work Options (paperback), Christine Ingham (London: Thorsons)

First-rate text examining the changing world of work, and the latest working practices. Read it to bring you up-to-date, if necessary.

The Kogan Page Careers Series (paperbacks) (London: Kogan Page Limited)
A series of practical guides detailing jobs across a wide range of sectors. Well worth checking out if you are planning a move into a new field.

Useful Contacts

Advisory, Conciliation and Arbitration Services (ACAS)
1–12 St James Square, London SW1Y 4LA
Telephone: 0171 210 3000

ACAS provides good solid advice on a whole range of employment issues. Well worth contacting for assistance. There are various regional offices around the country. Head office will supply details on request.

Central Office of the Industrial Tribunals
93 Ebury Bridge Road, London SW1W 8RE
Telephone: 0171 730 9161

Contact this body if you feel you have been discriminated against during the job-hunting process. Regional offices exist around the country.

Commission for Racial Equality
10–12 Allington Street, London SW1E 5EH
Telephone: 0171 828 7022

The Commission can help you if you have been discriminated against on racial grounds. This is THE organization to contact in these circumstances.

The Department of Employment
Caxton House, Tothill Street, London SW1H 9NF
Telephone: 0171 272 3000

A valuable source of information on all employment-related matters.

Equal Opportunities Commission
Overseas House, Quay Street, Manchester M3 3HN
Telephone: 0161 833 9244

If you believe you have had a raw deal because of your sex, race or age, talk to the Commission's staff for hands-on advice and guidance.

Executive Recruitment Association
36–38 Mortimer Street, London W1N 7RB
Telephone: 0171 323 4300.

This organization can put you in contact with agencies specializing in executive recruitment in your region.

Federation of Recruitment and Employment Services Limited
36–38 Mortimer Street, London W1N 7RB
Telephone: 0171 323 4300

Similarly, this body will provide details of other recruitment and employment agencies near to you.

Job Centres
For the address and phone number of your local office, look in the telephone directory under 'Employment Service'.
Without doubt, the best source of help and information available to job-seekers; from the current state of the jobs market through how-to advice to training schemes. Whatever your query, contact them first.

Occupational Pensions Advisory Service
11 Belgrave Road, London SW1V 1RB
Telephone: 0171 233 8080

This is an independent body which will explain the rules of any occupational pension scheme you are involved with and will negotiate on your behalf, if necessary.

Personal Investment Authority
7th Floor, 1 Canada Square, Canary Wharf, London E14 4LH
Telephone: 0171 538 8860

The PIA will put you in touch with independent financial advisers in your area. If you are thinking of taking out a personal pension plan you may wish to contact them.

Race Relations Employment Advisory Service
11 Belgrave Road, London SW1V 1RB
Telephone: 0171 834 6644

Excellent advice and support is available from this source, upon request.

Index

acknowledgements 105–6, 116
acceptance (of job offer) 139–42, 145–6
additional information (on application form) 89–91
advertisements 16–17, 26, 29, 30–1, 36, 38, 39, 40, 96–7, 98–9, 134
advertising media 16–17, 18–19, 134
age related questions 109–11
ageism 151–3
agencies 18–19, 24–6, 29, 35, 36, 57–8, 59
answering machine 36, 98, 102, 134
appearance 60–61, 112–13, 116, 152

application forms 79–93, 98–9, 134–5

body language 114
business 38–9, 130, 132

change 2–3, 4–5, 151–2
closed questions 108
clothes 112–3
colleagues 152
consultancies 18–19, 24–6, 29, 35, 36, 57–8, 59
contra indicators 8, 9, 42
curricula vitae 46, 47, 48, 52, 55, 57, 69–78, 134–5

decisions 5–8, 44
desirable criteria 8, 9, 42

diaries 29
dislikes 7–8, 44
drafts 65, 92–3
dress 112–13
driving licence 88

education 76–7
employee required 42–3, 130, 132
employee specification 43
employment agencies 18–19, 25
envelopes 60
essential criteria 8, 9, 42
executive search consultants 25
exercise 152
external notices 17, 18–19

face-to-face contact 21, 22, 68
facial expressions 114
fax machine 36, 68
files 36
final versions 66, 92–3
fitness 145, 152
formats 64
free time 37

general circumstances 12, 44
goals 8, 44

hair 112–13
handwriting 61
headhunters 25
health 87, 145, 152

health insurance scheme 123–4
house publications 17, 18–19
hygiene 113
hypothetical questions 108

in person 21, 22, 68
incoming calls 100–102
industry 37–8, 130, 132
in-house publications 17, 18–19
internal notices 17, 18–19
interviews 100–126, 133
invitations to interview 100–101

job 39–40
jobsearch schedule 26–9, 85, 128, 134–5
job centres 18–19, 25
job description 40, 41

layouts 61
leading questions 108
leisure activities 77, 87–8
letters 21, 22, 46–50, 51–3, 54–6, 57–8, 59, 61, 103–104, 125, 126–7, 134–5, 137
likes 7, 44
limited questions 108
listening 103

media 16–17, 18–19
memoranda 17, 18–19
multiple questions 108

negotiating 146–7
networking 20–23, 26, 29, 32–3, 36, 51–3, 59, 130, 132
notes 36
notices 17, 18–19

offers of employment 137–8
one-to-one interviews 106–107, 126
on-spec applications 23–4, 26, 29, 34, 46, 54–6, 57–8, 59, 130, 132
open questions 107–108
opportunities 2, 3, 4
outgoing calls 96–100

panel interviews 106–107, 126
paper 60–61
pensions 123, 148–9
personal information 75–6

standard of living 3
status 3
sticky labels 29
strengths 5–7, 10–11, 44, 130, 132, 134–5, 153

talking 113–114
team player 152
telephoning 21, 22, 76, 95–104, 134–5, 137
teletext 17, 18–19
television 17, 18–19
thank you letters 126–7, 144
trade 37–8, 130, 132
training 76–7, 124
training facilities 124
trial run 115
typing 61

up-to-date 151

wallcharts 29
weaknesses 5–7, 11–12, 44, 130, 132, 134–5, 153
word of mouth 18–19
working time 26–9
writing paper 60–61
writing style 64–5

younger colleagues 152

A GUIDE TO
MANSFIELD PARK

MARY HARTLEY
WITH TONY BUZAN

Hodder & Stoughton

ISBN 0 340 77561 0

First published 2000
Impression number   10 9 8 7 6 5 4 3 2 1
Year   2005 2004 2003 2002 2001 2000

The 'Teach Yourself' name and logo are registered trade marks of
Hodder & Stoughton Ltd.

Copyright © 2000 Mary Hartley
Introduction ('Revision for A-level literature success') copyright © 2000 Tony Buzan

All rights reserved. No part of this publication may be reproduced or transmitted in
any form or by any means, electronic or mechanical, including photocopy, recording,
or any information storage and retrieval system, without permission in writing from
the publisher or under licence from the Copyright Licensing Agency Limited.
Further details of such licences (for reprographic reproduction) may be obtained
from the Copyright Licensing Agency Limited, of 90 Tottenham Court Road,
London W1P 9HE.

Cover photograph: Frances O'Connor as Fanny Price in *Mansfield Park*
(Buena Vista), copyright © Disney Enterprises, Inc.
Mind Maps: Phil Chambers
Illustrations: David Ashby

Typeset by Transet Limited, Coventry, England.
Printed in Great Britain for Hodder & Stoughton Educational, a division of
Hodder Headline Plc, 338 Euston Road, London NW1 3BH by Cox and Wyman Ltd,
Reading, Berks.

Contents

Revision for A-level literature success　　v
How to use this guide　　xiii
Key to icons　　xv
Context　　1
The story of *Mansfield Park*　　5
Characterization　　7

- Fanny Price: serious, principled heroine who marries Edmund Bertram　　7
- Sir Thomas Bertram: upper-middle-class owner of Mansfield Park　　9
- Lady Bertram: Sir Thomas's self-centred wife　　9
- Mrs Norris: Lady Bertram's selfish, interfering sister　　10
- Tom Bertram: fun-loving elder Bertram son, heir to the estate　　11
- Edmund Bertram: steady, high-principled Bertram son, who becomes a clergyman　　11
- Maria Bertram: elder Bertram daughter who leaves her husband for Henry Crawford　　12
- Julia Bertram: younger Bertram daughter who elopes with Mr Yates　　13
- Mary Crawford: lively lady from London　　13
- Henry Crawford: Mary's sexy brother　　14
- Mrs and Dr Grant: the Crawfords' tolerant half-sister and her grumpy husband　　15
- Hon. John Yates: a London socialite, Tom Bertram's friend　　15
- Mrs Rushworth: head of the household at Sotherton, a neighbouring estate　　15
- Mr Rushworth: Mrs Rushworth's stupid son, married to, then deserted by, Maria Bertram　　16

- Mr and Mrs Price: Fanny's feckless father and struggling mother — 16
- William Price: Fanny's appealing brother — 17
- Susan Price: Fanny's younger sister who eventually takes her place at Mansfield Park — 17

Themes — 19

- Change and improvement — 19
- Family relationships — 21
- Love and marriage — 23
- Education and growth — 24
- Church and clergy — 24
- Money and materialism — 24

Language, style and structure — 27

Commentary — 30

Critical approaches — 94

How to get an 'A' in English Literature — 99

The exam essay — 100

Model answer and essay plan — 101

Glossary of literary terms — 105

Index — 109

REVISION FOR A-LEVEL LITERATURE SUCCESS

You are now in the most important educational stage of your life, and are soon to take English Literature exams that may have a major impact on your future career and goals. As one A-level student put it: 'It's crunch time!'

At this crucial stage of your life the one thing you need even more than subject knowledge is the knowledge of *how* to remember, *how* to read faster, *how* to comprehend, *how* to study, *how* to take notes and *how* to organize your thoughts. You need to know how to *think*; you need a basic introduction on how to use that super bio-computer inside your head – your brain.

The next eight pages contain a goldmine of information on how you can achieve success both at school and in your A-level English literature exams, as well as in your professional or university career. These eight pages will give you skills that will enable you to be successful in *all* your academic pursuits. You will learn:

- How to recall more *while* you are learning.
- How to recall more *after* you have finished a class or a study period.
- How to use special techniques to improve your memory.
- How to use a revolutionary note-taking technique called Mind Maps that will double your memory and help you to write essays and answer exam questions.
- How to read everything faster while at the same time improving your comprehension and concentration.
- How to zap your revision!

How to understand, improve and master your memory of Literature Guides

Your memory really is like a muscle. Don't exercise it and it will grow weaker; *do* exercise it properly and it will grow incredibly more powerful. There are really only four main things you need to understand about your memory in order, dramatically, to increase its power:

Recall during learning
– YOU MUST TAKE BREAKS!

When you are studying, your memory can concentrate, understand and recall well for between 20 and 45 minutes at a time. Then it *needs* a break. If you carry on for longer than this without one, your memory starts to break down. If you study for hours non-stop, you will remember only a fraction of what you have been trying to learn, and you will have wasted valuable revision time.

So, ideally, *study for less than an hour*, then take a five- to ten-minute break. During this break listen to music, go for a walk, do some exercise, or just daydream. (Daydreaming is a necessary brain-power booster – geniuses do it regularly.) During the break your brain will be sorting out what it has been learning and you will go back to your study with the new information safely stored and organized in your memory banks. Make *sure* you take breaks at regular intervals as you work through the *Literature Guides*.

Recall after learning
– SURFING THE WAVES OF YOUR MEMORY

What do you think begins to happen to your memory straight *after* you have finished learning something? Does it immediately start forgetting? No! Surprisingly, your brain actually *increases* its power and carries on remembering. For a short time after your study session, your brain integrates the information, making a more complete picture of everything it has just learnt. Only then does the rapid decline in memory begin, as much as 80 per cent of what you have learnt can be forgotten in a day.

However, if you catch the top of the wave of your memory, and briefly review what you have been revising at the correct time, the memory is stamped in far more strongly, and stays at the crest of the wave for a much longer time. To maximize your brain's power to remember, take a few minutes and use a Mind Map to review what you have learnt at the end of a day. Then review it at the end of a week, again at the end of a month, and finally a week before the exams. That way you'll surf-ride your memory wave all the way to your exam, success and beyond!

The memory principle of association

The muscle of your memory becomes stronger when it can **associate** – when it can link things together.

Think about your best friend, and all the things your mind *automatically* links with that person. Think about your favourite hobby, and all the associations your mind has when you think about (remember!) that hobby.

When you are studying, use this memory principle to make associations between the elements in your subjects, and to thus improve both your memory and your chances of success.

The memory principle of imagination

The muscle of your memory will improve significantly if you can produce big images in your mind. Rather than just memorizing the name of a character, imagine that character of the novel or play as if you were a video producer filming that person's life. The same goes for images in poetry.

In *all* your subjects use the **imagination** memory principle.

Throughout this *Literature Guide* you will find special association and imagination techniques (called mnemonics after the Greek goddess Mnemosyne) that will make it much easier for you to remember the topic being discussed. Look out for them!

Your new success formula: Mind Maps

You have noticed that when people go on holidays, or travel, they take maps. Why? To give them a general picture of where they are going, to help them locate places of special interest and importance, to help them find things more easily, and to help them remember distances and locations, etc.

It is exactly the same with your mind and with study. If you have a 'map of the territory' of what you have to learn, then everything is easier. In learning and study, the Mind Map is that special tool.

As well as helping you with all areas of study, the Mind Map actually *mirrors the way your brain works*. Your Mind Maps can be used for taking notes from your study books, for taking notes in class, for preparing your homework, for presenting your homework, for reviewing your tests, for checking your and your friends' knowledge in any subject, and for *helping you understand anything you learn*. Mind Maps are especially useful in English literature, as they allow you to map out the whole territory of a novel, play or poem, giving you an 'at-a-glance' snapshot of all the key information you need to know.

The Mind Maps in the *Literature Guide* use, throughout, **imagination** and **association**. As such, they automatically strengthen your memory muscle every time you use them. Throughout this guide you will find Mind Maps that summarize the most important areas of the English Literature guide you are studying. Study these Mind Maps, add some colour, personalize them, and then have a go at making your own Mind Maps of the work you are studying – you will remember them far better! Put them on your walls and in your files for a quick and easy review. Mind Maps are fast, efficient, effective and, importantly, *fun* to do!

HOW TO DRAW A MIND MAP

1 Start in the middle of the page with the page turned sideways. This gives your brain more radiant freedom for its thoughts.

REVISION FOR A-LEVEL LITERATURE SUCCESS

2 Always start by drawing a picture or symbol of the novel or its title. Why? Because *a picture is worth a thousand words to your brain.* Try to use at least three colours, as colour helps your memory even more.

3 Let your thoughts flow, and write or draw your ideas on coloured branching lines connected to your central image. The key symbols and words are the headings for your topic. The Mind Map at the top of the next page shows you how to start.

4 Next, add facts and ideas by drawing more, smaller, branches on to the appropriate main branches, just like a tree.

5 Always print your word clearly on its line. Use only one word per line.

6 To link ideas and thoughts on different branches, use arrows, colours, underlining and boxes.

HOW TO READ A MIND MAP

1 Begin in the centre, the focus of your novel, play or poem.

2 The words/images attached to the centre are like chapter headings; read them next.

3 Always read out from the centre, in every direction (even on the left-hand side, where you will read from right to left, instead of the usual left to right).

USING MIND MAPS

Mind Maps are a versatile tool – use them for taking notes in class or from books, for solving problems, for brainstorming with friends, and for reviewing and revising for exams – their uses are infinite! You will find them invaluable for planning essays for coursework and exams. Number your main branches in the order in which you want to use them and off you go – the main headings for your essay are done and all your ideas are logically organized!

Super speed reading and study

What do you think happens to your comprehension as your reading speed rises? 'It goes down!' Wrong! It seems incredible, but it has been proved – the faster you read, the more you comprehend and remember!

So here are some tips to help you to practise reading faster – you'll cover the ground much more quickly, remember more, *and* have more time for revision and leisure activities!

SUPER SPEED READING

1 First read the whole text (whether it's a lengthy book or an exam paper) very quickly, to give your brain an overall idea of what's ahead and get it working. (It's like sending out a scout to look at the territory you have to cover – it's much easier when you know what to expect!) Then read the text again for more detailed information.
2 Have the text a reasonable distance away from your eyes. In this way your eye/brain system will be able to see more at a glance, and will naturally begin to read faster.
3 Take in groups of words at a time. Rather than reading 'slowly and carefully' read faster, more enthusiastically. Your comprehension will rocket!
4 Take in phrases rather than single words while you read.
5 Use a guide. Your eyes are designed to follow movement, so a thin pencil underneath the lines you are reading, moved smoothly along, will 'pull' your eyes to faster speeds.

HOW TO MAKE STUDY EASY FOR YOUR BRAIN

When you are going somewhere, is it easier to know beforehand where you are going, or not? Obviously it is easier if you *do* know. It is the same for your brain and a book. When you get a new book, there are seven things you can do to help your brain get to 'know the territory' faster:

1 Scan through the whole book in less than 20 minutes, as you would do if you were in a shop thinking whether or not to buy it. This gives your brain *control.*

2. Think about what you already know about the subject. You'll often find out it's a lot more than you thought. A good way of doing this is to do a quick Mind Map on *everything you know* after you have skimmed through it.
3. Ask who, what, why, where, when and how questions about what is in the book. Questions help your brain 'fish' the knowledge out.
4. Ask your friends what they know about the subject. This helps them review the knowledge in their own brains, and helps your brain get new knowledge about what you are studying.
5. Have another quick speed read through the book, this time looking for any diagrams, pictures and illustrations, and also at the beginnings and ends of chapters. Most information is contained in the beginnings and ends.
6. If you come across any difficult parts in your book, mark them and *move on*. Your brain *will* be able to solve the problems when you come back to them a bit later. Much like saving the difficult bits of a jigsaw puzzle for later. When you have finished the book, quickly review it one more time and then discuss it with friends. This will lodge it permanently in your memory banks.
7. Build up a Mind Map as you study the book. This helps your brain to organize and hold (remember!) information as you study.

Helpful hints for exam revision

◆ To avoid **exam panic** cram at the *start* of your course, not the end. It takes the same amount of time, so you may as well use it where it is best placed!
◆ Use Mind Maps throughout your course, and build a Master Mind Map for each subject – a giant Mind Map that summarizes everything you know about the subject.
◆ Use memory techniques such as mnemonics (verses or systems for remembering things like dates and events or lists).
◆ Get together with one or two friends to revise, compare Mind Maps, and discuss topics.

AND FINALLY ...

- *Have fun while you learn* – studies show that those people who enjoy what they are doing understand and remember it more, and generally do better.
- *Use your teachers* as resource centres. Ask them for help with specific topics and with more general advice on how you can improve your all-round performance.
- *Personalize your* **Literature Revision Guide** by underlining and highlighting, by adding notes and pictures. Allow your brain to have a conversation with it!

Your amazing brain and its amazing cells

Your brain is like a super, *super, SUPER* computer. The world's best computers have only a few thousand or hundred thousand computer chips. Your brain has 'computer chips' too, and they are called brain cells. Unlike the computer, you do not have only a few thousand computer chips – the number of brain cells in your head is a *million MILLION*!! This means you are a genius just waiting to discover yourself! All you have to do is learn how to get those brain cells working together, and you'll not only become more smart, you'll have more free time to pursue your other fun activities.

The more you understand your amazing brain the more it will repay and amaze you!

Apply its power to this *Literature Guide*!

(Tony Buzan)

How to use this guide

This guide assumes that you have read *Mansfield Park*, although you could read 'Context' and 'The story of *Mansfield Park*' first. It is best to use the guide alongside the novel. You could read the 'Characterization' and 'Themes' sections without referring to the novel, but you will get more out of these if you do.

The sections

The 'Commentary' section can be used in several ways. One way is to read a chapter of the novel, and then read the relevant commentary. Keep on until you come to a test section, test yourself – then have a break! Alternatively, read the commentary for a chapter, then read that chapter in the novel, then return to the commentary. See what works best for you.

'Critical approaches' sums up the main critical views and interpretations of the novel. Your own response is important, but be aware of these approaches too.

'How to get an "A" in English Literature' gives valuable advice on how to approach a text, and what skills to develop in order to achieve your personal best.

'The exam essay' is a useful 'night before' reminder of how to tackle exam questions, though it will help you more if you also look at it much earlier in the year. 'Model answer' gives an example A-grade essay and the Mind Map and plan used to write it.

The questions

Whenever you come across a question in the guide with a star ✪ in front of it, think about it for a moment. You could make a Mini Mind Map or a few notes to focus your mind. There is not usually a 'right' answer to these: it is important for you to develop your own opinions if you want to get an 'A'. The 'Test' sections are designed to take you about 15–20 minutes each – time well spent. Take a short break after each one.

Page references

Page references in this guide are to the Wordsworth Classics edition.

KEY TO ICONS

Themes

A **theme** is an idea explored by an author. Whenever a theme is dealt with in the guide, the appropriate icon is used. This means you can find where a theme is mentioned by flicking through the book. Go on – try it now!

Change and improvement

Family relationships

Love and marriage

Education and growth

Church and clergy

Money and materialism

LANGUAGE, STYLE AND STRUCTURE

This heading and icon are used in the Commentary wherever there is a special section on the author's choice of words and imagery, and the overall plot structure.

CONTEXT

Jane Austen's life

EARLY INFLUENCES

Jane Austen's life was comparatively uneventful, but some of its circumstances and events are used to good effect in her novels. She was born in 1775 in Hampshire; her father was the village rector, and her mother was the daughter of a Church of England clergyman. Jane had one sister and five brothers.

Parts of her brothers' lives are reflected in *Mansfield Park*. One was adopted by wealthy relatives and inherited an estate, much in the same way as Fanny was sent to Mansfield Park. Two of her brothers became clergymen. This strong Church of England and clerical background is reflected in the detailed and confident handling of clerical matters in *Mansfield Park*.

The two other brothers had successful careers in the navy, their exploits providing Austen with many of the details for the naval aspects of the novel. Jane's brother Charles sent topaz crosses to Jane and Cassandra when he gained prize money after a successful capture at sea – an event reflected in the novel when William gives Fanny an amber cross.

Jane's brothers also put on plays in the Rectory barn, though not with the disastrous outcome of the theatricals in *Mansfield Park*!

COUNTRY AND TOWN

Jane was very close to her older sister Cassandra, and the two girls spent some time in boarding school together before being educated at home by their father. Austen's novels reflect her love of, and familiarity with, country life; she hated having to move to Bath in 1801, and was delighted when she finally returned to Hampshire, to Chawton, in 1809. In the meantime, though, her father had died, and she had stopped writing the novels she had worked on before the move to Bath.

Settled in Chawton, Austen started writing again. She revised her early work, *Pride and Prejudice*, *Sense and Sensibility* and what was to become *Northanger Abbey*, and wrote *Mansfield*

Park, *Emma* and *Persuasion*. Austen drew inspiration from her surroundings: *three or four families in a country village is the very thing to work on* (*Jane Austen's Letters*, ed. R.W. Chapman, 1932).

UNLUCKY IN LOVE

Austen never married. It is thought that she had a couple of attachments, but one man died and the other relationship came to nothing, possibly because the man's family objected as Jane was the daughter of a poor clergyman. She received a proposal from an old friend, accepted, then got cold feet and backed out. Cassandra was engaged at one time to a naval officer, but he died.

A BUSY LIFE

Austen's last years were spent writing and enjoying the company of her family and friends. In 1817 her health began to deteriorate and in July of that year she died in Winchester. She is buried in Winchester Cathedral.

Influences on Mansfield Park

WARS AND REVOLUTIONS

The American War of Independence started in 1775 and was fought during Austen's early childhood years. The French Revolution began in 1789; Marie Antoinette was executed when Austen was eighteen years old. The subsequent wars between England and France lasted until 1815. *Mansfield Park* contains references to war and the dangers faced at sea not only by William, a serving naval officer, but by travellers like Sir Thomas, whose voyage on business to the West Indies put him in danger of attack.

SOCIAL CHANGE

Agricultural workers (most of the population) suffered during the period of the wars with France. Other groups of workers displayed unrest; in 1812 the Luddite riots spread through northern England as protesters against unemployment destroyed the machinery that they saw as taking away their jobs. During this period, England still consisted of country towns and villages, but cities were growing and the canal network was being developed. Change was imminent as the new commercial and manufacturing classes became a challenge to the old landed gentry.

In the year after Austen started working on *Mansfield Park* the Prince of Wales became Prince Regent. Regency London was a flourishing centre of fashion, and towns such as Bath and Brighton became fashionable as well. However, the Regent was associated with decadent behaviour which brought him notoriety and disapproval. In *Mansfield Park*, London stands for unprincipled behaviour. Corruption spreads from the ruler and the capital, threatening to infect the Bertrams and undermine social values.

THE SLAVE TRADE

The anti-slavery movement, led by William Wilberforce, was at its height when *Mansfield Park* was being written. Many families in Jane Austen's society had some connection with slavery. The Abolition Act of 1807 outlawed Britain's slave trade; emancipation of slaves did not occur until about 1833. (See also 'Critical Approaches'.)

FEMINISM AND EDUCATION

In 1792 Mary Wollstonecraft published *A Vindication of the Rights of Woman*, championing education for women, and arguing that women received inadequate education because they were willing to be subservient to men. *Mansfield Park* looks critically at women's education, and explores the constraints experienced by dependent women.

BOOKS AND PLAYS

The novel was a popular form in the eighteenth century, especially **Gothic** novels such as Ann Radcliffe's *The Mysteries of Udolpho* (1794). This genre features melodramatic, passionate events which take place in settings such as haunted castles. Austen satirizes the genre in *Northanger Abbey*. In the same novel, Austen also defends the novel form against a charge of being frivolous and lightweight, saying that novels display 'the most thorough knowledge of human nature ... conveyed to the world in the best chosen language'. Austen read and enjoyed contemporary novelists such as Fanny Burney and Maria Edgeworth.

You might find it useful to read some of these works and compare them with Austen's. Try *The Mysteries of Udolpho*; explore the Gothic theme further with *The Monk* by Matthew Lewis (1796) and *Frankenstein* by Mary Shelley (1818). Also try Fanny Burney's *Evelina*.

Theatrical entertainment was a part of Austen's young life, and performances are enjoyed in the Bertram family. A performance of *Lovers' Vows*, however, is Austen's chosen vehicle for identifying principled and unprincipled characters. The play itself is a comedy which deals with some radical ideas about sexual mores and marriage contracts; Edmund has seen it performed in London. Why does Sir Thomas disapprove of the project? It could be because amateur dramatics had become somewhat disreputable. Two of the Prince Regent's mistresses took leading parts in plays put on by the Pic Nic Society, which was formed in 1802 by a titled woman who also ran a shady gambling club.

Lovers' Vows opens with Agatha, seduced and deserted by Baron Wildenheim and turned away from an inn because she has no money. She is helped by cottagers and by a soldier, Frederick, who turns out to be her long-lost illegitimate son. Frederick has to beg to help his mother. He also robs a man who, unknown to him, is the Baron, his father. Frederick is arrested and taken to the castle where the Baron's daughter Amelia has proposed to her former tutor Anhalt, rejecting her formal suitor, Count Cassell. Eventually Frederick's identity is revealed, the Baron is remorseful for his treatment of Agatha and marries her, Count Cassell is revealed as a cheat and a seducer, and Amelia is allowed to marry Anhalt.

RELIGION

Non-conformist religious groups flourished from the end of the eighteenth century onwards. These included the Quakers and John Wesley's Methodist movement. The anti-slavery campaigner William Wilberforce was a prominent member of an Evangelical group known as the Saints. As well as opposing slavery, this group disliked amateur theatricals and similar frivolity. It has been suggested that Fanny Price belongs to a sect of the Saints, whose beliefs prompt her question to Sir Thomas about slavery and her deep-rooted objection to the theatricals.

THE STORY OF MANSFIELD PARK

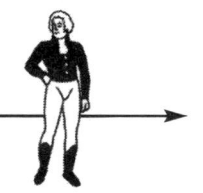

A *new home*

Fanny Price, just 10 years old, is adopted by her wealthy uncle and aunt, Sir Thomas and Lady Bertram, and taken from her home in Portsmouth to live with them at Mansfield Park in Northamptonshire. She is brought up with her cousins, Tom, Edmund, Maria and Julia. Fanny's other aunt, Mrs Norris, behaves spitefully towards her, but Edmund befriends her and helps her write to her favourite brother, William. Fanny settles at Mansfield Park, becoming indispensable to Lady Bertram.

N*ew influences*

Sir Thomas goes to the West Indies on business. He takes Tom with him to get him away from the bad influence of his friends. While he is away Maria becomes engaged to the wealthy heir to Sotherton Court, James Rushworth. Meanwhile, Mary and Henry Crawford, the half-sister and brother of the local clergyman's wife, Mrs Grant, visit the Parsonage. Henry, a womanizer, flirts with both Julia and Maria before deciding he prefers Maria; Maria, despite her engagement, reciprocates. Edmund falls for Mary, to the distress of Fanny, who now loves Edmund. However, Mary will not marry a clergyman, which Edmund is about to become.

W*hile the cat's away*

Tom returns from Antigua and, incited by his friend John Yates, draws everyone into a theatrical production at Mansfield Park. During the final rehearsal Sir Thomas turns up and puts a stop to the whole business. Henry, having led Maria on, makes off for Bath, and Maria marries Rushworth.

A *refusal*

Henry returns and decides to make Fanny fall in love with him. He then becomes genuinely drawn to her, and pleases her by helping William's career. Henry proposes, but Fanny refuses. Sir Thomas sends her to her impoverished family in Portsmouth to change her mind. Henry visits her there and makes a good impression.

*S*candal and illness

When Henry leaves Portsmouth he goes to London, where he meets again the newly-married Maria. Fanny receives news that Tom is ill, then hears that Maria has left her husband and is living with Henry Crawford. This is followed by the news that Julia has eloped with John Yates.

*H*ome at last

Fanny and her sister Susan are brought back to Mansfield Park. Fanny comforts the family. Mary Crawford's reaction to the affair makes Edmund realize her true character, and he soon realizes it is Fanny he loves. Maria leaves Henry and ends up living with Mrs Norris; Julia and Yates are gradually accepted; Mary Crawford lives with her aunt following the death of Dr Grant. Edmund and Fanny marry. At first they live in Edmund's parish, Thornton Lacey, but following the death of Dr Grant the couple move to the parsonage at Mansfield, where their happiness is complete.

CHARACTERIZATION

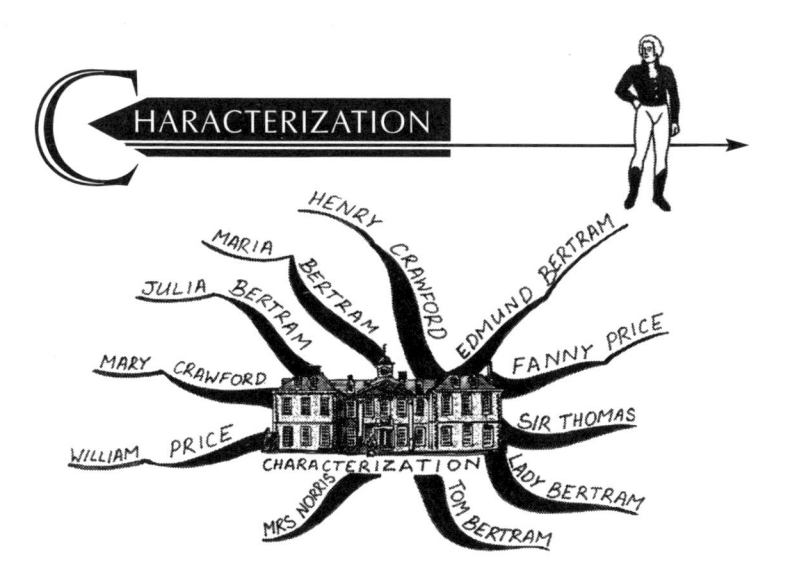

Mind map showing characters in Mansfield Park: Henry Crawford, Maria Bertram, Julia Bertram, Mary Crawford, William Price, Edmund Bertram, Fanny Price, Sir Thomas, Lady Bertram, Tom Bertram, Mrs Norris.

The Mini Mind Map above summarizes the main characters in *Mansfield Park*. When you have read this section, look at the full Mind Map on p. 18, then make a copy of the Mini Mind Map and try to add to it from memory.

Austen's characters are established and developed through their words and actions and through narrative comments. Austen's characteristic narrative tone is **ironic** (seeming to say what she does not really mean); it is occasionally **sympathetic** and often uncompromising in its judgement. Her attitude to the characters is clear. Particularly effective is the creation of individual voices: the main characters are identified by the content, rhythm and tone of their speech. There is little description of physical appearance.

Fanny Price

Central to *Mansfield Park* is Fanny's development from an unremarkable, timid and delicate child (Chapter 2) to the principled young woman who is strong enough to become the guardian of the best values associated with Mansfield Park.

NOT A VERY PROMISING BEGINNING

At her home in Portsmouth Fanny had a central place in the family. She happily looked after the younger children, and enjoyed close companionship with William. Removed to Mansfield Park, she is severed from these sources of security, and her ignorance and timidity (Chapter 2) result in her being treated as inferior by Maria and Julia and subjected to Mrs Norris's spite. Unhappy, homesick, humiliated, Fanny suffers in silence until befriended by Edmund. Attracted by his kindness and principles, she falls in love with him.

STRENGTH AND SUFFERING

Fanny's character is often described as weak and passive. Her qualities, such as modesty, shyness and sweet-temperedness, can seem insipid. However, Fanny's response to unpleasant experiences reveals her capacity for strong feeling, although it is rarely voiced. Her love for Edmund makes her vulnerable, and she suffers jealousy when she has to observe his infatuation with Mary Crawford. She feels angry at various points in the novel, such as at Sotherton, where she is *sorry for almost all that she had seen and heard, astonished at Miss Bertram, and angry with Mr Crawford* (Chapter 10).

Fanny is deeply unsettled and disturbed by the unwanted attentions of Henry Crawford. She refuses his proposal because she knows he lacks principle, and because she loves Edmund, neither of which she can admit. Fanny suffers the severest misery when criticized for refusing Henry, but she shows courage and conviction in withstanding pressure to accept him. Her strength is also seen in her stand against the theatricals.

FROM ISOLATION TO ACCEPTANCE

Fanny is isolated both physically and emotionally. The longest period of isolation is her stay at Portsmouth, where she can only be a passive recipient of the alarming news from Mansfield and London. This visit, intended to make her change her mind about Henry, in fact consolidates Fanny's allegiance to Mansfield Park. The dirt and chaos of Portsmouth makes her long not only for the physical comfort of Mansfield Park, but for its spirit of harmony and order. These values are restored to Mansfield Park when Fanny and Edmund marry and unite to uphold its traditions. Fanny's loyalty and resilience, and her sense of decorum and principle, are finally rewarded.

CHARACTERIZATION

Sir Thomas Bertram

Sir Thomas Bertram's social and family background is unclear – he is a member of the upper middle classes, but how he acquired his title is not revealed. He is a Member of Parliament, and takes care of his estates in England and Antigua. (See also 'Critical Approaches'.)

On the surface, Sir Thomas represents the ordered, dignified face of Mansfield Park. His authority is unquestioned; his high-spirited daughters find his regime repressive. However, under his rule unprincipled and destructive behaviour takes place at Mansfield Park. His elder son and heir is a self-indulgent wastrel and his daughters disgrace the family.

How far can Sir Thomas be blamed? You could say that he shows poor judgement in a number of areas. He married a self-centred woman of little sense and no judgement. He goes away for a long period, *leaving his daughters to the direction of others*. He trusts them to Edmund's care, but also has confidence in Mrs Norris's *watchful attention*. He is stern and remote with his daughters, unable to see their true characters and dispositions, and trusting too much in his sister-in-law's influence.

However, Sir Thomas does develop and acquire self-knowledge. He recognizes that the education he provided for his daughters was inadequate morally. He sees the value of *early hardship and discipline* (Chapter 48), and learns to appreciate the qualities of Fanny and of William. In reward for the charity and good intentions he extended to her as a child, Sir Thomas has the *rich repayment* of the estimable Fanny as his daughter. His experiences have led him to prize the *sterling good of principle and temper*, and he and Fanny enjoy a *mutual attachment*. He has learnt from his daughters' unfortunate marital experiences to reject *ambitious and mercenary connections* (Chapter 48).

Lady Bertram

Lady Bertam's indolence and self-centredness are a source of humour in the novel, but the ironic way in which she is presented implies criticism of her parenting and personal shortcomings. Unlike Mrs Norris, Lady Bertram is not in the least spiteful, but neither does she display positive qualities.

She made a good marriage, capturing a richer man than was expected, and spends her days occupying the sofa with her little dog. She has no ideas of her own, following Sir Thomas's lead in important matters and Mrs Norris's in others.

Lady Bertram pays little attention to her daughters' upbringing or to activities in the house during her husband's absence. She barely considers Edmund's doubts about the play: '*Do not act anything improper, my dear, Sir Thomas would not like it. Fanny, ring the bell; I must have my dinner*' (Chapter 15). Although never deliberately unkind to Fanny, Lady Bertram's relationship with her niece reveals her selfishness. Her need for Fanny's attentions is her first consideration whenever Fanny receives an invitation. She eventually relinquishes Fanny's companionship only because Susan Price takes her place.

Mrs Norris

Mrs Norris's preoccupations with economy and her interfering activities provide much amusement. She has no real place or influence at Mansfield Park, so gives the impression that she is indispensable. Mrs Norris is motivated by self-interest and the self-imposed necessity to save money. She suggests adopting Fanny, but makes it clear that she will not share in her maintenance, and on Mr Norris's death she moves to a small house to avoid accommodating Fanny. There are numerous examples of her petty economy: she 'sponges' a lapful of goodies on the visit to Sotherton, she makes off with the green baize curtain from the theatricals, and she decides not to visit her sister when she realizes she would have to pay her own fare home.

Amusing though she is, Mrs Norris does real damage. Her over-indulgence and flattery of Maria and Julia contribute to their downfall, and her desire to see her favourite, Maria, marry well leads her to promote the disastrous marriage to Rushworth *by every suggestion and contrivance* (Chapter 4). Her treatment of Fanny is despicable. From the beginning she bullies and belittles her niece, from preventing her having a fire in her room to viciously rebuking her for not taking part in the play.

CHARACTERIZATION

Tom Bertram

Tom has *easy manners and excellent spirits*. He is an agreeable, popular young man, but he feels *born only for expense and enjoyment* (Chapter 2). Tom's extravagance gets him into debt, and prevents Edmund from taking up the position of clergyman when Mr Norris dies. Tom does feel *shame and some sorrow* (Chapter 3) at this, but does not take the situation too seriously. Sir Thomas worries about Tom's way of life, and takes him to Antigua to separate him from the bad influence of his friends.

Tom's enthusiasm and determination persuade most of the Mansfield party to support the proposal to stage a play. He maintains that it will do no harm, and will not heed warnings of his father's disapproval. Tom is uncowed by Sir Thomas's return, and is highly amused by the sight of his astonished father coming face to face with the ranting Mr Yates.

Tom's frequent absences from Mansfield Park to attend race meetings and parties indicate his lack of stability. His illness, brought on by a fall at Newmarket, effects a change in his character. After his recovery he becomes less thoughtless and selfish, and reflects on the damage caused by *the dangerous intimacy of his unjustifiable theatre* (Chapter 48). Tom becomes steady and quiet, and is useful to his father.

Edmund Bertram

GOOD SENSE AND UPRIGHTNESS OF MIND

Edmund is the novel's high-minded hero, whose virtue and principled behaviour make him dull in the eyes of some readers. His clerical profession underlines his worthiness and makes him an unacceptable marriage choice for Mary Crawford, with whom he is infatuated.

Edmund probably appears at his best at the beginning of the book, before his feelings for Mary Crawford cloud his judgement. He is a serious young man, committed to his chosen profession. He is kind to Fanny during her early unhappy days at Mansfield Park, helping her write to William and arranging a horse for her to ride. He is always true to her interests and considerate of her feelings. Edmund recognizes Fanny's good qualities and potential, and becomes her guide and teacher.

BLINDED BY LOVE

Edmund's infatuation for Mary Crawford causes him much pain. Her admiration of Edmund's sincerity and integrity enhances his character in the reader's eyes, and his defence of his vocation is thoughtful and honest. However, Mary's opposition to his decision is a source of agony for Edmund, who begins to have doubts about Mary's attitudes and behaviour, while trying to convince himself that they are suited. Edmund makes some errors of judgement, in particular, his decision to act in the play after all, and his urging Fanny to accept Henry Crawford. Almost to the end, Edmund has to struggle with his strong attraction for Mary and his knowledge of her character. In the end he declares that '*the charm is broken*' (Chapter 47) and finds true happiness with Fanny.

TOO MUCH OF A PRIG?

Some readers find Edmund too dull to be a satisfactory hero, and find Henry Crawford more entertaining. You might think that Edmund is saved from smugness by his strong physical attraction to Mary and the shifts and compromises into which it leads him. Also, he has more range and scope than is sometimes acknowledged. He enjoys the theatre – Julia says '*Nobody loves a play better than you do, or can have gone much farther to see one.*' He goes hunting and shooting, and is not so pious that he cannot joke about the length of chapel prayers. Edmund's observation of Rushworth is pertinent and amusing: '*If this fellow had not twelve thousand a year he would be a very stupid fellow.*' (Chapter 4)

Maria Bertram

Maria is good-looking and confident, used to company and praise. Encouraged by Mrs Norris to think well of herself and admirably taught in everything but disposition, Maria develops into a spoilt young woman. She becomes engaged to Mr Rushworth for material and financial reasons, then proceeds to treat him very badly. She flirts outrageously with Henry Crawford, so that even the foolish Rushworth sees enough to become jealous.

When Henry makes it clear that he has no intention of proposing to her, Maria marries Rushworth to mask her disappointment by putting on a good face, and to escape from

Mansfield Park. The subsequent affair with Henry ends in disaster. He will not marry her, and Maria is socially ostracized and banished from Mansfield Park to live with Mrs Norris. Maria pays the price for lacking a sense of duty and decorum.

Julia Bertram

Julia is a year younger than Maria and her equal in looks and temperament. Like Maria, her upbringing has encouraged her vanity and wilfulness. She vies with her sister for Henry's attentions, gloating when she claims the seat beside him on the way to Sotherton, vexed when Henry disappears into the wilderness with Maria, and finally angry and bitter at having been treated so shabbily by Henry. Julia's elopement with John Yates is motivated by her fear of having to return to Mansfield Park and face her father's anger and lose her liberty. Julia fares better than her sister, being legitimately married and therefore socially acceptable. She is punished less because she has not been so spoilt by Mrs Norris: she has more self-control than Maria, and *education had not given her so very hurtful a degree of self-consequence* (Chapter 48).

Mary Crawford

Mary Crawford's wit and vitality make her an instantly attractive character, and a serious contender for Edmund's affections. Her self-confidence is seen in her jokes and light-hearted references, for example, to 'Rears and Vices', without any concession to context and audience. This disregard for the feelings and attitudes of others, which she can usually mask with wit, has detrimental consequences in her last interview with Edmund.

Mary has good points. She is sensitive to Fanny's feelings when Mrs Norris publicly criticizes Fanny, and she acknowledges her own cynicism and low opinion of human nature. However, it is important to the novel that her attraction lessens as the story progresses. Austen portrays Mary in an increasingly vulgar and self-centred light. The strikes against her mount up: her complicity in the plan to make Fanny fall in love; her tricking Fanny into accepting Henry's necklace; her crude reconsideration of Edmund as a marriage prospect should Tom die, and finally her response to the behaviour of Maria and Henry.

Mary is unprincipled, caring for appearances rather than inner worth. Her friendships are superficial, and she owes no loyalty. Edmund attributes her *faults of principle* to upbringing and background, but finally recognizes that she will not change. She has a *corrupted, vitiated mind* (Chapter 47). Nevertheless, her vibrant character enhances the novel, for some readers outweighing Fanny's merits and making the ending unsatisfactory.

Henry Crawford

Henry's charming manners make him a social asset. Like his sister, he brings vigour to the novel and to the company at Mansfield Park, and like her, he threatens and destroys order and decorum. His instability and lack of substance are illustrated by his restlessness and desire for novelty, and by his ability to act a variety of roles.

Henry is attractive to women. As his sister says, he is *the most horrible flirt that can be imagined*, who cares little about *the havoc he might be making in young ladies' affections* (Chapter 4). His treatment of Maria and Julia illustrates his selfish lack of principle. Henry is *thoughtless and selfish from prosperity and bad example* (Chapter 12), and sees no harm in indulging his vanity by playing with the feelings of the Bertram sisters.

Henry's plan to make Fanny fall for him leads to a real relationship. He becomes genuinely drawn to her, and she, against her will, notices his improved character. There is more to him than heartless philandering: he is clever, educated and generous. Although his helping William is a path to Fanny's heart, he honours the sailor's *warm hearted blunt* fondness (Chapter 14). He shows tact and sensitivity to the other members of the Price household.

How much of a challenge to Edmund is Henry? How genuine is his improvement? In the end, Henry's vanity and selfishness are confirmed when he cannot resist the challenge of overcoming Maria's coolness. However, tension is created through the possibility of Henry reforming and offering Fanny a genuine alternative. Some readers think that Austen had to strain to make the novel fit her intended pattern.

Mrs and Dr Grant

Mrs Grant is consistently good-humoured, preserving her even temper while dealing with her bad-tempered husband. She enjoys the company of the Crawfords and at the end of the novel offers Mary a home. She is warm-hearted and sincere. Dr Grant is an example of the worst kind of clergyman. Mary's description of a clergyman who is *slovenly and selfish* (Chapter 11) and quarrels with his wife could be based on her observation of Dr Grant. He is a scholar, and preaches well, but he is lazy and self-indulgent. He constantly nags Mrs Grant about food, and dies after eating three great institutionary dinners in one week.

Hon. John Yates

It is the Hon. John Yates who proposes the theatrical production at Mansfield. He is immediately identified as someone of whom Sir Thomas would not approve, being associated with the lax morals of sections of the aristocracy. Yates has little to recommend him *beyond habits of fashion and expense* (Chapter 13). His preoccupation with amateur theatricals reinforces this judgement and suggests a lack of respectability. His view that Sir Thomas's return is only *a vexatious interruption for the evening* (Chapter 19) illustrates his lack of perception. Sir Thomas views Yates as *trifling and confident, idle and expensive* (Chapter 19) and longs for him to leave. Yates's marriage to Julia is precipitated by her sense of *selfish alarm* (Chapter 48), but the match turns out reasonably well, with Yates showing a desire to be accepted into the Bertram family and to be guided by Sir Thomas.

Mrs Rushworth

Mrs Rushworth is the well-meaning, pompous mistress of Sotherton Court, one of the largest and finest estates in the country. She has learnt by heart from her housekeeper the history of the house, and, *never weary in the cause* (Chapter 9), delights in showing it off to her visitors. She is delighted when Maria marries her beloved son, and moves to Bath to allow the couple to move into Sotherton. She is full of bitterness at Maria's later treatment of her son, fuelled by the *personal disrespect* with which Maria had treated her.

Mr Rushworth

Mr Rushworth is a man of *not more than common sense* (Chapter 4), whose sole attraction for Maria is his income and estate. Edmund is the only one who recognizes Rushworth's foolishness, and feels that he is a poor prospect as a husband. Sir Thomas has reservations about the match, having *expected a very different son-in-law* (Chapter 21) and allows the marriage to go ahead, thinking that Rushworth will improve. Rushworth is a figure of fun during the theatricals, excited about his pink satin cloak and obsessed with his number of speeches, which he has difficulty in learning. Although Maria treats him badly, the author's voice allows him no sympathy: *The indignities of stupidity, and the disappointment of selfish passion, can excite little pity* (Chapter 48).

Mr and Mrs Price

Fanny is *sadly* pained (Chapter 38) when she meets her father, a retired naval officer, at the Portsmouth house. She dislikes his language and manner, and his smell of spirits. He pays her little attention, and is interested only in naval matters. Mr Price shows no concern for others. He neglects his family, and is *dirty and gross* (Chapter 39). He shows some social awareness, adapting his behaviour when meeting Henry Crawford, but Henry is struck by Mr Price's lack of attendance on his daughters as they walk to the dock-yard.

Fanny is even more disappointed in her mother. Mrs Price, though fond of Fanny, lacks the resources to develop a close relationship with her. She struggles to run a household in difficult living conditions, battling with noise, chaos and unbiddable servants. Fanny sees in her mother *a dawdle, a slattern ... whose house was the scene of mismanagement and discomfort from beginning to end* (Chapter 39). However, she feels some sympathy for her *poor mother*, being aware of her financial hardship. Had Fanny's mother made a more prudent marriage, she might have enjoyed a life like Lady Bertram's. Nevertheless, the children brought up in the Portsmouth environment turn out well, unlike some of those reared in the comfort of Mansfield Park.

CHARACTERIZATION

William Price

William is a likeable and pleasant young man who makes a good impression on those he meets. He has *good principles, professional knowledge, energy, courage and cheerfulness* (Chapter 24). He benefits from Sir Thomas's financial aid, but cannot progress in the navy without wealth or influential connections. Following Henry Crawford's recommendation, Admiral Crawford uses his influence to secure William's promotion to Lieutenant. William's career illustrates the difficulties faced by those who are poor and not well connected. The honest affection between Fanny and William is a contrast with the relationship between Mary and Henry, and William's unaffected warmth and spirited accounts of adventures at sea gain him affection and respect.

Susan Price

Susan, Fanny's younger sister, tries to bring some order to the chaos at the Portsmouth home. Fanny's stay at Portsmouth is made more bearable by her closeness to Susan, and Susan benefits from Fanny's guidance. When she is taken back to Mansfield Park, Susan adapts well to her new environment. She has a *more fearless disposition and happier nerves* (Chapter 48) than Fanny, and she copes well with the difficulties of her arrival and with Mrs Norris's antipathy. Susan is delighted to have escaped Portsmouth's *many certain evils* (Chapter 47), and eventually takes Fanny's place as Lady Bertram's companion.

Test yourself

- ? Copy the Mini Mind Map at the beginning of the chapter. Add to the map from memory. Compare your completed Mind Map with the one below.
- ? Draw a pie chart of the major characters. Divide it to show how sympathetic you find each character.
- ? Choose two male and two female characters. For each, think of (a) a colour, (b) a piece of music, and (c) an animal that represents their dispositions and personalities.

MANSFIELD PARK

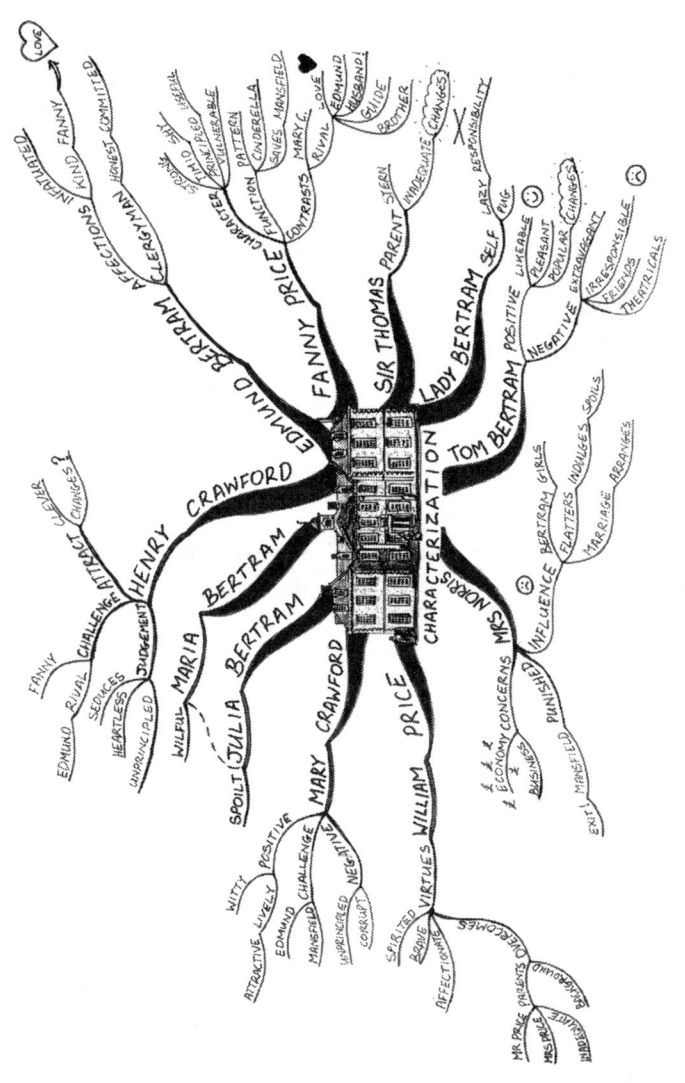

Take a break — *Now that you know who's who and who does what, it's time for a change. Take a short break before focusing on themes and ideas.*

THEMES

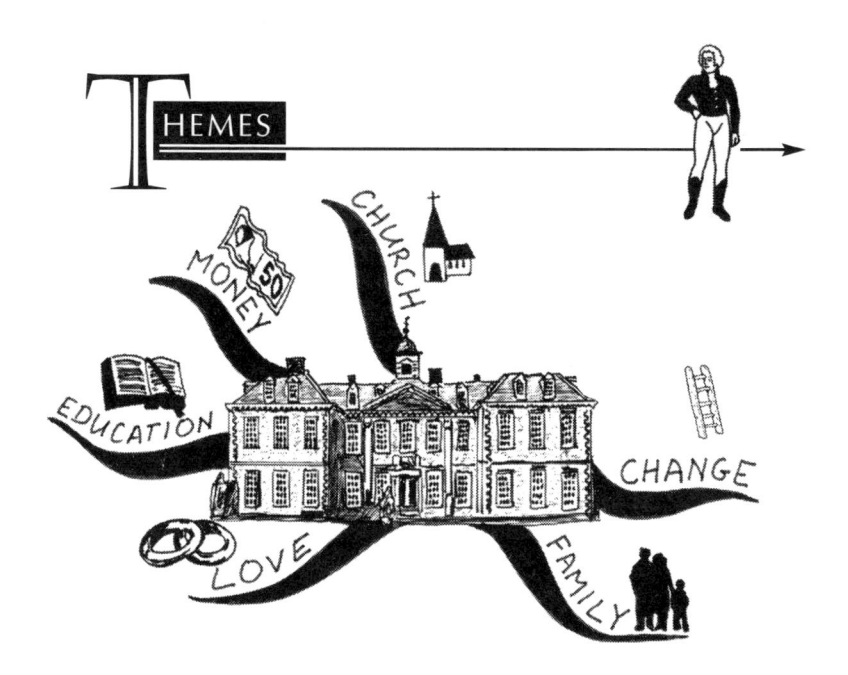

A **theme** is an idea which runs through a work and is explored and developed along the way. The Mini Mind Map above shows the main themes of *Mansfield Park*. Test yourself by copying it and then trying to add to it before comparing your results with the version on p. 25.

All the themes and ideas in *Mansfield Park* reflect the novel's central concerns: the establishment and defence of values and moral principles.

Change and improvement

In *Mansfield Park* Austen pitches the values of stability against the values of change, and presents the conflict through characters and concepts such as landscape gardening and the improvement of property.

CHANGE FOR THE GOOD
Some characters in the novel demonstrate the good effects of change and improvement. On his return from Antigua, Sir Thomas sees in Fanny *equal improvement in health and beauty*

(Chapter 19), and Fanny's growth and development is central to her role in the novel. The change and improvement in Sir Thomas is also significant. The fundamental malaise at Mansfield Park may be seen as partly caused by its master's authoritarian rule, applied with good intentions but with little human awareness or attention to morality. Sir Thomas's eventual realization of the deficiencies of this regime contributes to the improvement in Mansfield Park's moral health at the end of the novel.

The departure of Mrs Norris, the change in Tom's attitude and even the development of Mr Yates into a *less trifling* character (Chapter 48) signify healthy change at Mansfield Park, consolidated by the central position of Fanny. In all these cases, 'improvement' refers to intellectual and moral improvement. Characters who see 'improvement' in purely physical or aesthetic terms lack moral depth themselves. Henry Crawford, for example, notices *the wonderful improvement* in Fanny's looks (Chapter 24). Mary Crawford thinks that the cessation of family prayer in the chapel at Sotherton is an improvement; her comment highlights how different her values are from those of Fanny and Edmund.

ATTITUDES TO CHANGE

The attitude to change held by different characters is significant. The novel upholds the values of stability and tradition, while recognizing that tradition itself sometimes needs to be improved and regenerated. Opposed to these values are those which promote change and variety for the sake of novelty and excitement. Henry Crawford's and Tom Bertram's restlessness and Mary's need of the stimulus of the London social scene are presented critically. Characters who are in need of constant distraction are seen as morally lightweight, while those who value stability but can also encompass change are the moral centre of the novel.

Edmund sees the necessity for religious change. In Chapter 34 he applauds *the spirit of improvement* which is changing the content and style of sermons. His reference to the desirability of *distinctness and energy* in preaching and to the education of congregations hints at Wesleyism. (See 'Context', under the heading 'Religion'.)

THEMES

CHANGING HOUSES AND GARDENS

'Improvement' is used specifically in *Mansfield Park* to refer to the kinds of changes made to country houses and estates by landscape gardeners such as Capability Brown and Humphry Repton. The theme of improvement helps to define the different value systems explored in the novel.

In the discussion about Sotherton in Chapter 6 characters display their different attitudes to the subject. The foolish Mr Rushworth is all in favour of changing the house – *I never saw a place that wanted so much improvement* (Chapter 6) – but he has no idea what improvements are needed. Henry Crawford is enthusiastic about making improvements, and is disappointed that his Norfolk house needed so little attention. Mary Crawford, with her ready eye for fashion and novelty, supports the use of a professional landscape gardener. Although she is aware that change can upset the equilibrium, having experienced disruption when the Admiral's cottage was altered, she sees such disruption purely as a personal inconvenience. Mrs Norris's commendation of constant improvements reflects her love of bustle and business, particularly when she will not incur any of the expense.

Fanny is distressed that natural beauty, such as the avenue of oaks, may be destroyed. She is aware of the connection between nature and humanity, and appreciates the continuity of nature. Edmund's response to the matter of improvement, reiterated in Chapter 25 when Thornton Lacey is discussed, is that when modernization is advisable it should be effected for the owner's pleasure and comfort and suit his needs. Edmund, like Fanny, is not concerned with ornament (Chapter 25).

Family relationships

PARENTS AND GUARDIANS

The novel scrutinizes different kinds of families and the relationships within them. The role of parent and guardian is examined through the presentation of Sir Thomas and his proxy Mrs Norris. Sir Thomas takes seriously his responsibilities to his four children, and is fully resolved to be the *real and consistent patron* (Chapter 1) of the adopted Fanny Price. As a parent, he has faults. He is distant, seeming harsh, and knows little of his children's inner lives and real dispositions. He makes mistakes, such as allowing Maria to marry Rushworth and pressurizing Fanny to marry Henry Crawford; his confidence in Mrs Norris is misplaced. He also has a repressive effect on his daughters' behaviour.

However, the need for order is seen in what happens when Sir Thomas is absent: his household deteriorates and is shown to be vulnerable to outside influences. His return sees the re-establishment of order and the beginning of a renewal. Sir Thomas grows in self-knowledge, becoming conscious of errors in his own conduct as a parent (Chapter 47). In spite of the ambiguous way in which he is presented throughout the novel, he is finally commended for his growth in humanity and his willingness to change.

Mrs Norris is criticized and condemned for her poor guardianship. She shows no sense of responsibility or judgement. Her flattery and indulgence of Maria and Julia is ultimately destructive, and her malicious treatment of Fanny is inexcusable. She is so blinkered by her own preoccupations that she has no objections to the theatricals, and is so ineffective that she would not have been heard anyway. Not even Fanny regrets her departure from Mansfield Park, a telling indication of Mrs Norris's failure honourably to fulfil her role .

Admiral Crawford is another example of poor guardianship, whose dissolute behaviour has affected both Henry and Mary. A man of vicious conduct (Chapter 1), his example has shaped Mary Crawford's cynical attitude to marriage, and has spoilt Henry, who admits that few fathers would have been so indulgent. Mr and Mrs Price are also shown to be inadequate parents. Mr Price is feckless and negligent of his duties, and Mrs Price, though well-meaning, is over indulgent with her sons and unable to impose order and discipline.

Austen criticizes those who fail to provide the parental authority essential for children's physical, moral and emotional development.

THE INSTITUTION OF THE FAMILY

The novel presents a study of the conventions and relationships which shape families, particularly families of the class and status of the Bertrams, and shows the pressures that they experienced in the early eighteenth century. The family at Mansfield Park undergoes challenge and change, but has within it the resources to endure and continue.

Love and marriage

The importance of marriage for women is central to the novel. Their economic and social status is determined by marriage, which represents the only viable option for their happiness and development. In the context of *Mansfield Park* it is a woman's duty to marry appropriately. However, money and status do not guarantee a good marriage, and unions which are financially sound and emotionally or morally lacking are criticized. The novel suggests that a good marriage is based on a balance of equality, and leads to improvement and growth. However, this ideal is not recognized by all the characters in *Mansfield Park*.

Maria Bertram feels a *moral obligation* (Chapter 4) to marry Rushworth because he will provide her with status and a good income. Her feelings towards him develop from lukewarm to careless and cold, but piqued by Henry's rejection, she insists on going ahead with the marriage. Sir Thomas lets it happen in spite of his misgivings, persuading himself of the advantages of the match. He is genuinely baffled and shocked by Fanny's refusal of Henry Crawford, not understanding how she could sentence herself to a lifetime of dependency instead of welcoming financial security.

Imprudent marriages, that is, those contracted without regard for money, are also criticized. Mrs Price's miserable life is the result of marrying a naval officer without *education, fortune or connections* (Chapter 1). In this marriage, lack of money is seen to be the reason for the material and spiritual impoverishment of the household – but it could also be due to the irresponsible character of Mr Price and Mrs Price's lack of inner resources.

Fanny and Edmund achieve happiness because they are intellectually and emotionally suited. They share the same values and principles, and their happiness is *as secure as earthly happiness can be* (Chapter 48).

Education and growth

Mansfield Park explores ideas about the influence of education and upbringing on growth and development. Maria and Julia Bertram are given the traditional education of young women of the time. They learn a smattering of general knowledge, with the emphasis on names and dates, and acquire the expected accomplishments such as music and drawing. However, their expensive education does not teach them principles or a sense of moral duty. They mock Fanny's ignorance, yet Fanny is better educated than they. She reads widely and is interested in the world around her. In Portsmouth she joins a circulating library and encourages Susan's intellectual development. Fanny responds to Edmund's encouragement and guidance and shows that she has the capacity to learn and grow.

Church and clergy

Austen said that *Mansfield Park* is about 'ordination', referring to the ceremony in which a person becomes a minister of the Church. This indicates the importance of Edmund's interpretation of his role as clergyman. He sees himself as responsible for the well-being and improvement of those in his care; he has the *guardianship of religion and morals* (Chapter 9). He feels that a country clergyman should live in his parish and be involved with its moral welfare.

Dr Grant is an example of a poor clergyman. Although he is a scholar and preaches a weekly sermon, he shows little care for his parishioners.

Money and materialism

The material and financial basis of existence is well documented in *Mansfield Park*. We know the precise income of many of the characters, and the importance of income is made ironically clear in Chapter 1: *Miss Maria Ward of Huntingdon, with only seven thousand pounds, had the good luck ...* . The harmonious way of life at Mansfield Park is based on material prosperity, as is emphasized through the contrast with the Portsmouth household. However, those whose judgement is clouded by material concerns are criticized.

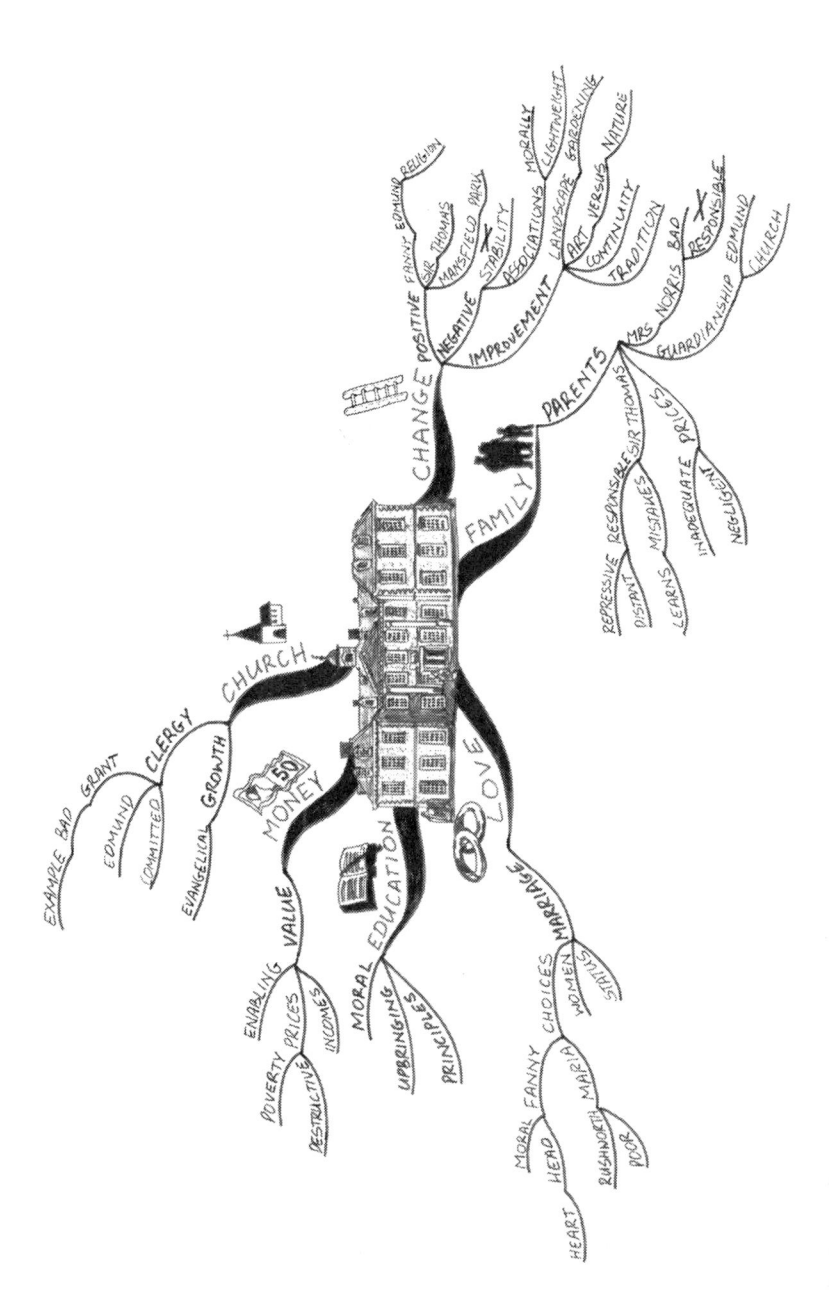

THEMES

CHANGE
- **Positive**: Fanny, Edmund, religion
- **Negative**: Sir Thomas, Mansfield Park
- **Stability**
- **Associations**
- **Improvement**
  - Morally
  - Landscape gardening
  - Lightweight
  - Art versus nature
  - Continuity
  - Tradition

FAMILY
Parents
- Mrs Norris bad
- Responsible Edmund
- Guardianship church
- Repressive
- Distant responsible Sir Thomas
- Learns mistakes
- Inadequate prices
- Negligent

CHURCH
Clergy
- Example bad grant
- Edmund
- Committed
- Evangelical growth

MONEY
Value
- Enabling
- Poverty prices
- Destructive incomes

EDUCATION
- Moral
- Upbringing
- Principles

LOVE
Marriage
- Moral Fanny
- Head choices
- Heart women
- Rushworth Maria status
- Poor

Try this

- ? Look at the Mini Mind Map at the beginning of this chapter. Develop it with your own ideas. Compare your finished Mind Map with the one opposite.
- ? Write sentences summarizing the importance of each theme.
- ? Write the key words of each theme on a large sheet of paper. At random, draw a line between two words. Explain how they are thematically connected.

LANGUAGE, STYLE AND STRUCTURE

An important aspect of Austen's language and style is her use of **irony**. This implies one thing while saying another, often using understatement and a balance of explicit statement and implied judgement. Its effect depends on shared understanding and assumptions between reader and author. Irony also implies the gap between expectation and outcome. For example, it could be ironic that Fanny, an outsider at Mansfield Park, turns out to be essential to its well-being. You will also become used to the **authorial voice** or **omniscient narrator's voice** in which Austen comments directly on the action and characters.

Characters are revealed through **direct speech**, when their actual words are quoted, and through **free indirect speech**, when the author's voice merges with that of the character. Characters are identified by their individual voices: Mary Crawford's characteristic tone is light and rather racy, whereas Fanny's is usually serious and considered.

Mansfield Park has many examples of **symbolism** – a literary technique in which one thing is used to represent something else. There are symbolic aspects to the card game of Speculation (see Commentary, Chapter 25). The cross and chain that cause Fanny such anguish also have symbolic applications (see Commentary, Chapter 27).

The novel is carefully **structured**, being divided into three volumes. The first volume (Chapters 1–18) assembles the characters and establishes the narrative and main themes. Tensions are set up between the pairs of lovers or would-be lovers, and set pieces such as the Sotherton visit and the theatricals provide a focus for themes and action. In the second volume (Chapters 19–31) Fanny becomes the central focus as she becomes an established member of the Bertram family. In the last volume (Chapters 32–48) Fanny retains centrality as pressure is put on her to marry Henry, and she is then exiled to Portsmouth to endure the period of time before she is finally claimed by Edmund and Mansfield.

Setting

Places in *Mansfield Park* have symbolic and thematic significance. The significance of each of the main settings – Mansfield Park, Sotherton and London – is outlined below.

MANSFIELD PARK

Mansfield Park itself gives the novel its name, emphasizing its centrality to the book's ideas. It is a spacious modern-built house set in five miles of parkland, and details of its rooms and furnishings emerge through the narrative. Fanny finds the grandeur of the house difficult to cope with, and is uncomfortable in its large rooms. The humble space allocated to Fanny in the house is indicative of her inferior position there.

The house may be seen to represent certain values: it is associated with orderliness, propriety, duty and decorum. However, these virtues are corrupted by its inhabitants, and the patriarchal rule of Sir Thomas is morally ambiguous. It is up to Fanny to energize and cleanse it with her strength and principles. The wealth and status of the household enable harmony and order, unlike the house at Portsmouth, where poverty and difficult circumstances create chaos and confusion. The order of a household has moral and social value, and there is a connection between moral worth and social privilege. However, the privileged family at Mansfield Park is not an example of virtuous living.

It has also been suggested that Mansfield Park, tainted by the moral laxness of the Crawfords and John Yates, represents the condition of England – tainted by its colonial activities and by instability in the ruling class. The madness of King George III, who suffered his final attack in 1811, and the scandalous life of the Prince Regent, created an atmosphere of moral uncertainty. The assassination of the Prime Minister, Spencer Perceval in 1812, added to the sense of instability.

SOTHERTON

This large Elizabethan house can be seen as reflecting issues to do with tradition and change. Sotherton represents a way of life which does not exist any more. The chapel remains, but is no longer used for family prayers; there is discussion about felling the centuries-old oak avenue. Tradition is weakened, and what is to replace it is uncertain.

LONDON

London is associated with corrupt modern values. In contrast to the order and stability valued at Mansfield Park, it is depicted as a place which encourages the self-indulgent pursuit of variety and excitement. London is the setting for sexual misdemeanours; it is where Maria's elopement with Henry Crawford takes place, and is the home of the dissolute Admiral Crawford. London is the spiritual and social home of Mary and Henry, and the Bertram sisters are drawn into its social whirl.

London, representing city life in general, is morally opposed to the country. Rural values are based on traditional social relationships and routines which are threatened by the shifting, superficial town life with its different standards of behaviour and different attitudes to money. The wealth of country people like Sir Thomas was tied up in land and farming, while the growth of urban trade was based on ready cash. The discussion about Mary Crawford's harp in Chapter 6 exemplifies the city person's lack of understanding of the country and the conflict between town and country values.

You will find more comments on language and style throughout the Commentary.

Get stylish

- ? Make a chart of the main events in each volume.
- ? Choose short speeches from each of the main characters. Speak each one aloud in the way that you think the character would speak. Work with a friend and take turns to guess which character is speaking.

Time for a short break — problems concerning marriage and money coming up!

COMMENTARY

Volume 1: Chapters 1–18
Chapter 1

The Ward sisters marry

(To p. 3, *Mrs Norris wrote the letters*.)

- Maria Ward marries Sir Thomas Bertram, a wealthy landowner.
- The oldest Miss Ward marries the Revd Mr Norris, a poor clergyman.
- The youngest Miss Ward marries Lieutenant Price, a man with few prospects.
- Sir Thomas appoints the Revd Norris to be rector at Mansfield Park.
- The sisters become estranged because of the imprudent Price marriage.
- Mrs Price, in financial difficulties, asks her rich sister for help.

The novel begins with a discussion of marriages that took place about thirty years before the start of the main narrative. The situations and characters of the three sisters are immediately established. Lady Bertram has married advantageously, having acquired wealth and rank; the Norrises have been set up in some comfort with the help of Sir Thomas; Mrs Price, however, is suffering the consequences of having a very low income and eight children, with another on the way.
✪ What does the passage suggest are the conditions for a happy marriage?

The description of Lady Bertram's *remarkably easy and indolent* character suggests a lack of engagement with anything outside her own concerns, and indeed she would easily sever all connection with her impoverished sister. Mrs Norris, on the other hand, is driven by her *spirit of activity* to point out to Mrs Price how foolish she was to enter into such a marriage. She also feels obliged to pass on to Lady Bertram disrespectful comments that Mrs Price makes about Sir Thomas. There is a

COMMENTARY

marked contrast between Lady Bertram's idle self-absorption and Mrs Norris's urge to interfere, cause trouble and impose her own critical views. Mrs Price's desperation is seen in her humble appeal to her wealthy sister. ✪ Look at the series of questions in her letter. What effect is created by the repeated enquiries about her eldest son's future?

Sir Thomas, who has *principle as well as pride*, wishes to help his relatives to positions of respectability, but has been prevented from assisting the Prices by the rift between the sisters. He is motivated partly by a general desire to do the right thing and partly by the desire that his family connections should be suitable and socially acceptable.

STYLE AND LANGUAGE

The author's ironic **tone** is heard in the opening sentence of the novel. The juxtaposition of *only seven thousand pounds* and *good luck to captivate* indicates that in the world of the novel, marital expectations are linked to financial assets. The fact that the future Lady Bertram is said to be *three thousand pounds short* of any rightful claim to this marriage underlines the irony. The diction of the passage emphasizes the idea of marriage as a lottery in which women strive for the highest prize. Maria Ward has the *good luck* to win Sir Thomas, and her success is applauded: *All Huntingdon exclaimed on the greatness of the match*. Her sisters, like many women, are not so lucky. There are not enough prizes to go round: *... there are certainly not so many men of large fortune in the world, as there are pretty women to deserve them.*

✪ Which words from the following list could describe the author's attitude to the values presented in the passage? You could add your own words and expressions.

shocked   amused   scandalized   tolerant   critical
deeply moved   indifferent   mocking

Fanny is sent for

(From p. 3, *Such were its immediate effects*, to end of chapter.)

◆ Mrs Norris suggests that one of the Price children should live at Mansfield Park.
◆ After discussion, Fanny is invited to Mansfield Park.

Mrs Norris's self-centred, interfering nature is further revealed in the way she urges Sir Thomas to give a home to Fanny Price. She claims to be generous – *I should be the last person in the world to withold my mite* – but her actual meanness may be seen in her excuses for not offering Fanny a home at the Parsonage. The only advantage of Mrs Norris's brutally casual arrangements for Fanny's journey is that they involve little expense. Mrs Norris is very ready to tell others how they should spend their money, and very reluctant to spend any of her own.

Sir Thomas's deliberations on the matter show him to be cautious and concerned to do the right thing. His desire that Fanny and the Bertram daughters should grow up together but that the difference in their status should be maintained, without arrogance on the Bertrams' part or a sense of inferiority on Fanny's, shows some confusion. Sir Thomas thinks that this uneasy mixture of equality and inequality reflects the social realism that their *rank, fortune, rights and expectations will always be different*, and also his awareness of the *delicacy* of the situation. ○ Look at the paragraph that begins 'Should her disposition be really bad ...'. What does the list of qualities that Sir Thomas anticipates in Fanny suggest about status and wealth?

Lady Bertram's contribution to the discussion about Fanny is characterized through easy acquiescence – *let us send for the child* – and through negatives: *Lady Bertram made no opposition*. Her main concern in the matter of adopting a niece is that Fanny might tease her little dog.

STYLE AND LANGUAGE

Notice how character is created through the characters' own words and actions and through comment in the **authorial voice**. With dry wit and caustic humour, the voice of the narrator reveals the nature and extent of Mrs Norris's self-interest. The style displays **balance**, as in *her love of money was equal to her love of directing*. The voice is that of an **omniscient narrator**, who has an overview of all the events and characters, including characters' thoughts and feelings.

COMMENTARY

Chapter 2

Edmund to the rescue

(To p. 16, ... *and laughed at her*.)

◆ Fanny arrives at Mansfield Park.
◆ Edmund comforts and befriends Fanny.

Fanny finds the Bertram family intimidating. She is *exceedingly timid and shy*, and is put off by Sir Thomas's stern and serious manner. To Fanny's 10-year-old eyes, the boys, Tom and Edmund, have the *grandeur of men*. Maria and Julia gain even more confidence from Fanny's total lack of it. They reveal their shallow values as they assess Fanny's worth by the number of sashes she owns and whether she has learnt French.

Fanny is overwhelmed with misery, loneliness and a sense of her own inferiority. The servants sneer at her clothes, the governess exclaims at her lack of education, her cousins comment on her smallness and her shyness. Fanny's lack of status is emphasized by her room in the attic, the province of the servants. The space allocated to Fanny shows her social inferiority; it is significant that she feels that the wider space of Mansfield Park is too large and too grand for her.

Edmund shows gentle consideration towards Fanny. Patiently he draws Fanny out, and discovers that she misses her brother William and wants to write to him. Edmund enables Fanny to write to William, and advises her about how to deal with Maria and Julia. With Edmund's help, Fanny becomes more integrated into the total space of Mansfield Park, and loses some of her fear and awkwardness. Edmund recognizes Fanny's strengths, including her *affectionate heart* and her *strong desire of doing right*.

Fanny settles in

(From p. 16, *As her appearance* ... to end of chapter.)

◆ Maria, Julia and education.
◆ Tom and Edmund.
◆ William visits.

MANSFIELD PARK

Maria and Julia disparage Fanny's lack of education. Encouraged by Mrs Norris's sycophantic praise of their cleverness and quickness, they assert their superiority, which is grounded in their grasp of snippets of information from a range of subjects and their ability to paint and play a musical instrument. These are the common acquirements of young ladies of the time; the authorial voice draws attention to the Bertram girls' lack of the *less common acquirements of self-knowledge, generosity and humility*.
✪ What does this comment suggest about the nature and purpose of education? Mrs Norris's attitude fosters the girls' complacency, and Lady Bertram does not involve herself with her daughters' education, being too busy sitting on the sofa doing needlework. Sir Thomas is distant, but what he sees of his daughters' development satisfies him. He is truly anxious about them, but sees little of what they are really like as his reserved manner *repressed all the flow of their spirits before him*.

Tom and Edmund have contrasting characters. Tom is lively and spirited, and feels that expense and enjoyment are his birthright. His careless and extravagant behaviour have already caused Sir Thomas some concern. Edmund, on the other hand, is honourable, with good sense and an upright mind. ✪ What does Edmund's decision to be a clergyman suggest about his character?

William's visit, before he goes to sea, gives Fanny a brief period of intense enjoyment. Edmund comforts Fanny during William's absence, and also encourages her educational and cultural development through suggested reading and conversation and discussion. As a result, Edmund becomes second only to William in Fanny's affections.

STYLE AND LANGUAGE

Notice Austen's choice of words in her description of Edmund's influence on Fanny: *... his attentions were otherwise of the highest importance in assisting the improvement of her mind.*

Improvement is linked with education and with intellectual improvement. ✪ Look for the different ways in which the word is used, and for the different values placed on it.

COMMENTARY

Chapter 3

The master departs

- The Revd Mr Morris dies.
- Because of Tom's extravagance, the Norris living (the area from which a church minister obtained his income) is leased to Dr Grant.
- Fanny faces living with Mrs Norris.
- Sir Thomas goes away to Antigua with Tom.

Five years on, Sir Thomas is seen to be in some financial difficulty, partly caused by Tom's extravagance, as a result of which Edmund will not be able to take over as rector at the Parsonage, but will have to take up a living in a less attractive situation. In addition, Sir Thomas has incurred losses on his estate in West India. He assumes that Mrs Norris will now relieve him of the financial burden of providing for Fanny, but Mrs Norris is quick with her excuses. A year later, Sir Thomas has to visit Antigua himself, probably for twelve months.

Some critics see Sir Thomas's interests in Antigua as crucial to an understanding of the novel. They assert that the Bertram wealth comes from sugar plantations worked by slaves, and build a critical theory based on the idea of England as a slave-owning society. (See 'Critical Approaches' for more on this.) The nature of Sir Thomas's wealth is also a matter of speculation. He is rich enough to send his sons to Eton and Oxford, as would be expected, but his assets are so dented by Tom's debts that Edmund's future income is more than halved. Sir Thomas can be of some help to William's career, but his influence will not be as great as Admiral Crawford's. ✪ As you read the novel, mark all the references to Sir Thomas's money and influence. How conclusive is the evidence? Is Sir Thomas's wealth hereditary? In terms of the pattern of the novel, does it matter?

Lady Bertram's calm lack of engagement may be seen in the way she approaches Fanny about the proposed move to a small house in the village, Mrs Norris's new abode. Her one concern is that Fanny should still help her with her patterns. Her response to Mrs Norris's desire to save a little money at the end of the year – '*I dare say you will. You always do, don't you?*' – serves to illuminate Mrs Norris's lack of self-knowledge, but is without malicious intention. Lady Bertram shares Mrs Norris's dislike of the newcomer Mrs Grant, for a different reason: as a good-looking woman herself, she feels aggrieved that the plain Mrs Grant should have made a financially sound marriage. Mrs Norris complains about Mrs Grant's extravagant housekeeping.

Edmund offers rational support to Fanny in her distress over the suggested move. He reassures her that she is neither foolish nor awkward, and commends her good sense and sweet temper. Fanny's declaration, '*I love this house and everything in it*', shows how far she now aligns herself with Mansfield Park.

Sir Thomas leaves his daughters to Mrs Norris's watchful attention, and Edmund's judgement. ✪ What do you think about his own judgement in this? Maria and Julia feel that their father's departure releases them from restraint; Lady Bertram does not like to have her husband leave her, but feels no concern for his comfort or safety, since only her comfort and safety matter; Fanny regrets that she cannot grieve more at the departure of someone who has done so much for her and her family. Sir Thomas's departure marks the removal of authority from Mansfield Park. ✪ What effect might his absence have on the family? Who is most likely to take advantage of it? Who is least likely to do so?

Time for a test

? Who –

(a) married to disoblige her family?
(b) had a temper *remarkably easy and indolent*?
(c) teaches Maria and Julia Bertram?
(d) has only two sashes?
(e) is a Member of Parliament?
(f) has not been half as much in debt as some of his friends?

(*Answers on p. 93.*)

COMMENTARY

> ? What are Sir Thomas's strengths and weaknesses as a parent? Make a Mini Mind Map of your ideas. Do the same for Lady Bertram.
>
> ? How do you see Fanny at this stage in the novel? Put a mark on the sympathy scale. Write a sentence explaining your response.

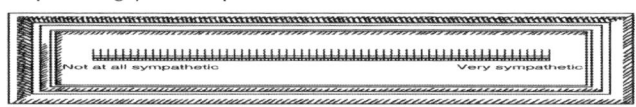

|||||||||||||||||||||||||||||||||||||||||||||||||||||||||
Not at all sympathetic   Very sympathetic

> ? How does the information that Edmund is to be ordained affect your view of him?
> ? Start a Mind Map of each of the main characters.

With Sir Thomas out of the way, treat yourself to a break, then go on to enjoy a potent mixture of love, sex and the devastating Crawfords!

Chapter 4

Without Sir Thomas

(To p. 38, ... *before the end of the summer*.)

◆ Fanny as companion.
◆ Fanny's horse.
◆ Maria's engagement to Mr Rushworth.

Fanny's role in the household is consolidated as she becomes Lady Bertram's companion, being particularly useful to her ladyship in the evenings when Maria and Julia attend a ball or a party. Lady Bertram does not attend these functions because she is too indolent even to enjoy the spectacle of her daughters' social success. ✪ Why does Fanny not attend?

When Fanny's horse dies, she is left without access to suitable exercise. She may ride one of her cousins' horses when they are not needed, but the girls enjoy riding every day and have no intention of *carrying their obliging manners to the sacrifice of any real pleasure*. Edmund recognizes the bad effect on

Fanny's health, and shows judgement and tact in his arrangement to provide her with a horse. Fanny's gratitude is inexpressible, and her feelings towards Edmund are combined of everything that is *respectful, grateful, confiding and tender*.
✪ Who do you think shows least regard for Fanny in the matter of the horse?

Mr Rushworth, who has recently inherited one of the largest estates and finest houses in the country, is impressed by Maria's beauty, and being ready for marriage, *soon fancied himself in love*. Maria considers Rushworth to be suitable because she feels it is her duty to marry, and marriage to Rushworth will bring her a larger income than her father's and a house in town. ✪ Underline the key words in the passage. What do they suggest about Maria's motives for marrying Rushworth? The match is encouraged by Mrs Norris. Only Edmund has doubts about the engagement, disliking Maria's financial motivation and recognizing that Rushworth's is not a distinguished character: '*If this man had not twelve thousand a year, he would be a very stupid fellow.*'

Enter the Crawfords

(From p. 38, *Such was the state of affairs*, to end of chapter.)

◆ Henry and Mary Crawford arrive.
◆ They are the half-brother and sister of Mrs Grant.

The Crawfords are the well-to-do children (Henry has a good estate in Norfolk and Mary has twenty thousand pounds a year) of Mrs Grant's mother by a second marriage. Following Mrs Crawford's death, the Admiral moves his mistress into the house, and his *vicious conduct* obliges Mary to find another home. Mary is remarkably pretty, lively and sophisticated, and used to London life. She good-naturedly receives Mrs Grant's plan that she should marry Tom Bertram; she intends to marry well, feeling that everyone should marry if they can do so to advantage.

Henry dislikes permanence and being confined to narrow society. He has a pleasing presence and engaging manners, like his sister, and Mary's response to Mrs Grant's suggestion that he should marry Maria Bertram reveals that Henry is widely regarded as a good marriage prospect but chooses to indulge in flirtations and delay marriage for as long as possible. ✪ What do you think of the Crawfords' attitudes to marriage?

COMMENTARY

Chapter 5

Getting to know you

- ◆ The Bertrams and Crawfords meet.
- ◆ Maria and Julia find Henry attractive.
- ◆ Mary considers Tom Bertram (returned from Antigua) as a marriage prospect.
- ◆ Fanny's social position is discussed.

Maria and Julia are both drawn to Henry, but because Maria is engaged he is in *equity the property of Julia*. ✪ What does this assumption suggest about Julia and Maria? What do the words used reveal about their attitude to marriage? Maria is thrown into confusion by her attraction to Henry, and her self-delusion and self-centredness are revealed in the mixture of bravado and justification in her comments that there could be no harm in her liking him.

Henry's teasing conversation with his sister reveals that he prefers Maria. He responds flippantly to Mary's warning that Maria is already engaged, but his ironic remark, '*I think too well of Miss Bertram to suppose she would ever give her hand without her heart*', suggests that he recognizes Maria's lack of emotional commitment to Rushworth. Mary's view of marriage is cynical and bitter: people are deceived when they marry, and marriage is a *manoeuvering business*. In contrast, Mrs Grant offers a sanguine view of marriage and of the tendency of human nature to recover from disappointment. ✪ Does the novel so far endorse any particular view of marriage? In spite of her negative attitude to marriage, Mary concludes that Tom Bertram's personality and prospects make him suitable husband material. ✪ In your text, underline the key words in Mary's assessment of Tom's position.

Mary is curious to identify Fanny's status in the household. She lightens her curiosity with style and wit – '*Pray, is she out, or is she not?*' – and pursues the matter to the end of the chapter, returning to it after Tom's anecdote. Perhaps Mary, sharp enough to see the ambiguity of Fanny's situation, has sensed the closeness between her and Edmund. Fanny's Cinderella-like position is highlighted by Mary's question. Fanny's status is obscure; although she is a member of the Bertram family she does not enjoy the same social activities as her cousins, and neither she nor the family find this situation remarkable.

○ Why does Austen introduce the Crawfords while Sir Thomas is away? What effects (good and bad) are they likely to have on the Bertram family?

STYLE AND LANGUAGE

One of the ways in which Austen establishes character is by reporting the characters' own thoughts and words in direct speech, and by reporting their thoughts and words in indirect speech. Direct speech is when the actual words of the speaker are reported, within speech marks; for example, *'Mary, how shall we manage him?'* Indirect speech is when the speaker's thoughts and words are reported, not repeated precisely, sometimes but not always introduced by a phrase such as 'He said/thought that ...'; for example, *He could allow his sister to be the best judge of her own happiness.*

A technique Austen uses very effectively is to mix authorial reporting with a character's own rhythm and choice of words. This technique of using a blend of first and third person narrative is known as **free indirect speech**. You will find a good example in this chapter in the passage where we hear Maria and Julia discuss Henry: *Her brother was not handsome; no, when they first saw him, he was absolutely plain, black and plain; but still he was the gentleman, with a pleasing address.*

Chapter 6

Dinner at Mansfield Park

◆ Improvements to estates.
◆ Mary Crawford's harp.
◆ A visit to Sotherton is planned.

In Tom's absence (he has gone away to a race meeting) Edmund takes the role of host at a dinner party. Mary anticipates finding Edmund a dull substitute. However, she is impressed by his tactful response to Rushworth's suggestions, observing that Edmund is *a well bred man*.

COMMENTARY

Mr Rushworth discusses improvements that have been made to a friend's house, and contemplates making similar changes at Sotherton Court. Mrs Norris enthusiastically supports his plans, declaring her delight in continual *improving and planting*, and Lady Bertram adds her recommendation of a shrubbery because there is one at Mansfield Park. Mrs Grant implies that Sotherton will be improved by Maria's presence as its mistress. Maria feels no obligation to humour Rushworth, but enjoys being connected with the large estate. Mr Rushworth's confusion as he tries to respond appropriately to all contributions shows his foolishness.

The discussion focuses on the destruction of an avenue of oak trees, and on the employment of a professional improver. Rushworth is very impressed with the work of Humphry Repton, a fashionable landscape gardener. However, Henry is the kind of improver of whom Repton disapproved. Although Repton was part of the Naturalist tradition that rejected structure and formality, he did not support the destruction of avenues just because of their line: '... the change of fashion in gardening destroys the work of ages, where lofty avenues are cut down for no other reason than that they were planted in straight lines' (from *An Enquiry into the Changes of Taste in Landscape Gardening*, 1806).

Fanny and Edmund dislike the idea of professional improvements. Fanny is sentimentally moved to quote the poet William Cowper and to regret the loss of natural beauty and tradition; Edmund would rather work out his own ideas. Mary suffered inconvenience when Admiral Crawford 'improved' his house, and would like to see the finished product without the intervening upheaval. Henry, on the other hand, has already effected 'improvements' on his own estate and regrets having completed them so quickly. He offers to advise Rushworth.

✪ How do individuals' responses to the question of 'improvements' reflect their characters? How is the kind of 'improvement' discussed in this chapter different from that noticed in Chapter Two? How does the novel present change and development?

Mary's harp is being delivered from London, and she plans to hire a horse and cart to collect it. Her surprise that such an action is impossible at harvest time shows her lack of understanding of country life. Mary tells the story amusingly, beginning with the roundabout way she heard that the harp had arrived, and disarmingly acknowledges that she has the London idea that everything can be bought for money, but its effect is to emphasize her different values. Town is set against country, the former embodying selfishness and moral laxity. Mary also jokes disparagingly about her uncle's fellow-admirals, the Rears and Vices, making a pun that to Edmund's ears at least seems coarse and inappropriate. Edmund also disliked Mary's previous public criticism of the Admiral.

Chapter 7

Mary and Fanny – rivals

- Fanny and Edmund discuss Mary.
- Edmund falls for Mary.
- Edmund lends Fanny's horse to Mary.
- Fanny suffers from lack of exercise and from being in the heat.
- Edmund feels guilty for neglecting Fanny.

Edmund uses Fanny as a sounding board for his feelings about Mary. After drawing praise for Mary from Fanny, he probes her response to Mary's conversational improprieties. Edmund, under Mary's spell, tries to justify her behaviour and to steer Fanny towards agreeing with him. He jumps to Mary's defence when Fanny complains peevishly about Mary's comments on Henry's letter-writing. It is to be expected that Edmund and Fanny will agree most of the time, since he has formed her mind and gained her *affections*. Edmund thinks that Mary is *perfectly feminine*. She shows no ill humour, roughness, sharpness, loudness or coarseness.
○ What is Edmund's idea of what a woman should be? Is he right about Mary? Who has the qualities that he admires?

Mary is attracted to Edmund although he is not conventionally appealing and does not comply with the *common rule* of flirtatious behaviour. Mary is struck by his sincerity, steadiness and integrity. ○ What do you think about their suitability for each other?

COMMENTARY

Fanny cannot agree with Edmund about Mary Crawford. Mary's beauty, wit and good humour are enhanced by her musicality and the attractive surroundings in which she plays the harp. Edmund is now *a good deal in love*, and approaches Mary with sincerity, steadiness and integrity. We hear Fanny's pique in the comment that she is surprised that Edmund could spend so long with Mary and not see more of the kind of fault that he has already observed. Fanny does not recognize that she is jealous, an idea which is presented poignantly in the description of Fanny at a distance watching Edmund and Mary riding together and hearing the sounds of their merriment wafting up to her.

Fanny watches Edmund's actions, and imagines what she cannot see, and asks herself what could be more natural than Edmund making himself useful. She has to listen to one of the servants compare her horsewomanship unfavourably with Mary's. At the end of the chapter we are told that Fanny has been *struggling against discontent and envy for some days past*. The reader can identify the source of these feelings, but Fanny is unwilling to acknowledge the changes in her relationship with Edmund.

The contrast between Fanny's self-effacing manner and Mary's confidence may be seen when Mary apologizes to Fanny for keeping her waiting to ride her horse. Mary offers apologies and acknowledges that she has behaved thoughtlessly, but at the same time she claims to be above the law: '*Selfishness must always be forgiven, you know, because there is no hope of a cure.*'

Fanny's lack of consequence is further seen in her being thoughtlessly sent on unnecessary errands in the hot sun, resulting in a bad headache. Edmund's insistent questioning of his mother and his aunt reveals that Fanny cut roses and walked twice across the park in heat that was *enough to kill anybody*. In self-justification, Mrs Norris remarks that Fanny has not been taking regular exercise, so pricking Edmund's conscience that for four days he has neglected Fanny's needs.
✪ Is Fanny's headache caused only by the heat?

Over to you

? Underline the words and phrases that apply to Mary, and circle those that apply to Fanny. Underline in another colour any that apply to both.

lively   low self-esteem   witty   sophisticated   timid
vivacious   critical   good judgement   cynical
reserved   observant   sensitive   clever

? How does Edmund's reaction to Mary Crawford affect your view of him?
? Think of a short diary entry that might be written about Henry by (a) Maria, (b) Julia, (c) Fanny.
? Where is Fanny on your sympathy scale now? Go back and mark it in.
? What is the significance of these objects?

? Who says the following?
(a) *Everybody is taken in at some period or other.*
(b) *She has the age and sense of a woman, but the outs and not outs are beyond me.*
(c) *I am inclined to envy Mr Rushworth for having so much happiness yet before him.*
(d) *It was very wrong – and very indecorous.*
(e) *You should learn to think of other people.*
(f) *Sitting and calling to Pug, and trying to keep him from the flowerbeds, was almost too much for me.*

(*Answers on p. 93.*)

Not only the weather becomes hot at Sotherton — take a break, then read on!

Chapter 8

The road to Sotherton

- ◆ The visit to Sotherton is set.
- ◆ Edmund arranges for Fanny to be part of the visit.
- ◆ Julia and Maria vie to sit next to Henry – Julia wins.
- ◆ Maria gains some consolation from being the future mistress of Sotherton.

Mrs Norris opposes Fanny's inclusion in the visit to Sotherton, and is vexed when her arrangements are thwarted through Edmund's intervention. Mrs Norris's behaviour towards Fanny consolidates Fanny's inferior and dependent role. ✪ Why might Mrs Norris behave in this way towards Fanny? How does Mrs Norris see her own role at Mansfield Park? Mrs Norris's urge to impose her own arrangements is ironically presented in her insistence that one carriage will be enough for the Sotherton trip – she does not realize that her comments about the possible damage to the Mansfield coach apply just as much to Henry's barouche.

Maria and Julia emerge as rivals for Henry's attention. Julia gains and hangs on to the favoured seat next to Henry, and their laughter and conversation irritate Maria throughout the journey. ✪ How does the rivalry between Maria and Julia compare with that between Fanny and Mary? Maria recovers some good humour on the approach to Sotherton, indulging her *vanity and pride* as she speaks with authority about the house and the estate, although she had previously been unable to offer Mr Rushworth any opinion on such matters (see Chapter 6). ✪ What are the differences between this occasion and that one?

Fanny and Mary are united on the journey only in the way they look out for Edmund's appearances as he rides behind them on his horse. Fanny takes in the details of the countryside, seeing it is a complex working entity that sustains lives and livelihoods, while Mary observes little of the natural surroundings.

STYLE AND LANGUAGE

Austen's ironic tone and diction mocks Maria's and Julia's jockeying for position. The use of inflated language – *The place of all places, the envied seat, the post of honour* – contrasts with the image of Julia nipping smartly into her seat and the neat deflating ending of the sentence, as the carriage drives off to the accompaniment of *the barking of pug in his mistress's arms.*

Chapter 9

So near the altar

(To p. 88, ... *that they had been there long enough.*)

◆ The chapel at Sotherton.
◆ Mary hears that Edmund will be ordained.

The party is taken on a tour of the house, ending in the chapel. The chapel may be seen as the spiritual centre of the house, representing tradition and religion. ✪ What other feature of the grounds at Sotherton may be seen as symbolic of tradition? The chapel, however, is no longer used. This could suggest that the old values represented by estates such as Sotherton (and Mansfield Park) are in decline.

Fanny's initial reaction to the chapel is one of disappointment. Her expectations of a more dramatic and atmospheric building demonstrate Fanny's tendency to **Romanticism** (a literary and artistic movement associated with the expression of emotion and freedom) as she quotes from Walter Scott's *The Lay of the Last Minstrel*. Fanny is also disappointed that the family prayers in the chapel have been discontinued, again demonstrating her support of order and tradition.

Mary Crawford sees the decline of the custom as an improvement, and laughs at the idea of the household staff being forced to attend prayers. She speaks disparagingly of the clergy. Her light-hearted banter shows her wit, her imagination, her entertaining personality and her total disregard for taste and propriety. ✪ Mary is scathing about an aspect of religion. Are there topics which you think should be sensitively handled in modern social situations?

Edmund responds gravely to Mary's comments. He presents the idea of being distracted from prayer as a weakness, and stresses the importance of the heads of the household setting an example. ✪ How are Edmund and Mary different? Do you think that either appears in a better light than the other? What kind of confusion does Edmund experience through his relationship with Mary?

Julia draws attention to the position of Maria and Mr Rushworth in front of the altar. ✪ What reason may Julia have for pointing this out? What does Henry's response reveal about his character and intentions? Mary Crawford is disconcerted to hear that Edmund is to be ordained. Fanny feels sympathy for the embarrassment that she imagines Mary must feel. ✪ What do you think Mary feels at this point?

Into the wilderness

(From p. 88, *The lower part of the house ...* to end of chapter.)

◆ Henry, Maria and Mrs Rushworth discuss improvements.
◆ Fanny, Mary and Edmund walk into the wilderness.
◆ Mary and Edmund discuss the clergy.
◆ Fanny rests on a seat.
◆ Edmund and Mary go on together.
◆ Julia is left behind with Mrs Norris and Mr Rushworth.

The character grouping is significant. Henry and Mr Rushworth are placed with Maria, signifying their underlying rivalry; similarly, Fanny and Mary are placed with Edmund, underlining the women's competing claims on his affection; Julia is marginalized to some extent, being left to accompany the older women.

The details of the grounds at Sotherton and of the day's heat emphasize the idea of the characters being removed from their normal environment to an alien setting which will intensify their emotional entanglements and affect their usual patterns of behaviour. ✪ You could compare this part of the novel with Shakespeare's *A Midsummer Night's Dream*. Look for patterns of pairings and pursuit.

MANSFIELD PARK

Mary continues the discussion about Edmund's ordination, reiterating her low opinion of a clergyman's social status, although the thrust of her questioning makes it clear that she is considering Edmund as a possible husband. Edmund's reply, that a clergyman has *the guardianship of religion and morals*, links the themes of ordination, improvement and guardianship. Society will be improved by behaviour based on good principles as promoted through the work of the clergy. ◯ Who are the guardians at Mansfield Park? How well do they perform their duties?

Chapter 10

The locked gate

- Maria, Mr Rushworth and Henry join Fanny.
- Mr Rushworth goes to get the key of the iron gate.
- In his absence, Henry and Maria pass around the edge of the gate.
- Julia arrives and follows them.
- Mr Rushworth returns and follows.
- Fanny goes in search of Mary and Edmund.
- Fanny finds them returning to the wilderness.
- The party returns to Mansfield Park.

The conversation between Maria and Henry in Rushworth's absence is intimate, in spite of Fanny's presence, and reverberates with hidden meanings. Their talk of 'improvements' and 'prospects' refers not only to landscaping but to the union of Maria and Rushworth, and Maria's perception that the iron gate imposes restraint implies her impatience with the restraints of her engagement. Henry's offer to help Maria pass around the edge of the gate suggests that he is also challenging her to escape from her marriage. Maria's determination to get past the gate and over the ha-ha shows her wilful desire to ignore her duty to Rushworth and to indulge her flirtation with Crawford.

Fanny warns Maria not to go into the park through that route, offering also, although she does not realize it, a warning of the moral danger threatening Maria. Julia's pursuit of the couple is fired by her impatience to get away from the Rushworth family and her desire to be with Henry and thwart Maria. Fanny, the

COMMENTARY

observer, is sorry for Mr Rushworth and would like to offer some consolation. He blames Henry Crawford for the situation: *... these Crawfords are no addition at all. We did very well without them.* Fanny and Rushworth both suffer as a result of the Crawford fascination – Henry has appropriated Maria, and Mary has visited with Edmund the avenue that Fanny had longed to visit with him.

On the return journey, Julia reclaims the favoured seat next to Henry. ◎ Why is Maria less disturbed by this arrangement than she was on the outward journey? How does Rushworth respond to this arrangement?

STYLE AND LANGUAGE

In the Sotherton chapters the use of **symbolism** intensifies the significance of the characters' actions. They are dazed by the heat and glare of the day and wander into a wilderness with winding serpentine paths. The suggestions of temptation and danger are enhanced by the references to the iron gate, which assumes symbolic dimensions as a representation of Maria's being restrained by marriage and convention. Henry's awareness of this application is seen in his weighted suggestion that Maria cannot '*get out without the key and without Mr Rushworth's authority and protection*'. Maria's flight into the park with Crawford prefigures their later elopement. ◎ Maria chafes against the kind of restraint suggested by the gate. Why does she not legitimately free herself from her engagement? What value does the novel as a whole place on the concept of restraint?

Snap your synapses

- ? Remind yourself of the conversation between Edmund and Mary (p. 92); look back at the conversation about Mary's harp on pp. 56–7. Start a Mind Map of town and country values.
- ? Who had the most enjoyable day at Sotherton? Put these characters in order: Fanny, Edmund, Mary Crawford, Henry Crawford, John Rushworth, Maria Bertram, Julia Bertram, Mrs Norris, Mrs Rushworth.

> ? Draw an outline of Mansfield Park, and one of Sotherton. (If you like, you could cut out pictures from magazines.) Inside each outline, write the values associated with the houses. Circle any values that you think are shown to be in a weakened form or under threat.
>
> ? Skim Chapters 1–10, marking references to Fanny's and Edmund's literary knowledge and tastes. Start a Mini Mind Map of literary references in the novel. Add to it as you read on.

Time for a break, and to prepare for more than one kind of drama at Mansfield Park!

Chapter 11

The black month

- Sir Thomas to return.
- Edmund and Mary disagree again about Edmund's ordination.
- Edmund joins Fanny to contemplate the beautiful evening, but is drawn back to Mary.

The news that Sir Thomas will come home in November, in about thirteen weeks, casts an air of gloom. His daughters do not look forward to the re-establishment of their father's repressive regime, and Maria does not look forward to her wedding being arranged.

Mary Crawford is alerted to the fact that on Sir Thomas's return Edmund will be ordained. She jokes that Sir Thomas is like an ancient hero, offering sacrificial lambs – Maria and Edmund – to the gods in thanks for a safe journey. The real object of her barbed jest is, of course, Edmund. Mary assumes that Edmund's decision has been influenced by the fact that his father has provided him with a clerical position. She sees clerics in general as idle and self-indulgent, an opinion formed partly through her observation of Dr Grant. ✪ What impression have you gained of Dr Grant?

COMMENTARY

Edmund counters Mary's criticisms with serious, measured arguments. He accepts that he may have been swayed by the provision of a living, but denies that he will be a worse clergyman as a consequence. Edmund's response to Mary's blanket condemnation of the clergy – '*Where any one body of educated men, of whatever denomination, are condemned indiscriminately, there must be a deficiency of information, or (smiling) of something else*' – suggests that he may be aware of some shortcoming in Mary's character. ❂ Why does Edmund smile before saying that there may be some other deficiency in Mary? What kind of deficiency might he mean? How good a judge of Mary's character is he at this point?

Fanny defends Edmund and Dr Grant, although she is clear-sighted about the latter's faults, and sees that his temperament may have caused more damage in another profession. Edmund speaks affectionately of Fanny's good nature, and Mary's remark that Fanny seldom hears herself praised shows her appreciation of Fanny's qualities. Fanny's pleasure in the harmony and repose of the unclouded night has a moral dimension. She feels that reflection on the natural world frees people from selfish concerns. Fanny and Edmund are united in their delight in nature and the stars, and his pleasure in Fanny's enthusiasm, a characteristic which in other contexts can seem naïve, indicates the strength of the bond between Fanny and Edmund and their suitability for each other. However, Edmund is in an *ecstasy of admiration* for Mary, and Fanny is soon the solitary observer once more.

STYLE AND LANGUAGE

Austen's presentation of Fanny is not entirely partisan. Although we are led to sympathize with her and see events from her perspective, there is irony in the depiction of Fanny. Her interjection about the kindness William received from the chaplain of his ship is described as being *very much to the purpose of her own feelings, if not of the conversation*. Fanny is not exempt from authorial mockery.

Chapter 12

Fanny's first ball

- Tom returns to Mansfield Park.
- Henry goes to Everingham (his estate) but soon returns.
- An impromptu ball at Mansfield.

This chapter helps to establish Tom's thoughtless, charming character. He enjoys the kind of social whirl he has had at Weymouth and is used to having to please no-one but himself. At the ball he subjects Fanny to conversation about his sick horse, then turns his attention to the newspaper. His offer to dance with Fanny is offhand until it suits him to take to the floor to avoid playing cards with Mrs Norris and the Grants. Mary decides that she prefers Edmund to Tom. ○ Why is this a *vexatious* situation for Mary? What are the main reasons for her preference?

Henry misses the social pleasures of Mansfield, in particular flirting with Maria and Julia. Austen's moral tone is stern as she comments that Henry's absence *ought* to have given him an opportunity of examining his behaviour towards the women. Henry, however, is *thoughtless and selfish from prosperity and bad example* and is not given to reflection and self-examination. Julia and Maria are similarly blind to the dangers of their situation, and each believes that she is Henry's favourite. ○ Why does each believe this?

Fanny is concerned about the situation with Henry, Maria and Julia, but is not sufficiently confident of her judgement to do more than hint to Edmund. Edmund believes that a *serious attachment* will cure any faults that Henry possesses, and is convinced that Julia is Henry's choice. As Fanny overhears at the ball, this view is shared by Mrs Norris, who discusses the financial suitability of the marriage with Mrs Rushworth. Mrs Norris also believes that Maria is happy with Mr Rushworth. She attributes Maria's seeming indifference to her *delicacy and propriety*. ○ What different kinds of blindness are shown in this chapter? What examples of irony do you find?

COMMENTARY

Chapter 13

Let's do the play here!

- The Hon. John Yates arrives, full of enthusiasm for amateur theatricals.
- Tom suggests that they create a theatre at Mansfield Park.
- Edmund and Fanny disagree with Tom's plan, but it goes ahead.

John Yates is a recently acquired friend of Tom's, who has just left a house party which was about to stage a production of *Lovers' Vows*; the presentation had to be abandoned because of a family death. He represents the raffish, slightly disreputable face of the aristocracy. ✪ What do you think about his comment that the news of the death could have been kept quiet for three days to allow the performance to go on? What is the author's attitude to John Yates?

✪ Which characters would you expect to be excited by the *novelty* of acting? Edmund shows his opposition in the first place through a heavily ironic description of how Mansfield Park could be adapted to stage a complicated performance. He is seriously disturbed when Tom suggests turning the billiard room into a theatre. His objections to the whole scheme are moral and ethical. He feels that his father's sense of decorum would be offended by the enterprise and his daughters' participation in it, and that Tom should not take liberties with his father's house. ✪ In what sense is Edmund using the word *house*? In what sense does Tom use the word when he replies '*His house shall not be hurt. I have quite as great an interest in being careful of his house as you can have*'? For the sake of avoiding a family quarrel, Edmund decides to let things run their course.

Tom's arguments are forceful and varied. He laughingly acknowledges the lack of justification in his attempt to present the scheme as likely to distract Lady Bertram from her anxiety about her husband's journey, as he and Edmund observe their mother falling into a tranquil doze on the sofa. But he goes on to claim that Sir Thomas supports activities associated with acting, and sarcastically refutes Edmund's comment about expense. He points out that the scheme will keep the estate manager busy. Tom feels that Edmund is being self-righteous

MANSFIELD PARK

and interfering: '*Manage your own concerns. Don't imagine that nobody in this house can see or judge but yourself.*'
✪ How is Tom fulfilling his role as temporary guardian of the family?

Maria and Julia support Tom, and the Crawfords are keen to be involved in the scheme. Mary's desire to act in the play confuses Edmund, as he wishes to interpret all her actions favourably. Mrs Norris supports the plan because it will satisfy her urge for bustle and involvement without costing her anything – in fact, she will save money because she will have to move into Mansfield Park to be on hand to help. Fanny supports Edmund, but her hope that Mrs Norris will not support the scheme is soon dashed, and her wish that they will not find a suitable play is about to be realized.

STYLE AND LANGUAGE

Different styles of dialogue in this chapter enhance the characters' representations of their ideas. The argument between the brothers, presented in direct speech, shows the contrast between Tom's impetuous, vigorous manner of speaking, punctuated by dashes and parentheses, and the rhythms of Edmund's calmer yet equally intense observations.

The use of free indirect speech to show the response of Maria and Julia highlights their rivalry. They begin by countering Edmund's arguments with one voice: *There could be no harm in what had been done in so many respectable families*; but then they split into separate representations, each attempting to show her own suitability to act in the play, and her sister's unsuitability to do so: *Julia did seem inclined to admit ... Maria evidently considered her engagement as only raising her so much more above restraint.*

Chapter 14

Who's going to be Agatha?

◆ Tom suggests that they perform *Lovers' Vows*.
◆ Maria and Julia compete to play opposite Henry.
◆ Maria gets the part.

COMMENTARY

- Julia refuses an alternative part and withdraws from the production.
- Fanny reads the play and is shocked.

The discussion of how parts should be allocated reveals the characters' barely-masked selfishness. The argument over the part of Agatha reflects the personal drama between Henry, Maria and Julia. Henry's choice of Maria for the part suggests that she is the one he prefers, making Julia jealous and encouraging Maria to believe that Henry genuinely loves her.

Fanny is shocked by the female roles: *the situation of one and the language of the other, so unfit to be expressed by any woman of modesty.* Agatha (Maria Bertram) has an illegitimate son, and Amelia (turned down by Julia, now to be Mary Crawford) has passionate love scenes with her tutor. ◯ See 'Context' for details on the play.

Try this

? Make a Mind Map of the significant new arrivals at Mansfield Park. What kind of effect does each have?

? Imagine the conversation between Henry and Mary about the proposed production. You could write it as dialogue, or improvise it out loud. Better still, get together with a friend and enjoy creating the roles of Henry and Mary!

? How sympathetic do you find Edmund at this point?

? Who –
(a) met with great kindness from the chaplain of the *Antwerp*?
(b) wrote to the gamekeeper, then to Edmund, announcing his return?
(c) was on the brink of stardom at Ecclesford?
(d) could be fool enough to undertake any character that was ever written?
(e) saved three quarters of a yard of green baize?
(f) is too tall and robust to play Amelia?

(*Answers on p. 93.*)

Now that you have enjoyed some dancing and some drama, take a short break. After the interval, the curtain unexpectedly descends.

Chapter 15

Edmund objects

- John Rushworth joins the cast.
- Edmund voices his objections to the choice of play.
- Mary tries in vain to persuade Edmund to play Anhalt, Amelia's tutor.
- Fanny refuses to take a part.
- It is decided to ask an 'outsider' to play Amelia's tutor.

John Rushworth's slow and limited character may be seen in his preoccupation with his costume and the number of lines he has to memorize. We see Tom's determination to get his own way and his ability to alter facts to suit himself as he tries to persuade Fanny to take the part of the Cottager's wife: '*it is a nothing of a part ... and it will not much signify if nobody hears a word you say.*' Previously he had tried to persuade Julia that '*it is a very pretty part*' and that the character has '*a good deal of spirit*' (Chapter 14).

Edmund's plea to Maria not to take part in the play is passionate and sincere, but unsuccessful. Maria is strongly motivated by the knowledge that if she surrenders her role, Julia will take it. Lady Bertram halfheartedly expresses the wish that Maria should not act anything improper, and Mrs Norris's main concern is how she got the better of a young boy who she thought was trying to get a free dinner with the servants. Only Edmund and Fanny oppose the play. Fanny's objections to acting in it are overruled until Edmund intervenes.

COMMENTARY

Mary Crawford shows good feeling and sensitivity when she hears Mrs Norris call Fanny a *very obstinate, ungrateful girl* for refusing to take part. Mary joins Fanny and tries to raise her spirits, admiring her needlework and enquiring about William. In spite of her dislike of Mary, Fanny is touched by her kindness. Mary is aware of Fanny's inferior position in the household. You might have noticed the comment earlier in the chapter that the household was still in the habit of sending Fanny on errands, in spite of all that Edmund could do.

○ How does Mary feel about an outsider playing the part opposite her? Edmund maintains a *determined gravity* in the face of the idea. What might his inner feelings be?

Chapter 16

A room of her own

◆ Fanny is upset by the argument about her refusal to act.
◆ She goes to the East Room and considers whether she was right to refuse.
◆ Edmund has decided to take the part of Anhalt after all.

We are introduced to the space that Fanny has appropriated for herself, the former schoolroom, which she had filled with her plants and books and uses as an escape and a refuge. In this room, which does not even have a fire (on Mrs Norris's instructions), Fanny constructs a world of her own to combat *the pains of tyranny, of ridicule and neglect* that have been her lot at Mansfield Park. In this room, where she continues to educate herself and to develop her knowledge and taste, it is possible for Fanny to find consolations arising from her suffering.

Among the objects from which she draws comfort is a transparency of Tintern Abbey, the subject of a poem by William Wordsworth celebrating solitary contemplation. There is also a sketch of William's ship, a reminder of affectionate ties that contrast with the feelings represented by the Bertram family portraits. ○ How much has Fanny changed from the girl whose only space was the little white attic, and who found something fearful in every person and place (Chapter 2)? How does the description of her room affect your view of her?

Edmund wants Fanny to approve his decision to act in the play. He will take the part in order to prevent an outsider becoming part of the enterprise and to spare Mary Crawford the embarrassment of having to act a romantic part with a stranger. Edmund claims that by this action he can limit the damage that the play might cause, but it is clear to Fanny that he has sacrificed a principle because of Mary's influence.

Edmund's behaviour contrasts with Fanny's own struggle with her conscience as she probes the correctness of her action in refusing to take part, which will spoil the pleasure of those people to whom she owes a great deal. Fanny explores the uncomfortable motives for her decision, unlike Edmund, who acknowledges that he will be seen to have descended from the moral high ground, but does not really admit that he has done so. ✪ What do you think of Edmund's decision? How does it affect your view of him?

Chapter 17

The green-eyed monster

- Maria and Tom see that jealousy has caused Edmund to change his mind.
- Julia is angry and jealous of Maria.
- Mrs Grant and Mary discuss Henry's flirtatious behaviour.
- Fanny is left isolated by Edmund's moral desertion.

Maria and Tom see Edmund's submission as a triumph. They enjoy his display of *jealous weakness*, and attribute his decision to *selfish inclinations* only. ✪ Where do your sympathies lie at this point?

Now that Julia's hopes of capturing Henry are dashed she feels angry and ill-used. She rebuffs Henry's short-lived attempts to mollify her with *gallantry and compliments*. The sisters are now emotionally estranged from each other, lacking the affection and principle that would enable them to deal with the situation with honour and tolerance. Maria revels in her triumph and Julia hopes that her sister is heading for disaster. ✪ What does this suggest about the education and development of the Bertram sisters?

COMMENTARY

Mrs Grant is not entirely reassured by Henry's claim that he and Julia were never serious about each other. When Mary remarks that Mr Rushworth would not stand a chance if Henry stepped in before the wedding, Mrs Grant determines to talk to Henry when the play is over. Mary is sarcastic about Sir Thomas's return. ✪ Look at Mary's parody and circle the words that she has substituted. What do you think of her assessment of Sir Thomas's character and the likely effect of his return? The parody gives another example of Mary's quick wit and lively mind.

Fanny feels *sad and insignificant*, removed from the bustle and activity of the production. Like Julia, she is experiencing intense misery, and is full of jealousy and agitation. Unlike Julia, she gives no outward sign of her inner turmoil. She is disturbed by Edmund's desertion of his principles, and can hardly bear Mary Crawford's expressions of friendliness and good humour. ✪ How does Fanny's suffering affect your response to her?

Chapter 18

'My father is come!'

◆ Edmund becomes alarmed as the preparations become more elaborate.
◆ Fanny becomes involved in the play as everybody's help and confidante.
◆ Mary and Edmund rehearse a love scene in front of Fanny.
◆ Mrs Grant is ill for the first full rehearsal.
◆ Fanny is persuaded to read Mrs Grant's part.
◆ Sir Thomas returns unexpectedly.

Fanny becomes both a spectator and a participant as she watches rehearsals, hears lines and sews materials for the play. She likes being useful and becomes more reconciled to the situation. In her *pity and kindheartedness* Fanny sympathizes with *poor* Mr Rushworth, whose tendency to find it easier to count his speeches rather than to learn them is made worse by the sight of Maria's and Henry's spirited rehearsing. ✪ What differences are there in the author's view of Rushworth and Fanny's view of him?

MANSFIELD PARK

We are drawn into Fanny's turbulent feelings as she watches the love scene between Edmund and Mary. Her spirits sink, and she feels herself becoming insignificant to both Mary and Henry. Fanny acknowledges that her emotional involvement and her disapproval of the situation impair her judgement. Fanny is severely tested, first by having to observe Edmund performing the love scene with gusto, then by the request to read Mrs Grant's part. Fanny feels that her difficult position is a punishment for her neglecting her duty to stay away from the rehearsal. ○ Why does Fanny agree to read the part? What do you think of her decision? How does it compare with Edmund's earlier change of heart about acting?

Try this

- ? Make a chart or Mind Map to show how the theatricals divide the characters. What qualities are associated with those who support the enterprise? What qualities are associated with those who oppose it?
- ? Make a Mind Map showing how the idea of **acting** is explored in the novel.
- ? During the period of the theatricals, which character most engages your sympathy? Give a brief explanation.
- ? Draw a graph of the tension generated in Chapters 15–19.

Fanny is saved from one ordeal by Sir Thomas's return — but another lies ahead! Have a break before going on.

COMMENTARY

Volume 2: Chapters 19–31
Chapter 19

Curtain down

- Tom, Edmund, Julia, Maria and Mr Rushworth go to meet Sir Thomas.
- The Crawfords slip away home.
- Fanny joins the family gathering and is warmly greeted by Sir Thomas.
- Sir Thomas comes face to face with Mr Yates in full flow on the stage.
- Sir Thomas puts a stop to the production.

The characters are further defined by their immediate reactions to the arrival of Sir Thomas. Both Maria and Julia, in different ways, gain courage to face their father from the way that Henry hangs on to Maria's hand. We see the Crawfords' quick understanding and social awareness as they agree on the *propriety* of returning home. ✪ What do you think about the association of this word with the Crawfords? Mr Yates shows his lack of tact, sensitivity and understanding by assuming that the interruption is only temporary, and in his later regaling Sir Thomas with details of the theatrical project. Mr Yates thinks little of parental claims or *family confidence*. ✪ In terms of principles and attitudes, with which characters would you group Mr Yates?

Fanny steels herself to perform the *dreadful duty* of facing her uncle, but is pleasantly surprised by his declarations of pleasure at seeing her. Sir Thomas is impressed by the *improvement in health and beauty* in his *little Fanny*, and Fanny, warmed by his kindness, is touched with compassion and tenderness for her uncle. She is stung by his reproachful glances at Edmund and longs to defend her cousin.

Sir Thomas values *domestic tranquillity* and a home which *shuts out noisy pleasures*. He gravely surveys the damage to the billiard room, but as yet is unaware of the extent of the real damage to the stability of Mansfield Park.

STYLE AND LANGUAGE

There is a variety of effects in this chapter. The meeting of Sir Thomas and his family is surrounded by **tension**. The **comic** effects range from the moment of near **farce** when Sir Thomas comes face to face with the ranting Mr Yates to the **comic irony** in Lady Bertram's response to her husband's unexpected arrival, which almost flusters her for a few moments.

Chapter 20

Order restored?

- ◆ Edmund apologizes for his involvement in the play and insists that Fanny alone should not be blamed.
- ◆ Sir Thomas criticizes Mrs Norris for allowing the enterprise.
- ◆ Sir Thomas gets rid of every trace of the theatre.
- ◆ Mr Yates, attracted to Julia, hangs on for a few days then leaves.
- ◆ Henry departs for Bath.

Sir Thomas removes all sign of the theatricals and the house is *restored to its proper state*. He does not investigate further, assuming that his children felt their error. His remonstrations with Mrs Norris have little effect as she evades his criticisms by turning the conversation to focus on how helpful she has been to the family through her practice of economy and through her role in bringing together Maria and Mr Rushworth. Sir Thomas's return restores order. ☉ What do you think of the way he deals with the situation?

Maria realizes that Henry will not propose marriage, but in the restrained environment of the breakfast room she has to hide the *tumult of her feelings*. ☉ Why is Henry leaving Mansfield Park at this point? What do you think of his behaviour?

COMMENTARY

Chapter 21

Maria and Rushworth marry

- The house has become quieter since Sir Thomas's return.
- Fanny is embarrassed by compliments about her looks.
- Sir Thomas, unimpressed by Rushworth, offers to help Maria break the engagement.
- Maria determines to go ahead in order to show Henry that he cannot influence her.
- The marriage takes place.

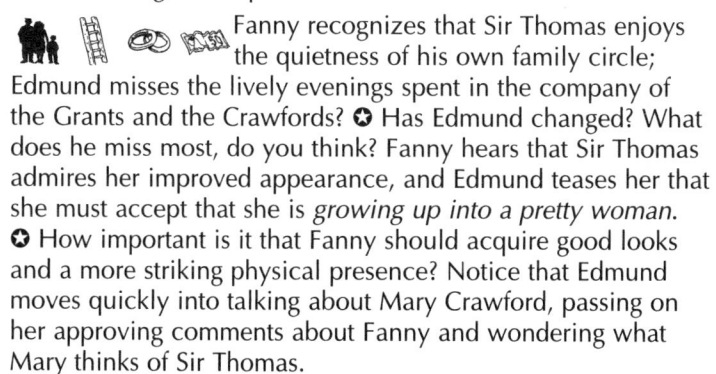

Fanny recognizes that Sir Thomas enjoys the quietness of his own family circle; Edmund misses the lively evenings spent in the company of the Grants and the Crawfords? ✪ Has Edmund changed? What does he miss most, do you think? Fanny hears that Sir Thomas admires her improved appearance, and Edmund teases her that she must accept that she is *growing up into a pretty woman*. ✪ How important is it that Fanny should acquire good looks and a more striking physical presence? Notice that Edmund moves quickly into talking about Mary Crawford, passing on her approving comments about Fanny and wondering what Mary thinks of Sir Thomas.

Sir Thomas realizes that Rushworth is an *inferior young man*, and that Maria's manner to him is *careless and cold*. He feels that her happiness should not be sacrificed for an advantageous alliance, and speaks seriously and kindly to her about her choice of husband. He is satisfied with Maria's declaration that she wishes to proceed with the marriage, and finds reasons to justify it. ✪ What does the author think of Sir Thomas's response?

Maria craves independence and liberty, and longs to escape the restraint of her father's authority at Mansfield Park. The wedding is arranged quickly and Maria and Rushworth set off for the *novelty, amusement and pleasures* of Brighton, accompanied by Julia. ✪ What does the author think of Maria's attitude to marriage? How does the Rushworth marriage compare with the other marriages in the novel?

MANSFIELD PARK

STYLE AND LANGUAGE

Look at the paragraph that begins 'To such feelings ...'. What is suggested by the use of words such as *hatred, restraint, misery, disappointed* and *contempt* in a description of wedding preparations?

Chapter 22

An unlikely friendship

- Fanny and Mary begin to spend time together.
- Mary and Edmund again discuss Edmund's chosen way of life.
- Mrs Grant invites Edmund and Fanny to dine.

Fanny and Mary have little in common, and become closer acquaintances only because Fanny is the only young woman left at Mansfield Park, and Mary has a *desire of something new*. Fanny is motivated to visit Mary by *a kind of fascination*, but she has no affection for her rival. The contrast between the two is illustrated in their conversation in the shrubbery. Fanny's remarks about nature and memory exemplify her breadth of interests and her tendency to philosophize, while at the same time revealing her *naïveté* and awkwardness. Mary is *untouched and inattentive*, her response displaying her superior wit and sophistication as she identifies herself as a town dweller whose sole source of wonder in the countryside is finding herself in it.

The women also disagree about Edmund's title. Fanny likes the use of his Christian name – one which has heroic and honourable associations – while Mary prefers public titles such as *Mr, Lord* and *Sir*, which imply status and social worth.

The conversation between Edmund and Mary reveals her desire for wealth: '*A large income is the best recipe for happiness I ever heard of.*' Edmund is clearly satisfied with the prospect of being a country clergyman earning an honest living in the *middle state of worldly circumstances*. ❂ How important are the differences between Edmund and Mary?

COMMENTARY

Chapter 23

Dinner with the Grants

- ◆Fanny goes to dinner at the Parsonage.
- ◆Henry Crawford has returned and dines with the party.
- ◆Mary is angry with Edmund for going ahead with his ordination.

We focus on Fanny's uncertain position at Mansfield Park as the suitability of her dining with the Grants is discussed. Mrs Norris spitefully and arrogantly objects. She rattles off reminders that Fanny is being asked only to compliment the family and because Julia is absent, criticizes the Grants' dining arrangements, tells Fanny to remember her place as the least significant of the party, and warns that Fanny cannot expect to travel in the carriage.

Mrs Norris complains of *'The nonsense and folly of people's stepping out of their rank and trying to appear above themselves'*. ✪ What is Mrs Norris's own 'rank'? Why is she so keen to remind Fanny of her perceived status? Sir Thomas sees Fanny's invitation as properly reflecting her status as a member of his family. To Fanny's grateful surprise, he arranges for her to travel in the carriage.

Henry tries to ingratiate himself with Fanny, but her replies to his attempts are *as short and indifferent as civility allowed*. Fanny dislikes his references to the Rushworths and his suggestion of a liaison between Julia and Mr Yates. Throughout the conversation Henry adapts his tone to suit the context. He adopts one of *gentle gallantry* when he addresses Fanny, and employs a *calmer, graver tone* when he encounters her opposition to his remarks. Fanny speaks out angrily in defence of her uncle and the cessation of the theatricals, and is amazed at her daring in doing so. It is significant that Henry was so happy when the play was being prepared. He loves the life and interest it provided. ✪ How appealing do you find Henry? How far do you sympathize with Fanny's dislike of him?

65

MANSFIELD PARK

Mary is upset by the information that Edmund is to be ordained in a few weeks. She had not thought that her influence would count for so little with him, and decides that from now on she will pursue the relationship for amusement only.

Chapter 24

A small hole in her heart

- Henry decides to stay another fortnight and to make Fanny fall in love with him.
- William comes to visit.
- Henry is touched by the affection between William and Fanny.
- Henry lends William his horse.

Henry, struck by the improvement in Fanny's looks, plans to *make a small hole* in her heart. Mary points out that his changed view of Fanny stems from his own *idleness and folly*, and that Fanny is a challenge to Henry because she has hurt his pride by not responding to his charm. Mary shows some concern for Fanny in not wanting her to be unhappy, but in the end she *left Fanny to her fate*. ✪ What does the conversation between Mary and Henry reveal about their relationship? What do you think of Henry's plan?

Henry begins to behave in a way that is appealing to Fanny's gentle and delicate nature, and is so entertaining and polite that she is civil towards him. Perhaps she would be more susceptible were she not already emotionally attached to Edmund. Henry realizes that he can get to Fanny through William. He brings her news of the arrival of William's ship, and lends him his hunter; his kindness to William touches Fanny. Henry is impressed by William's *warm hearted, blunt fondness* and by Fanny's capacity for affectionate feelings. His feelings for Fanny develop: *She interested him more than he had foreseen.*

✪ How does Henry's response to William affect your view of him? Are Henry's motives always self-interested? Why is it important that Henry should be more than a cold-hearted flirt?

COMMENTARY

William's personal qualities and impressive career history make him popular at Mansfield Park. ✪ Why do you think he is introduced at this point in the novel?

Over to you

- ? What are Sir Thomas's strengths and weaknesses? Make a Mind Map or notes.
- ? How do Yates and Rushworth compare? What is the function of each character?
- ? With which of these characters is the reader led to sympathize the most in these chapters? Put them in order: Mrs Norris; Mr Rushworth; Maria; Edmund; Fanny; Mary; Henry.
- ? Compare the relationship between Edmund and Mary with that between Henry and Fanny.
- ? What ideas does the novel portray about the relationships between brothers and sisters? Make a rough essay plan.

Time for a break – there's a ball and a declaration of love coming up.

Chapter 25

A gathering at the Parsonage

- ◆ Sir Thomas notices Henry's attentions to Fanny.
- ◆ A game of Speculation at the Parsonage.
- ◆ Henry and Edmund discuss improvements to Thornton Lacey.
- ◆ William's prospects, or lack of them.

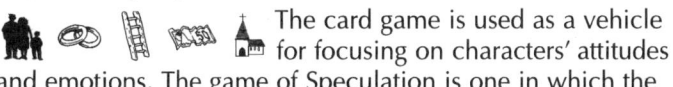

The card game is used as a vehicle for focusing on characters' attitudes and emotions. The game of Speculation is one in which the players bet on the buying and selling of trump cards. The word 'speculation' also means guessing the future, and, in another context, describes a kind of business venture in which money is invested in a financial venture that involves some risk.

○ What different kinds of 'speculation' are the characters involved in?

Henry has come across Thornton Lacey, where Edmund is to live as a clergyman, and is impressed not by its present state but by the amount of improvement he thinks it needs. ○ What do you already know about Henry's attitude to improvement? Henry's improvements would turn the house into a gentleman's residence unconnected with the local agricultural life (the farmyard, for example, he sees as a *terrible nuisance*). Edmund would be thought of as a great landowner. Mary urges Edmund to follow Henry's proposals, indulging pleasant fantasies of Thornton Lacey as the occasional abode of a man of independent means, all trace of church and clergy having been obliterated. Sir Thomas's words dispel all such illusions. He draws attention to Edmund's duty as a clergyman.

The importance of position and influence may be seen in William's complaint about his lack of promotion. Fanny hopes that Sir Thomas may be able to use his influence to help her deserving brother.

STYLE AND LANGUAGE

The card game has **symbolic** value. The description of the game may be read on more than one level. For example, in teaching Fanny how to play, Henry has to *sharpen her avarice and harden her heart*. Mary Crawford says '*I will stake my last like a woman of spirit.*' ○ What different meanings may be interpreted? Find some more examples and explain their significance.

Chapter 26

The gold chain

◆ Sir Thomas arranges a ball at Mansfield Park.
◆ Fanny would like to wear a cross that William gave her.
◆ Edmund wonders whether Mary would marry him.
◆ Mary offers Fanny a gold necklace for the cross.
◆ The necklace had been bought by Henry.

COMMENTARY

Sir Thomas makes the arrangements for the ball without deferring to Mrs Norris. ✪ How has Sir Thomas's return affected the position of Mrs Norris?

Edmund is pondering two important events: ordination and marriage. He is unsure of Mary's feelings, and is particularly perturbed by her deep dislike for the kind of quiet life she would have as a country clergyman's wife. Edmund looks for indications that her love for him would outweigh her preference for London life. Edmund recognizes that Mary might require him to change his life in ways that go against his conscience. ✪ How clear-sighted is Edmund about Mary? How significant are the differences in their attitudes and values?

The cross that William gives Fanny is associated with religious faith and with the love between the brother and sister. Mary Crawford's offer of a necklace for the cross at first seems to be the kind gesture of a real friend, but Fanny realizes that she has been manouevred into accepting a gift that will place her under an obligation to Henry. Mary cleverly pre-empts Fanny's objections by laughingly listing and dismissing Fanny's possible reservations in such a way that Fanny has to give in. Fanny is the victim of collusion between Mary and Henry. She suspects that Henry intends to *cheat her of her tranquillity* as he did Maria and Julia. ✪ How does this incident affect your view of Mary and of Fanny?

Chapter 27

Edmund's chain

- Edmund gives Fanny a gold chain for the cross.
- Fanny realizes that Edmund wants to marry Mary.
- Henry invites William to travel with him and meet Admiral Crawford.
- Mary will not marry – or even dance with – Edmund when he is a clergyman.
- Fanny decides to wear both the necklace and the chain.

Edmund's gift is a *plain gold chain perfectly simple and neat*, very suitable for the cross. Fanny is delighted with the gift and the giver.

MANSFIELD PARK

○ How are the two chains different? How are the characters of Henry and Edmund apparent in their different choices? What is significant about the different ways in which the gifts are offered? Edmund is pleased by what he sees to be a mark of Mary's regard for Fanny, and he persuades Fanny not to return the necklace. Fanny decides to wear both the necklace and the chain.

We are drawn into Fanny's consciousness as she struggles with the idea that Edmund will marry Mary Crawford, who she believes does not deserve Edmund. In spite of her *heroism of principle* and her attempts to persuade herself that Edmund and she can never be more than friends, Fanny pores emotionally over the note accompanying Edmund's gift.

Henry continues his kindness to William. His plan is approved by William because of the pleasure it will afford, by Fanny because it will spare William fatigue, and by Sir Thomas because he thinks that Admiral Crawford might be able to help William. ○ What does this suggest about Sir Thomas's own sphere of influence?

STYLE AND LANGUAGE

There is **irony** in the description of Fanny reading Edmund's note. Sentences such as *Never were characters cut by any other human being, as Edmund's commonest handwriting gave!* gently mock Fanny's indulgence in romantic excess. Fanny is comforted by a *happy mixture of reason and weakness.*

Chapter 28

Fanny's first ball

- Fanny makes a good impression at the ball.
- Henry's continued attentions upset Fanny.
- Mary and Edmund disagree again about his choice of profession.

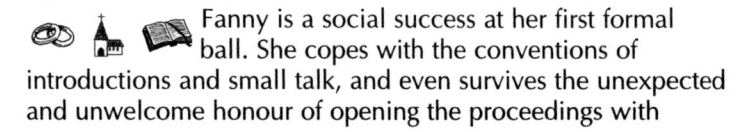

Fanny is a social success at her first formal ball. She copes with the conventions of introductions and small talk, and even survives the unexpected and unwelcome honour of opening the proceedings with

COMMENTARY

Henry as her dance partner. Fanny takes her place in society as a member of the Bertram family, successfully taking on the role left vacant by Maria and Julia. Her enjoyment of the occasion is marred by Henry's pointed glance at the necklace, by his continued attentions and Mary's assumption that she enjoys them. ✪ Does Fanny actively dislike Henry? What pleasing qualities does he display?

Sir Thomas is proud of the improvement in Fanny, and is gratified that her *education and manners* have been developed through her upbringing at Mansfield Park. ✪ How do you think Mansfield Park has contributed to Fanny's education and development? How is her education different from Maria's and Julia's? The ambiguity of the last paragraph of the chapter draws attention to Sir Thomas's perception of Crawford's interest in Fanny.

For Fanny, the best part of the ball is dancing with Edmund. Their compatibility is seen in their easy enjoyment of the *luxury of silence* and the *solemn tranquillity* with which they dance. The onlookers' assumption that they were not intended for each other ironically intensifies our awareness of how well they are suited, and highlights Edmund's lack of awareness of this.

STYLE AND LANGUAGE

The tension between Edmund and Mary with regard to his ordination is seen in the terse summary of their argument. The use of dashes, as in *They had talked – and she had been silent – he had reasoned*, indicates the force of their reciprocal arguments.

Chapter 29

A quiet house

- Edmund and William leave in the morning.
- Mary is unsettled by Edmund's prolonged absence.
- Mary is suspicious and jealous of the sisters of Edmund's friend.

MANSFIELD PARK

William sets off with Henry Crawford, as planned, and Edmund goes to stay with his friend Mr Owen, who is also about to be ordained. Mansfield Park is very quiet without them, a condition emphasized by Julia's request not to return home, but to go to London with her sister and her husband. Fanny's position in the house changes; Sir Thomas and Lady Bertram depend on her and see her as a *valuable companion*. Sir Thomas intimates that they may one day lose Fanny to marriage, but Lady Bertram does not understand what he says. ○ What does this tell you about Lady Bertram's attitude to Fanny?

After her initial misery, Fanny adjusts to the absence of Edmund and William. In contrast, Mary Crawford is restless and agitated, missing Edmund's company and angry at the reason for his absence. She fishes for information about Edmund and about the Owen sisters, showing her jealousy of the girls and their potential threat to her hold over Edmund. ○ Does Mary have any reason to feel jealous? What does her reaction suggest about her character? Fanny's calm replies and lack of concern about Edmund's proximity to the Miss Owens shows her to be a more stable character than Mary.

Chapter 30

'A sweet little wife'

◆ Henry returns from London.
◆ Henry tells Mary that he intends to marry Fanny.

Henry's announcement takes Mary completely by surprise. Her pleasure in his decision is tinged with personal considerations and a touch of malice – she likes the idea of Henry marrying a little beneath him. Mary does speak warmly of Fanny's good qualities, in spite of the patronizing comment '*You will have a sweet little wife; all gratitude and devotion*'. Like Henry, she assumes that Fanny will wish to marry him.

Henry declares that his feelings for Fanny are genuine, and that he repents of his *wicked project* of making her fall in love with him. Now that he knows her better he appreciates the *gentleness, modesty and sweetness of her character*. ○ How

COMMENTARY

does Austen prepare the reader for the change in Henry? Mary thinks that Henry's proposed marriage will remove him from the Admiral's influence, but Henry speaks affectionately of his uncle. ✪ What is the main reason for Mary's dislike of the Admiral? What do you think of Henry's response to her comments?

Chapter 31

Pleasure and pain

- ◆ Henry tells Fanny that William has been promoted.
- ◆ Henry reveals his love for Fanny.
- ◆ Fanny is distraught and runs out of the room.
- ◆ Mary writes to congratulate Fanny.
- ◆ Fanny writes a dismissive reply, hoping to end the matter.

Henry takes great pleasure in telling Fanny about William's promotion and his own part in securing it. Fanny's delight in William's good fortune turns to unease as Henry reveals that his love for her motivated him to help William. Fanny is greatly distressed by Henry's declaration. She is torn between her dislike for what she sees as Henry's demeaning and offensive behaviour, and her obligation and gratitude to him for his friendship to William.

Mary's note increases Fanny's confusion. She cannot believe that Henry's proposal is sincere, but is ashamed of her doubts. Her reply to Mary's letter indicates her wish that the matter should be dropped. Fanny is not convinced that Henry is any more than the selfish philanderer who toyed with the affections of her cousins. ✪ What do think about Fanny's response to the proposal and to the note? What aspects of her character does it reveal?

Try this

? Make a Mini Mind Map of the Crawfords' life before they came to Mansfield Park. Explain how their life with the Admiral has influenced them.

? The plain gold chain that Edmund gives Fanny is more to her taste than Henry's more ornate necklace. Design a piece of jewellery or personal accessory to suit Mary

Crawford, Henry Crawford, William Price and Julia Bertram.
- ? Write a sentence about Henry Crawford that might be spoken by Fanny, Edmund, Mary, Maria and Julia.
- ? Remember to add to your Mind Maps

After the break, a proposal, pressure, persuasion and Portsmouth.

Volume 3: Chapters 32–48
Chapter 32

Pressurizing Fanny

(To p. 315, '... that I should be miserable myself'.)

◆ Sir Thomas tells Fanny that Henry has asked for her hand.
◆ Fanny says that she will not marry Henry.

Sir Thomas begins his approach to Fanny by enquiring why there is no fire in her room, and assuring her that any inferior treatment she may have received at Mansfield Park was not meant unkindly. He suggests that Mrs Norris may have applied the principle of an unindulgent upbringing too severely in Fanny's case. ✪ Why does Sir Thomas make such observations at this point?

Sir Thomas is taken aback by Fanny's refusal. He satisfies himself that it has nothing to do with Tom or Edmund, then expresses his extreme displeasure and bafflement at Fanny's behaviour. Fanny is *wilful and perverse*; she is not considering the benefits to her family that marriage to Henry would bring, nor is she considering that such an opportunity of being *nobly settled* is unlikely to come her way again. Although Fanny does not owe Sir Thomas *the duty of a child*, she is guilty of ingratitude. Sir Thomas would have been glad had Henry wished to marry either of his own daughters.

Fanny is distressed and tearful. She cannot reveal her observations of Henry's behaviour, and her conviction of his

COMMENTARY

lack of principle. ✪ What is the effect of Sir Thomas referring to his 'own' daughters? What do you think of the way he speaks to Fanny? How reasonable are his comments? How do they reflect Sir Thomas's view of the world and of women's roles?

Fanny sticks to her guns

(From p. 315, *Another burst of tears* ... to end of chapter.)

◆ Sir Thomas thinks that Fanny might be persuaded.
◆ Fanny's aunts are not to be told of the situation.
◆ Fanny is summoned to speak to Henry.

Sir Thomas softens a little and does not insist that Fanny should speak to Henry, who is waiting downstairs, at that moment – partly because her tearful appearance does not show her in the most flattering aspect. His decision to keep the matter from Lady Bertram and Mrs Norris shows tact and kindness, and his arrangement for a regular fire in Fanny's room shows concern for her well-being. ✪ Or is it part of Sir Thomas's persuasive technique to give Fanny cause for gratitude? How far does Sir Thomas understand Fanny's reasons? Is it reasonable to expect him to understand?

Fanny hates being out of favour with Sir Thomas, and in Edmund's absence feels isolated and helpless. At dinner she has to endure Mrs Norris's unfounded criticisms of her secrecy and love of her own way. ✪ How does Sir Thomas react to these criticisms? Fanny recovers her spirits as she reflects that her uncle, basically a good man, will not want her to marry without affection, and convinces herself that when Henry leaves Mansfield Park the matter will be forgotten. ✪ What do you think of Fanny's refusal to be persuaded? What aspect of her character is revealed?

Chapter 33

Every young woman's duty

◆ Henry intends to persevere in his courtship of Fanny.
◆ Lady Bertram and Mrs Norris are informed of the situation.

MANSFIELD PARK

Fanny's refusal makes Henry all the more determined to marry her. He overrides Fanny's objection that she does not love him and that their characters are incompatible, but Fanny's gentle manner conceals the strength of her feelings. Furthermore, she now sees Henry in a different light: he speaks honourably and sincerely, and of course, he has brought about William's promotion. ✪ What effect does Fanny's manner have on Henry?

Mrs Norris, constantly trying to demean Fanny, begrudges her elevation and sees it as an insult to the much more deserving Julia. Lady Bertram feels that Henry's proposal reflects well on her, and is sure that it was precipitated by her generous offer in sending her maid to help Fanny to dress for the ball so that she looked her best. The fact that Mrs Chapman arrived too late to help emphasizes the exceedingly narrow range of Lady Bertram's awareness and understanding. Lady Bertram misses the urgent undertone in Fanny's plea for support, and intimates that it is Fanny's duty to accept the offer. This is the only guidance that Lady Bertram has ever given to Fanny. ✪ What do you think of Lady Bertram as a parent and as a guardian?

Chapter 34

A masterly performance

- ◆ Edmund thinks that Fanny should accept Henry's proposal.
- ◆ A Shakespeare reading.
- ◆ A discussion about preaching.

Edmund thinks that Henry has not given Fanny time to become attached to him. He hopes that Fanny will overcome her doubts and that she and Henry may become *blessed in each other*. Edmund and Sir Thomas are on the same side in this matter. ✪ Who else is usually on their side? What does this suggest about the present situation?

At the evening gathering, Henry gives an entertaining and talented reading from Shakespeare's *Henry V*. ✪ How does Fanny respond to Henry's performance? The ease with which Henry assumes different roles enhances our awareness of his ability to play parts in real life. ✪ How do Henry's conversations with Fanny reinforce this? Henry also has

COMMENTARY

sudden enthusiasms for trying new roles – William's stories of the Navy inspired a fleeting desire to be a sailor (Chapter 24) and in this chapter he plays with the idea of being a clergyman. ✪ What are the positive and negative aspects of Henry's gift for acting?

Edmund and Henry discuss the art of reading prayers out loud and of preaching; Edmund applauds the *spirit of improvement* that is leading the clergy to acknowledge the importance of a *clear manner and good delivery*. Henry admires effective preaching that is stimulating without being offensive and that is eloquently delivered. He would like to preach such a sermon, but only to an educated, sophisticated London audience, and only now and again. He dislikes *constancy*. ✪ Who do you think would be the better preacher, Edmund or Henry? What does Fanny think of Henry's comments? Fanny is finally pressed into responding and comments on Henry's awareness of his lack of stability, and his lack of self-knowledge in other respects.

Chapter 35

More pressure

◆ In support of Sir Thomas, Edmund encourages Fanny to accept Henry.
◆ Edmund thinks that Fanny and Henry are well suited.
◆ Mary is upset at Fanny's refusal and wants to talk to her.

Fanny is momentarily comforted by Edmund's assurance that he would not wish her to marry without love, but Edmund urges her to think favourably of Henry. He points out that despite the difference in their temperaments, Fanny and Henry have much in common. ✪ Why is it important that Henry should be convincing as a possible husband for Fanny? What does Henry's role in this respect contribute to the design and structure of the novel? Edmund rather skates over Fanny's references to the poor light in which Henry appeared during the theatricals. ✪ Why does Edmund respond like this?

Both Fanny and Edmund are influenced by feelings which lie behind their words. Fanny speaks, with *a warmth which quite*

77

astonished Edmund, about her inability to love Henry; Edmund, of course, is unaware that it is Fanny's feelings for him which prevent her from accepting Henry. Edmund himself is influenced by his hope that he may have a future with Mary Crawford. Edmund behaves towards Fanny with the *kind authority of a privileged guardian*. ✪ What do you think of the way Edmund is fulfilling his role as guardian?

Chapter 36

A persuasive sister

◆ Mary talks to Fanny about the proposal.
◆ Mary reveals that the gift of the necklace was Henry's idea.
◆ The Crawfords leave for London.

Mary begins her efforts to persuade Fanny by reminiscing about rehearsing *Lovers' Vows* with Edmund in the very room in which she and Fanny are now sitting. ✪ Why does Mary remind Fanny of this? Mary declares that she loves Fanny in particular, and the Bertrams in general, because they have so much more heart than is generally found. She sees Mrs Grant as an ideal wife, and Sir Thomas as an ideal husband, favourably comparing the *conjugal manners* at Mansfield Park with the marriages of her London set. ✪ How far do you think that Mary means what she says? To what extent has her view of family life changed? Mary compares the friendships she has enjoyed at Mansfield Park with those she will resume in London, which are not based on affection. Her description of her life in London includes references to women who are in love with Henry and the jealousy that Fanny will evoke in them. Mary continues her attempt to manipulate Fanny by reminding her of Henry's kindness to William. ✪ What do these strategies reveal about Mary's character?

When Fanny realizes that the necklace was a gift from Henry she is moved to voice her criticisms of Henry's flirtatious behaviour. Mary makes little of the fact that in the past Henry has toyed with ladies' affections, but when Fanny refuses to acknowledge that his behaviour is harmless, Mary emphasizes Henry's true attachment to Fanny. ✪ How strong does Fanny appear in this conversation? How strong does Mary seem?

COMMENTARY

STYLE AND LANGUAGE

Mary's values are revealed through the content and tone of her conversation with Fanny. The description of her London life is racy and a little vulgar. Her account of the marriages of her friends and acquaintances includes expressions such as *'She could not do otherwise than accept him for he was rich'*, *'my friend Flora who jilted a very nice young man in the Blues, for the sake of that horrid Lord Stornaway'* and *'there was no want of foresight. She took three days to consider his proposal'*. Mary also asserts, *'I look upon the Frasers to be about as unhappy as most married people.'* ✪ Why does Austen present Mary in this light at this point in the novel?

Chapter 37

Going home

◆ Fanny is convinced that Edmund and Mary will marry.
◆ William is to visit.
◆ Sir Thomas arranges for Fanny to visit her home, accompanied by William.
◆ Edmund delays a visit to London.

Fanny fears that marriage between Edmund and Mary is inevitable, and that Edmund's proposed visit to London will seal the matter. Edmund's unselfish decision to postpone his visit so that his parents will not be left alone increases Fanny's tension. She anticipates the dread with which she will receive Edmund's letter with the news of his engagement.

Sir Thomas believes that a period of time spent in Portsmouth will correct Fanny's thinking. Absent from the elegancies and luxuries of Mansfield Park, Fanny will learn *the value of a good income* and reconsider her attitude to Henry Crawford. Sir Thomas uses his authority to persuade Lady Bertram to let Fanny go. ✪ What do you think of the way Sir Thomas uses his authority?

Fanny is delighted at the prospect of seeing her family and she hopes that the visit will *heal every pain* caused by her forced separation from them. Fanny anticipates enjoying feeling loved

MANSFIELD PARK

and being equal to those around her. ◯ How does this description of her feelings affect your attitude to Fanny? What is the effect of William's comment that the Portsmouth home lacks Fanny's *nice ways and orderliness*?

Fanny and William are spared Mrs Norris's company because she realizes in time that although she could travel free with William and Fanny, she would have to pay her own fare home. ◯ Think of three other references to Mrs Norris's love of economy.

Time for a test

- ? Skim the conversations about the proposal that Sir Thomas, Edmund and Mary have with Fanny. (Give a mark out of 5 for Fanny's level of discomfort in each case. Write a sentence for each explaining your mark.)
- ? Make a Mind Map of the novel's examples of acting and playing parts.
- ? What qualities does the novel suggest are desirable in a guardian? How far do Sir Thomas, Lady Bertram and Edmund demonstrate these qualities? Mind Map your ideas.
- ? Who said each of the lines below?

(a) *… you have now shown me that you can be wilful and perverse.*
(b) *The next time pug has a litter you shall have a puppy.*
(c) *I thought it was a pity you did not always know yourself as well as you seemed to do at that moment.*
(d) *Our liturgy has beauties which not even a careless, slovenly style of reading can destroy.*
(e) *The time of the play is a time which I hate to recollect.*
(f) *You all give me a feeling of being able to trust and confide in you.*

(Answers on p. 93).

More discomfort for Fanny on the way – and a significant visit. Have a break first.

COMMENTARY

Chapter 38

Fanny meets her family

- ◆William is expected on his ship, the *Thrush*, immediately.
- ◆The household is full of discussion of naval matters.
- ◆Little notice is taken of Fanny.
- ◆Fanny is shocked by the house and by manner of her father and her siblings.

The reunion of Fanny and the Price family is not a moving, emotional occasion. She is ignored as the news of the departure of the *Thrush* and the movements of other ships and naval personnel is excitedly relayed by the maidservant, Mrs Price and Mr Price. ✪ What is the effect of the inclusion of so much new information about new topics? How is the world of Portsmouth distinguished from the world of Mansfield Park? When prompted by William, Mrs Price does acknowledge Fanny and offer hospitality, and also when prompted by William, her father does greet Fanny cordially before ignoring her again.

Fanny is taken aback by her father's behaviour and language. His speech is punctuated with oaths, he smells of alcohol and the boys take no notice of his attempts to regulate their behaviour. ✪ How does Mr Price compare with Sir Thomas in their roles as parent and guardian? When the girls quarrel over a silver knife (Betsey wanting to play with it although it was left to Susan by their deceased sister Mary), it is clear that they take little notice of their mother's instructions. Mrs Price does not manage the house efficiently and finds it difficult to get the servants to do their jobs properly.

The house is small and cramped, full of *confusion and noise*. It is different from Mansfield Park both in its lack of physical comfort and orderliness, and in the manners of its inhabitants. The lack of interest in Fanny and Mansfield Park and its inhabitants shows a lack of propriety and social awareness. ✪ What do you think of Fanny's response to Portsmouth? Draw a rough family tree showing Fanny's parents and brothers and sisters.

Chapter 39

All noise and discomfort

- Fanny is severely disappointed in her home and her parents.
- The children are disagreeable and quarrelsome.
- Fanny longs for Mansfield Park.

Fanny enjoys being useful by getting Sam ready to join the ship, but with him and William gone she is painfully aware of the deficiencies of her home and family. ✪ How is Mrs Price similar to Lady Bertram? Mrs Price has been forced into a life of *exertions and self-denials* because of her *imprudent marriage*. ✪ What is suggested about the importance of money in marriage? What is the significance of the fact that neither Edmund nor Henry is poor?

Fanny longs for the peace and tranquillity of Mansfield Park; she finds the noise at Portsmouth particularly jarring and unpleasant. ✪ Does Fanny idealize Mansfield Park?

STYLE AND LANGUAGE

We see Portsmouth through Fanny's consciousness: *She did feel that her mother was a partial, ill-judging parent, a dawdle, a slattern ... whose house was the scene of mismanagement and discomfort ... .* ✪ How far do you feel that these words reflect Fanny's own thoughts? How far do you think that the expression is a fusion of Fanny's observations and the author's judgement? Think of incidents where Fanny has thought or spoken in such stern critical tones.

The examples of life at Portsmouth are constructed to provide a contrast with Mansfield Park. Portsmouth is shown to be noisy, uncomfortable, lacking propriety and order and full of disharmony. ✪ What are the opposite qualities associated with Mansfield Park?

COMMENTARY

Chapter 40

Improving Susan

- ◆ A letter from Mary Crawford.
- ◆ Fanny and Susan become close.
- ◆ Fanny helps Susan to improve.
- ◆ Fanny waits in dread for Edmund's letter from London.

Mary Crawford's letter reveals that Maria was *wanting in self-possession* when she heard about Henry's love for Fanny, and that Mr Yates is still in pursuit of Julia, although Mary considers him to be *no catch*. ✪ Find in the letter examples of Mary's wit, her manipulativeness and her worldliness. The letter establishes that Henry is in Norfolk and that Edmund is still in Northamptonshire.

Susan emerges as a strong character, desirous of making things better at home. Fanny takes on the role of guide and mentor, assuming responsibility for Susan's development. Used to receiving gifts, Fanny is now able to give, and her offer of money for Betsey to buy her own silver knife paves the way for a close relationship with Susan. Fanny and Susan find a room upstairs where they talk and sew; Fanny joins a circulating library and longs to pass on her love of reading to Susan. ✪ Who guided Fanny's development? Susan has *good notions* in spite of having been brought up in *negligence and error*. ✪ What does this suggest about the environment at Portsmouth? Does it have any strengths? What did Fanny miss when she first came to Mansfield Park?

On hearing from Lady Bertram that Edmund has finally gone to London, Fanny waits for news of Edmund's engagement. ✪ At this point, how likely is it that the engagement will take place?

Chapter 41

A visit from Henry

- ◆ Henry Crawford turns up.
- ◆ Henry, Fanny and Susan go for a walk.
- ◆ Henry meets Mr Price.
- ◆ Fanny finds Henry greatly improved.

MANSFIELD PARK

Henry behaves tactfully and courteously. His manner towards Mrs Price is a perfectly judged mixture of politeness and friendliness, and his good manners towards Mr Price bring out the best in Fanny's father. Henry is agreeable and amusing to Susan, although her presence prevents intimate conversation with Fanny. To Fanny's great relief, he delicately refuses an invitation to dine with the family. ○ What do you think about Fanny's attitude to her family? How far do you sympathize with her? What is your impression of the Portsmouth household in this chapter?

Fanny is embarrassed by Henry's hints about his hopes for their future, but in general finds him *decidedly improved,* and *more gentle, obliging and attentive to other people's feelings* than before. She approves of his recent involvement with the tenants on his estate and his new awareness of his responsibilities as a landlord. ○ How far has Henry changed? What are Fanny's feelings for him at this point?

Chapter 42

Henry is concerned

◆ Henry accompanies the Prices to church.
◆ A walk with Fanny and Susan.
◆ A talk with Fanny.

Fanny's family appear in a good light in their Sunday best. Henry is attentive to the females in church, and escorts Fanny and Susan for a walk along the ramparts. Henry is concerned about Fanny's health, noticing her tiredness and general lack of bloom. He offers to escort her back to Mansfield Park at a moment's notice, accompanied by Susan, should Fanny request it. He is convinced that Fanny needs country air and regular exercise to restore her health. ○ What is significant about Fanny's failure to thrive at Portsmouth? What do you think about Henry's offer? Why does he include Susan in the arrangement? Look at the paragraph beginning *Their daily fare ...* . What does the description add to your awareness of Fanny's state of health and spirits?

Henry confides in Fanny about his problems with the land agent, and asks her advice. Although she refuses to give an opinion, Fanny is struck by the *wonderful improvement which she still fancied in Mr Crawford.* However, she hopes that in

COMMENTARY

his new sensitivity he will respond to her distress at his advances and stop pestering her to marry him. ✪ How successful is Sir Thomas's plan? How far does the Portsmouth environment enhance Henry's appeal?

Chapter 43

Mary writes again

◆ Another letter from Mary.
◆ Susan continues to improve.

Mary's letter reveals that as yet Edmund has not proposed. Her references to the *people and parties* that take up her time, and expressions such as *Mrs Fraser is mad for such a house* emphasize her shallowness, her love of a hectic social life and her slight vulgarity. Fanny dislikes Mary's reports of her friends' favourable responses to Edmund's appearance. ✪ Why is Fanny *ashamed* of Mary's attitude? Mary plans to delay Henry's return to his estate so that he can meet the Rushworths at a party. ✪ Why is Fanny appalled by this arrangement?

Fanny enables Susan's continuing growth and development. Fanny supports herself through this period of anxiety and isolation by sharing her cultural interests with Susan and telling her about Mansfield Park. ✪ Could Susan develop her taste for the *genteel and the well-appointed* in Portsmouth?

For you to do

? Make a Mind Map of the positive and negative aspects of the Price household.
? Rate each of the following statements according to how far you agree with them, on a scale of 1–10.
  • Fanny's reaction to Portsmouth and her family is snobbish.
  • Fanny's desire for order and harmony shows that she is better than her parents.
  • Good qualities will not develop in an unencouraging environment.
  • Good qualities will emerge in spite of an unencouraging upbringing.

MANSFIELD PARK

> ? Draw a graph showing Fanny's changing attitude to Henry.
>
> ? Compare Henry and William. You could make a Mind Map of your ideas.

Time for a break before lots of letters and a conclusion.

Chapter 44

The long-awaited letter and many more

- ◆ Edmund writes from Mansfield Park.
- ◆ He did not propose to Mary in London, but still intends to do so.
- ◆ Crawford and the Rushworths have met.
- ◆ Fanny's return to Mansfield Park is to be postponed.
- ◆ Frequent letters from Lady Bertram.

Edmund is disturbed by Mary's behaviour in London. He is torn between his conviction that she is the *only woman in the world* he could ever marry, and his dislike of her manner and her friends. The London society which Mary enjoys so much is a bad influence, encouraging *habits of wealth* and supporting the weaknesses of her character and her *too lively mind.* ✪ What do you think of Edmund's judgement that Mary's mind is 'too lively'? He makes excuses for Mary, saying that her friends have been *leading her astray for years.* ✪ What do you think of Edmund's determination to marry Mary in spite of his doubts about her character and behaviour? How does his letter affect your view of him?

Edmund reports that Maria was very cool to Henry Crawford when they met, and that they scarcely spoke. ✪ From his previous behaviour, how might Henry respond to Maria's coolness? Check your response against the paragraph beginning *Had he done as he intended ... .*

Lady Bertram's letter brings news that Tom is suffering from a fever brought on by a fall and a good deal of drinking. Edmund has gone to nurse him and bring him home. ✪ How do Tom's friends react to his illness? Which characters in the novel show genuine warmth and affection? In another letter, Lady Bertram conveys her distress and fright at Tom's appearance when he was brought home. ✪ How does the news about Tom affect Fanny?

Chapter 45

Delays and longing

- ◆ Continued isolation.
- ◆ Tom continues to be seriously ill.
- ◆ Edmund delays his proposal.
- ◆ Fanny's stay is prolonged.
- ◆ A letter from Mary.

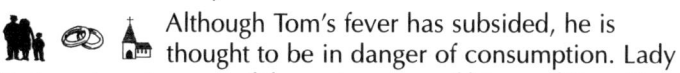

Although Tom's fever has subsided, he is thought to be in danger of consumption. Lady Bertram is not aware of the seriousness of his condition. Sir Thomas makes no move to collect Fanny, whose sense of isolation and longing to be at Mansfield is intensified with the onset of spring. She wishes she could be of use in the place she now considers to be her home. ✪ How does Fanny deal with informing her parents that Mansfield Park is her home? What does this reveal about her character? Fanny is surprised that Tom's sisters remain in London. ✪ What do you think of this?

Mary writes to ask about Tom's illness. She indicates that Edmund would be an acceptable marriage prospect if Tom dies and he became the Bertram heir. It seems that money can overcome Mary's objections to marrying a clergyman. The arch tone of Mary's comments and her attempts to draw Fanny into colluding smiles are tasteless and ill-judged. Mary's letter reveals that Maria and Henry have met in Twickenham; her assurances that this is not significant cut little ice with Fanny. Fanny is tempted to accept the Crawfords' repeated offer to convey her home, but her disgust at their behaviour and her dread of displeasing Sir Thomas prevent her. Fanny is repulsed by Mary's *cold-hearted ambition* and Henry's *thoughtless vanity*. ✪ How attractive do the Crawfords appear now?

Chapter 46

Two scandals

- Fanny hears in a letter from Mary of a scandalous rumour involving Henry and Maria.
- A newspaper report confirms that Henry and Maria have run off together.
- A letter from Edmund – Julia has eloped with Mr Yates.
- Fanny is to return to Mansfield the next day.

Fanny is alarmed to receive Mary's letter with its guarded references to scandal and rumour and its insistence on secrecy. The facts are unclear from Mary's agitated and hasty note, but the newspaper item that Fanny's father points out states that Maria has left her husband and gone away with Henry Crawford. Fanny is shocked by the event and by Mary's attempts to defend her brother and keep the matter hushed up. She is distressed at the possible consequences of the couple's behaviour and the pain it will cause others – particularly Sir Thomas and Edmund. ✪ How does Austen convey the enormity of what Henry and Maria have done? Read the paragraph that begins *Fanny seemed to herself never to have been shocked before*. Underline the key words that express Fanny's response.

Edmund's letter results in mixed feelings – Fanny is aware of the further pain that Julia's elopement will bring, but is delighted to be returning home. The invitation to Susan to stay at Mansfield Park is an added source of joy. On the journey she feels Edmund's suffering, of which he speaks little because of Susan's presence, but at the same time she derives great pleasure from the sight of nature in its early summer beauty. ✪ Look back at the paragraph that begins *She was deep in other musing*. How does Fanny respond to nature and the environment when in Portsmouth?

Lady Bertram's affectionate welcome establishes Fanny's importance to Mansfield Park. Once an outsider, she is now central to its well-being.

COMMENTARY

Chapter 47

Consequences

◆ Mrs Norris is stunned by the end of the Rushworth marriage.
◆ Lady Bertram tells Fanny details of the affair.
◆ Edmund talks to Fanny about Mary Crawford.

Mrs Norris has the wind taken out of her sails with the ending of Maria's marriage, which she had been so proud to arrange. She is so overwhelmed that she cannot vent her irritation with Fanny, who she believes is to blame for not having married Henry, and Susan, the newcomer, with her usual spiteful vehemence. ✪ How has your impression of Mrs Norris developed? Susan is happy to be left to herself and to explore her new surroundings.

Fanny is a consolation to Lady Bertram, and is able to distract her to some extent. ✪ What is Lady Bertram's view of the affair? Fanny is acutely sorry for Sir Thomas, all of whose children other than Edmund are causing him pain. In fact, Edmund has also been a source of anxiety for his father. Sir Thomas, assuming that Edmund's hopes of marrying Mary Crawford are now dashed, and aware that Edmund's conversation with Mary had caused him distress, had sent Edmund out of town to fetch Fanny and Susan. ✪ What does Sir Thomas know of Mary's character? Underline the authorial comment that tells us how he would react if he knew the details of the conversation between Mary and Edmund.

After a few days, Edmund tells Fanny about his last interview with Mary. He is shocked by Mary's attitude and by the way she expresses it. Mary thought that Henry and Maria were guilty only of *folly*, and that had they not been discovered no harm would have been done. ✪ Compare Mary's words with Fanny's (p. 439). Edmund is appalled by Mary's recommendation that the Bertrams should acquiesce in the affair and persuade Henry to marry Maria so that eventually they would achieve some social acceptance. Edmund and Fanny apply the laws of morality; Mary is worldly and pragmatic. Mary makes a final attempt to win back Edmund's affections. ✪ How does she behave? How successful is her enticement?

Edmund finally acknowledges Mary's *faults of principle,* her *blunted delicacy* and her *corrupted, vitiated mind.* ✪ Does Edmund find reasons or excuses for Mary's character? Why does Fanny tell Edmund that Mary's attitude to him was influenced by the possibility of Tom's death?

Chapter 48

Rewards and punishments

(To p. 468, ... *put Edmund Bertram sufficiently out of her head.*)

- Fanny is happy.
- Sir Thomas regrets.
- The Rushworths divorce.
- Maria and Mrs Norris live together in exile.
- Henry the loser.
- Exit the Grants.

Fanny has a lot to be pleased about. Edmund is free from Mary Crawford's clutches; she is free from Henry's attentions; she has Sir Thomas's esteem and affection; and she has a central role at Mansfield Park. ✪ Which of these circumstances gives Fanny most pleasure?

Sir Thomas feels that he has been an inadequate parent. He regrets having allowed Maria to marry John Rushworth, and realizes now that the upbringing and education of his daughters has failed to instil ideas of *active principle* and the *necessity of self-denial and humility.* Sir Thomas faces the painful truth that the combination of his repression and Mrs Norris's indulgence and flattery has been detrimental to the girls' moral development and to his knowledge of their characters and personalities. ✪ What do you think of the way Sir Thomas has performed his role as parent and guardian? However, there is pleasure in the fact that Tom gets better, and becomes a changed person, *steady and quiet,* and Edmund's improved spirits provide comfort.

Following the realization that Henry will never marry her and the divorce instigated by John Rushworth, Maria settles with Mrs Norris at some distance from Mansfield Park. Sir Thomas offers Maria protection and material comfort, but will not have her living at Mansfield Park. He is pleased to be rid of Mrs Norris, whose bad influence he now sees. ✪ How satisfying do

COMMENTARY

you find this outcome for Maria and Mrs Norris? Why does Julia receive a better fate than Maria?

Because he is a man, Henry is not socially ostracized for his behaviour as Maria is. However, he has to live with *self-reproach and wretchedness* that he lost Fanny and harmed the Mansfield Park family. The authorial voice comments sternly that Henry may receive *a juster appointment hereafter*. ✪ How strongly does the author disapprove of Henry's behaviour? How do you compare his behaviour with Mary's?

Dr Grant is appointed to a position in Westminster Abbey, and the Grants offer Mary a home with them, an arrangement which continues after Dr Grant's death. ✪ What prevents Mary from finding a husband?

Married at last

(From p. 468, *Edmund had greatly the advantage of her ...* to end of chapter.)

◆ Edmund falls in love with Fanny.
◆ Sir Thomas is delighted with the match.
◆ Susan takes Fanny's place at Mansfield Park.
◆ On Dr Grant's death, Edmund and Fanny move into the Parsonage.

Edmund soon realizes that Fanny is ideal for him; already emotionally attached to her and aware of her moral and mental superiority, he comes to prefer her *soft light eyes* to Mary Crawford's *sparkling dark ones*. Sir Thomas welcomes Fanny as a daughter, and finds pleasure in Susan's usefulness to Lady Bertram and in William's continued success. The Prices benefited from *early hardship and discipline, and the consciousness of being born to struggle and endure*. ✪ How does Susan adapt to Mansfield Park? How is she different from Fanny?

In the end, Fanny is the heir to Mansfield Park. She embodies its values and upholds its traditions. ✪ How are the values held by Fanny and Edmund different from those of the previous generation?

MANSFIELD PARK

Pull it together

- ? Make a Mind Map or chart showing the position of each main character at the beginning of the novel, and how they end up.
- ? Write a modern 'lonely hearts' advertisement that (a) Mary; (b) Henry might place.
- ? Put these items in the order in which they appear:

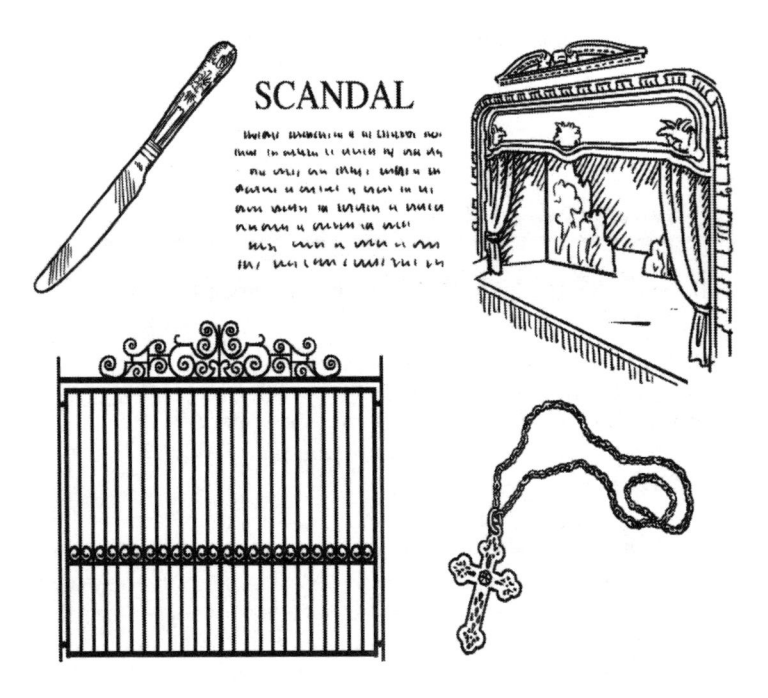

SCANDAL

- ? Choose three scenes that involve gatherings of people. Make notes of the instructions you would give to someone filming each scene.

Now you've reached the end of the Commentary, take a well-earned break.

Answers to Commentary tests

CHAPTER 3 (p. 36)

(a) Frances Ward (Mrs Price); (b) Lady Bertram; (c) Miss Lee; (d) Fanny Price; (e) Sir Thomas; (f) Tom Bertram.

CHAPTER 7 (p. 44)

(a) Mary Crawford; (b) Edmund Bertram;
(c) Henry Crawford; (d) Edmund Bertram; (e) Mrs Norris;
(f) Lady Bertram

CHAPTER 14 (p. 55)

(a) William Price; (b) Tom Bertram; (c) John Yates;
(d) Henry Crawford; (e) Mrs Norris; (f) Julia Bertram.

CHAPTER 37 (p. 80)

(a) Sir Thomas; (b) Lady Bertram; (c) Fanny Price;
(d) Henry Crawford; (e) Edmund Bertram;
(f) Mary Crawford.

CRITICAL APPROACHES

Since its first publication in 1814 *Mansfield Park* has attracted a great deal of critical attention. Throughout the nineteenth and twentieth centuries opinions have been divided about the novel, with critics who dislike some aspects of the text being scathing about what they see as its deficiencies. A particular criticism which was expressed strongly by Charlotte Brontë in 1848 and repeated in various ways by other critics in every era since is that Jane Austen's work is limited in scope, dealing with a narrow social class and displaying limited moral and emotional range. ✪ What is your immediate reaction to this criticism?

Early views

The first critics of *Mansfield Park* were Jane Austen's family and friends. The comments of this group focus mainly on plot and character, and their observations pinpoint some of the aspects of the text that have continued to be controversial. The points offered by these readers and by others in the 1800s include:

- admiration for Fanny's high principles
- dislike of Fanny's insipid, weak character
- annoyance with the unrealistic elopement of Maria and Henry
- appreciation of the realism and effectiveness of the Portsmouth scenes
- liking for the sound treatment of the clergy
- praise for its realistic portrayal of everyday life and ordinary people.

✪ Think of arguments to support and to counter each of the above points. Use evidence from the text. You could start a Mind Map and add to it as you work through this chapter.

CRITICAL APPROACHES

MORAL READINGS

Some nineteenth-century criticism takes the debate beyond issues of plot and character. In 1821 the critic Richard Whatley drew attention to the didactic purpose of Jane Austen, and approved of the points made in *Mansfield Park* about the education and upbringing of young women. Another important critic, Richard Simpson, wrote in 1870 that the themes of the novel and its didactic purpose are woven into the plot and characterization. He saw Austen as a social critic who uses irony as a weapon of attack.

✪ Which of the following statements describes your own reading of Mansfield Park? Think of arguments for and against each point of view:

- A snobbish, dull story with a limited social range.
- Its analysis of a restricted social world offers universal moral judgements.

Twentieth-century views

WOULD YOU ASK FANNY ROUND FOR THE EVENING?

Some critics in the early twentieth century were particularly virulent about the characterization of Fanny Price. D. W. Harding, writing in 1940, developed the idea of Austen as a satirist, one who cloaks her criticisms in comedy to mask what he called in the title of his essay 'Regulated Hatred'. Harding condemns Fanny as a priggish and uninteresting heroine. In 1970, Kinglsey Amis took the attack further in his essay 'What Became of Jane Austen?' He found Fanny 'morally detestable' and 'lacking in self-knowledge, generosity and humility'.
✪ Which characters in the novel are described as lacking these virtues? What point is being made by relating these qualities to Fanny? Amis pointed out the social limitations of Fanny and Edmund, and that to invite them round for the evening 'would not be lightly undertaken'. ✪ Who, by comparison, would provide good company for an evening? What serious point is being made? How does this comment reflect, or show a misunderstanding of, the novel's themes?

FANNY OR MARY? – A LIBERAL HUMANIST VIEW

The liberal humanist critic Lionel Trilling wrote about *Mansfield Park* in *The Opposing Self* (1955). Trilling's liberal approach focused on issues of the self and human identity. His discussion of Fanny Price and Mary Crawford highlighted one of the controversial aspects of the text: the wit and energy of Mary Crawford must be rejected in favour of Fanny's sickliness and virtue. Mary represents the kind of worldliness and egotism that threaten the stability and strength of the Christian values associated with Fanny, but Mary may be seen as the more attractive character. In spite of this, the Crawfords' glamour must emerge as inferior to the intrinsic worth of Fanny and Edmund.

Trilling pointed out that Mary's appeal is based on external concepts of fashion and style, whereas Fanny's sincerity, though less attractive, expresses the integrity of her true self.
❍ How strongly are you drawn to Mary Crawford's character? Does the opposition of Fanny and Mary present any particular problems for a modern-day reader?

A SLAVE-OWNING SOCIETY – A VIEW FROM A NEW HISTORICIST

In his book *Culture and Imperialism* (1993), the critic Edward Said offered a reading of *Mansfield Park* as an exploration of the position of England as an imperial power. Sir Thomas Bertram's estate, it is claimed, depends on income from West Indian sugar plantations worked by slaves. There are several textual references which could support this approach. In the first chapter, Mrs Price wonders if William could be useful to Sir Thomas *in the concerns of his West Indian property*. Sir Thomas's absence during the first part of the novel is caused by *some recent losses on his West Indian estate*, and Mrs Norris comments that the Antigua estate is making poor returns. Sir Thomas's unexpected early return is made possible by *prosperously rapid* business in Antigua.

Said argued that the order and comfort of Mansfield Park is made possible only by financial returns from slavery. There is one reference to slavery when Fanny says how she loves hearing her uncle talk of the West Indies, and says to Edmund, '*Did you not hear me ask him about the slave trade last night?*' (Chapter 21). Fanny's question is greeted by complete silence.

○ What would be Fanny's likely views on the slave trade? How likely is it that Sir Thomas's West Indian property is a sugar plantation?

UNDER THE SURFACE – DECONSTRUCTION

Edward Said and similar critics approach the text through a process of deconstruction – they look for gaps in the text and explore its hidden meanings. This school of thought proposes that readers are so aware of novelists' attempts not to mention certain subjects that these very matters, through their absence, assume great importance. ○ What mention is there in *Mansfield Park* of wars and political events?

THE ROLE OF WOMEN – FEMINIST APPROACHES

Feminist approaches to *Mansfield Park* explore the novel in terms of gender roles in relation to the structure of society. Sir Thomas, Edmund and Henry may be considered as examples of male authority, particularly with reference to their dealings with Fanny Price. ○ What kind of pressure does each of these men put on Fanny? What is each one's idea of what a woman should be? The limited possibilities for women are explored through Mary and Maria, for example. Mary's lively and unprincipled behaviour presents a challenge to accepted ideas about women's behaviour. ○ How strong a challenge does Mary represent?

Maria's challenge to accepted behaviour has a sorry outcome; the author attributes her failure to conform to a conventional role to the inadequate education received by her and her sister. Fanny, on the other hand, is rewarded. Her story may be seen as that of a young woman growing up and developing intellectual and social maturity; it may be seen as a fantasy like *Cinderella* in which her innate qualities are finally recognized as she takes her rightful place as mistress of the house.

Your own views

Some of the critical views outlined above support each other; others are contradictory. Remember that critics present their own interpretations based on the cultural positions they represent. Your own reading and close work on the text will enable you to form your own views, and to respond to and compare different critical interpretations.

How to get an 'A' in English Literature

In all your study, in coursework, and in exams, be aware of the following:

- **Characterization** – the characters and how we know about them (e.g. speech, actions, author description), their relationships, and how they develop.
- **Plot and structure** – story and how it is organized into parts or episodes.
- **Setting and atmosphere** – the changing physical scene and how it reflects the story (e.g. a storm reflecting chaos).
- **Style and language** – the author's choice of words, and literary devices such as imagery, and how these reflect the **mood**.
- **Viewpoint** – how the story is told (e.g. through an imaginary narrator, or in the third person but through the eyes of one character – 'She was furious – how dare he!').
- **Social and historical context** – the author's influences (see 'Context').
- **Critical approaches** – different ways in which the text has been, or could be, interpreted.

Develop your ability to:

- Relate **detail** to **broader content, meaning and style**.
- Show understanding of the author's **intentions, technique and meaning** (brief and appropriate comparisons with other works by the same author will gain marks).
- Give **personal response and interpretation**, backed up by **examples** and short **quotations**.
- **Evaluate** the author's achievement (how far does she/he succeed – give reasons).

Make sure you:

- Use **paragraphs** and **sentences** correctly.
- Write in an appropriate **register** – formal but not stilted.
- Use short, appropriate quotations as **evidence** of your understanding.
- Use **literary terms** correctly to explain how an author achieves effects.

THE EXAM ESSAY

Planning

You will probably have about 45 minutes for one essay. It is worth spending 5–10 minutes planning it. An excellent way to do this is in the three stages below.

1 **Mind Map** your ideas, without worrying about their order yet.
2 **Order** the relevant ideas (the ones that really relate to the question) by numbering them in the order in which you will write the essay.
3 **Gather** your evidence and short quotes.

You could remember this as the **MOG** technique.

Writing and checking

Then write the essay, allowing five minutes at the end for checking relevance, spelling, grammar and punctuation.

Remember!

Stick to the question and always **back up** your points with evidence – examples and short quotations. Note: you can use '…' for unimportant words missed out in a quotation.

Model answer and plan

The next (and final) chapter consists of an answer to an exam question on *Mansfield Park*, with the Mind Map and plan used to write it. Don't be put off if you think you couldn't write an essay like this yet. You'll develop your skills if you work at them. Even if you're reading this the night before the exam, you can easily memorize the MOG technique in order to do your personal best.

The model answer and plan are good examples to follow, but don't learn them by heart. It's better to pay close attention to the wording of the question you choose to answer, and allow Mind Mapping to help you to think creatively and structurally.

Before reading the answer, you might like to do a plan of your own to compare with the example. The numbered points, with comments at the end, show why it's a good answer.

MODEL ANSWER AND ESSAY PLAN

QUESTION

Do you agree that *Mansfield Park* is too concerned with moral messages to be enjoyable?

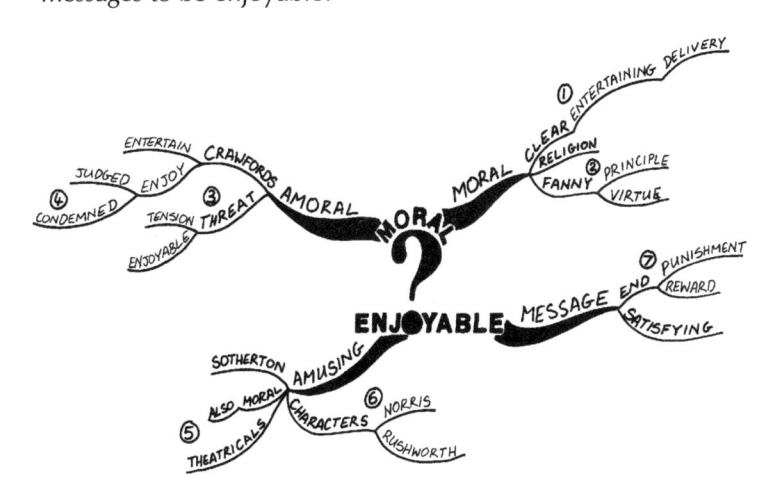

PLAN

- Clear moral message: virtue rewarded, lack of principle punished – but entertaining.
- Fanny's virtue.
- Crawford threat – enjoyable tension. Henry almost succeeds. Mary attractive almost to the end. Crawford appeal lessens.
- Crawfords judged and condemned.
- Sotherton and theatricals amusing and revealing.
- Rushworth and Mrs Norris – satirized.
- Clear message, but rewarding. Authorial comment.

ESSAY

In 'Mansfield Park' moral messages abound. Religion and moral virtues are central to the novel's development. Fanny Price, the moral centre of the novel, is well principled and religious and is eventually rewarded for her virtue, whereas the Crawfords are punished for their lack of principle. The moral message is clear, but it is presented in such an entertaining and absorbing way that it is accepted by the reader, and its delivery is made enjoyable through drama, comedy and ironic comment.[1]

The Crawfords present a threat to the values of Mansfield Park, and in keeping with the moral pattern of the novel, they cannot be allowed to prevail.[2] However, there is a strong danger that they might. Enjoyable tension is created through the presentation of the seductive, attractive Crawfords. Edmund is captivated by Mary's 'smiles and liveliness' so that he overlooks and excuses her faults to the extent that he no longer sees them. The tug of her sexual attraction is there to the end of the relationship. Even after her fatal response to the Henry and Maria affair, which shows her 'corrupt, vitiated mind', Edmund admits the occasional regret that he did not go back to her. Henry Crawford almost works his way into Fanny's heart; had she not been in love with Edmund, he might have succeeded.[3]

Austen carefully structures the novel so that the appeal of the Crawfords lessens. In the reader's eyes, if not in Edmund's, Mary seems increasingly vulgar as the novel progresses, her letters to Fanny in particular displaying superficiality and crassness. (Her comment about Tom's possible death is a good example.) Henry's behaviour to Maria finally marks him down as selfish and unprincipled.[4] In a way, the moral message is quite a relief to the reader; like Fanny and Edmund, we have been seduced and beguiled, and the sense that order is being restored is quite pleasurable.[5] The visit to Sotherton and the episode of the theatricals put the various couples under moral scrutiny while affording amusement and entertainment.[6]

At Sotherton, the growth of intimacy between Mary and Edmund, in a conversation which focuses on religion and morality, and the pairing up of Henry and Maria with an angry Julia left to look on are enjoyably presented. The seductive art of Henry is revealed as he persuades Maria to feel herself 'more at large' by slipping past the gate without the legitimate key. The use of the words 'authority' and 'prohibited' remind us of the moral aspect of the scene, while the whole dialogue, including Fanny's warning not to slip into the ha-ha, has a comic aspect.[7]

MODEL ANSWER AND ESSAY PLAN

During the theatricals the sense of moral danger is imminent as the tension between Henry and Maria and Edmund and Mary mounts, but at the same time Mr Rushworth's delight in his satin outfit and concern for his two-and-forty speeches is amusing. Mrs Norris too, although morally wrong in condoning the activities, provides much entertainment through her money-saving actions, such as moving into Mansfield Park to be more useful, and whisking away the green baize curtain for her own use.[8]

The final chapter of the novel leaves us in no doubt about its moral message. Rewards and punishments are distributed, and there is an allusion to divine justice in the hope that Henry may find 'a juster appointment hereafter'. The authorial comment at the beginning of the chapter expresses a wish to have everybody not greatly at fault 'restored to tolerable comfort, and to have done with all the rest'. The tone is stern at times, but on the whole expresses order, harmony and forgiveness. The moral message is clear but not unwelcome, and the journey towards its establishment has been enjoyable.[9]

WHAT EARNED THE MARKS?

1 Good beginning – addresses question and establishes argument.
2 Awareness of structure and intention.
3 Point clearly illustrated and discussed.
4 Argument developed with pertinent illustration.
5 Refers to question – personal response.
6 Focus on argument.
7 Awareness of style.
8 Good choice of example and illustration.
9 Draws argument to a conclusion – good textual reference.

This is one approach to the essay question; you may choose to answer it differently. You may feel that the moral messages spoil the novel. There is no right answer to the question – what is important is that you base your answer on textual knowledge and structure and express it convincingly.

GLOSSARY OF LITERARY TERMS

alliteration   the repetition, for effect, of consonant sounds.

allusion   the use of literary, cultural and historical references.

assonance   the repetition, for effect, of vowel sounds.

authorial voice   *see **narrator**.*

caricature   exaggeration and simplification of character traits.

characterization   the way in which characters are presented.

context   the background of social, historical and literary influences on a work.

dialect   regional form of language varying from the standard in vocabulary and grammar.

diction   choice and arrangement of words.

didactic   intended to instruct; in literary criticism, often used in negative sense.

discursive   presenting a logical argument, step by step.

epistolary novel   genre of fiction in which the plot unfolds through letters.

feminist criticism   critical approach developed in the 1960s, based on assessing the role of gender in texts. A particular issue is the subordination of women in a patriarchal society.

free indirect speech   technique of blending a character's words and thoughts with those of the narrator.

genre   type of literary work conforming to certain expectations; e.g. tragedy.

Gothic novel   genre of fiction popular in the eighteenth century, in which eerie and supernatural events take place in sinister settings.

idiom   a characteristic expression of a language or ***dialect***.

image   a word picture bringing an idea to life by appealing to the senses.

industrial novel novel dealing with the issues of the Industrial Revolution, often set in the north of England; e.g. *North and South* by Elizabeth Gaskell.

irony a style of writing in which one thing is said and another is meant, used for a variety of effects, such as criticism or ridicule.

magical realism a fiction style which combines mythical elements, bizarre events and a strong sense of cultural tradition; e.g. *Midnight's Children* by Salman Rushdie.

Marxist criticism critical approach which sees literature in relation to class struggle, and assesses the way texts present social realities.

melodrama sensational dramatic piece appealing to the emotions, usually ending happily.

metaphor a compressed *simile* describing something as if it were something else.

narrator in a novel, a character who tells the story. An *omniscient* narrator has complete knowledge of everything that takes place in the narrative; an *unreliable* narrator is one whose knowledge and judgements are limited and biased.

onomatopoeia use of words whose sound imitates the thing they describe.

paradox an apparently contradictory statement which contains some truth; e.g. 'I hear her hair has turned quite gold from grief' (*The Importance of Being Earnest*).

parody an exaggerated copy (especially of a writer's style) made for humorous effect.

persona an assumed identity.

personification an *image* speaking of something abstract, such as love, death or sleep, as if it were a person or a god.

picaresque type of novel popular in the eighteenth century, featuring the adventures of a wandering rogue; e.g. *Tom Jones* by Henry Fielding.

plot the story; the events that take place and how they are arranged.

GLOSSARY OF LITERARY TERMS

polemical   (of style) making an argument.

rhetorical   expressed with a view to persuade (often used in negative sense).

satire   literature which humorously exposes and ridicules vice and folly.

signifiers   verbal signs.

simile   an *image* comparing two things similar in some way but different in others, normally using 'like' or 'as'.

standard English   the particular form of English, originally based on East Midlands' dialect, most often used by educated speakers in formal situations.

stream of consciousness   technique exploring the thought processes and unconscious minds of characters; used by writers such as Virginia Woolf and James Joyce.

structure   the organization of a text; e.g. narrative, plot, repeated images and symbols.

symbolism   the use of an image or object to represent an idea.

subplot   subsidiary plot coinciding with the main plot and often reflecting aspects of it.

tone   the mood created by a writer's choice and organization of words; e.g. persuasive.

viewpoint   the way a narrator approaches the material and the audience.

INDEX

Page references in bold denote major character or theme sections.

Bertram, Edmund **11–12**
  authority 97
  clergyman 11, 34, 47, 48, 64, 68, 69, 71
  consideration 11, 33, 37
  infatuation 11, 12, 42, 43, 51, 86
  integrity 12, 42
  judgement 12, 86
  patience 33
  principles 11
  theatricals 52, 56, 58, 60, 62
Bertram, Julia **13**
  education 34
  elopement 88
  jealousy 55, 58
  rivalry 45, 47, 54
  theatricals 54, 55
  values 33
  wilfulness 13
Bertram, Lady **9–10**
  calmness 35
  guidance 76
  indolence 9, 30, 37
  selfishness 10, 31
  theatricals 56
Bertram, Maria **12–13**
  affair 13, 88
  challenge 97
  divorce 90
  education 34
  engagement 12, 48
  flirtation 12, 48
  marriage 63
  ostracism 13
  rivalry 45, 47, 54
  self-centredness 39
  theatricals 54, 55, 56
  values 33
Bertram, Sir Thomas **9**
  Antigua 9, 35, 96
  authority 9, 79, 97
  background 9
  departure 36
  distant 34
  Henry's proposal 74, 75
  judgement 9, 36
  kindness 75
  Portsmouth 79
  principles 31
  regret 90
  return 59
  self-knowledge 9, 22
  sternness 9, 33
Bertram, Tom **11**
  absences 11
  charm 52
  extravagance 11, 34
  fever 86
  improvement 90
  stability, lack of 11
  theatricals 11, 53

Change and improvement **19–21**
  intellectual and moral 20
  landscaping 19, 21, 41, 48
  Mansfield Park 20
  nature 21, 41
  novelty/variety 20, 21, 29
  religion 20

109

stability 19, 20, 28
Thornton Lacey 67, 68
tradition 20, 29
Church and clergy **24**
  Dr Grant 24, 35, 50
  Evangelicalism 4
  guardianship 48
  Methodism 4
  ordination 24
  prayers 46, 47, 77
  preaching 77
  Quakers 4
  religion 48
  sermons 20
Crawford, Admiral 37, 38, 41, 42, 73
Crawford, Henry **14**
  acting 76–7
  affair 88
  attraction 14, 38
  authority 97
  charm 14
  flirtatiousness 14, 38, 52, 58, 66, 78
  improvement 14, 83, 84, 85
  instability 14, 37, 38
  marriage 38, 62, 72
  Portsmouth, visit 83–5
  proposal 72, 73, 76
  selfishness 14, 52
  self-reproach 9
  sensitivity 14
  theatricals 54, 55, 59, 65, 77
  William 66, 70, 73, 76, 78
Crawford, Mary **13–14**
  attraction 96
  clergy 46, 47, 48, 50, 64, 66, 68, 71
  corruption 14
  harp 41
  kindness/friendship 57, 59, 64
  letters to Fanny 85, 87, 88
  London 38, 42, 78
  marriage 39, 78, 79, 87
  selfishness 43, 96
  sophistication 38
  unprincipled 14
  wit 13, 39, 42, 46, 59
  worldliness 96

Education and growth **24**
  Bertram, Edmund 11, 24
  Bertram, Maria and Julia 12–13, 24, 34, 58, 90
  Bertram, Sir Thomas 3
  Price, Fanny 1, 24, 34, 57, 71

Family relationships **21–2**
  brothers and sisters 13, 17
  family 22–3
  parents/guardians 16, 21, 22, 48, 50, 76, 81, 90

Grant, Dr **15**
Grant, Mrs **15**

Language, style and structure **27**
  authorial voice 27, 32, 91
  balance 32
  comedy 62
  dialogue/speech 27, 40, 52
  diction 46
  irony 46, 51, 52, 70, 95
  narrator 32
  structure 27
  symbolism 27, 49, 68
  tone 31, 46, 79
Love and marriage **23**
  ideal 23
  imprudence 23, 82
  money 23, 36, 38
  security 23
  status 23, 30
  values 23
Lovers' Vows 4, 54, 78

INDEX

Mansfield Park
  change 20
  malaise 20
  order 28, 29, 62, 96
  space 28, 33, 57
  stability 61
  values 28, 91
Money and materialism
  income 24, 31, 35, 38, 64, 79
  status 32
  wealth 28, 29, 32, 35, 64

Norris, Mrs **10**
  activity 30, 54
  economy 10, 32, 35–6, 54, 80
  indulgence 22, 90
  interference 10, 32, 45
  self-interest 10, 32
  spite 65

Portsmouth
  chaos 28
  noise 82
  poverty 28
Price, Fanny **7–8**
  amber cross 68, 69
  anger 8
  ball 68, 70
  courage/strength 8, 78
  decorum 8
  gold chain 65, 70
  horse 37, 43
  improvement 61, 63, 66, 71
  isolation 8, 58, 75, 85, 87
  jealousy 8, 43, 59
  letters from Mary 85, 87, 88
  modesty 72
  necklace 68–70, 78
  observer 49, 51, 59
  passivity 8
  Portsmouth 79, 81, 84, 85
  priggish 95
  proposal 73–7
  sweet temper 36, 72
  theatricals 54–6, 58–60
  unhappiness 8, 33, 59
  values 96
Price, Mr **16**
Price, Mrs **16**
Price, Susan **17**
Price, William **17**
  affection 17
  good impression 17
  navy 17
  Portsmouth 81
  principles 17
  promotion 73
  visit to Mansfield Park 34, 66

Romanticism 46
Rushworth, Mr **16**
  divorce 90
  foolishness 16
  income 16
  marriage 63
  theatricals 16, 56, 59
Rushworth, Mrs **15**

Setting **28–9**
  London 29
  town and country 29, 42
slavery 3, 4, 35, 96
Sotherton, visit 45–9

Yates, John **15**

BUZAN TRAINING COURSES

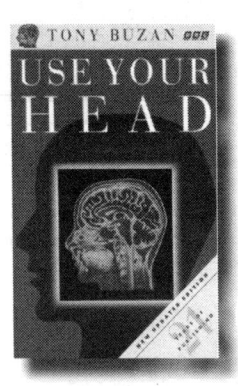

For further information on books, video and audio tapes, support materials and courses, please send for our brochure.

Buzan Centres Ltd, 54 Parkstone Road, Poole, Dorset BH15 2PX
Tel: 44 (0) 1202 674676, Fax: 44 (0) 1202 674776
Email: Buzan_Centres_Ltd@compuserve.com